PUBLIC THEOLOGY FOR CHANGING TIMES

John Atherton has been Canon Theologian of Manchester Cathedral since 1984, and Honorary Lecturer in the Department of Religions and Theology in the University of Manchester since 1975. He has ministered in the inner cities of Glasgow, Aberdeen and Manchester, was a consultant to Faith in the City (1985), and is currently a director of the Youth Justice Trust and the William Temple Foundation, patron of Jubilee 2000, and vice-chair of the Manchester Diocesan Board for Church and Society. He has been married to Vannie for 36 years, and enjoys hill walking in the Scottish Borders and Highlands several times a year. His previous publications include *The Scandal of Poverty* (1983), *Faith in the Nation* (1988), *Christianity and the Market* (1992) and *Social Christianity: A Reader* (1994).

PUBLIC THEOLOGY FOR CHANGING TIMES

JOHN ATHERTON

Published in Great Britain in 2000 by
Society for Promoting Christian Knowledge
Holy Trinity Church
Marylebone Road
London
NW1 4DU

Biblical references are from
The Revised Standard Version of the Bible © 1971 and 1952.

British Library Cataloguing-in-Publication Data

A catalogue record for this book is available from
the British Library

ISBN 0-281-05209-3

Typeset by WestKey Ltd, Falmouth, Cornwall
Printed in Great Britain by The Cromwell Press,
Trowbridge, Wiltshire

Contents

Acknowledgements

I have been fortunate in being able to test out much of this material with a variety of groups. For two years, an Extra Mural Department class from the University of Manchester explored the development of churches and theology in north-west England from 1750 to the present. Some material in Chapters 2 and 4 emerged from that experience, and is published in *The Church in Cottonopolis*. Other lectures allowed me to explore other themes, including issues of debt and Jubilee 2000, at Bradford Cathedral, Humberside University, and the Weatherill lecture at Croydon; USPG published one of these lectures. Reflections on the global context in Chapter 2 were developed more fully in the Winton and Basingstoke lectures, and published by ICF. Material on the Youth Justice Trust and marginalization in Chapter 5 was first elaborated at a training conference for Manchester magistrates, and the section on the welfare state in Chapter 6 will be published, in a revised form, by *Crucible*. Members of my Christian social ethics course at the University of Manchester, and my research students, continue to be another important arena in which to develop interpretations of contemporary society. Malcolm Brown's recent doctoral work is a good example of the value of such academic partnerships.

My particular thanks must go to my colleagues on the Chapter of Manchester Cathedral for their friendship and support since 1984, and for agreeing to a sabbatical in 1999. Canon Paul Denby read the manuscript and made helpful suggestions for its improvement. My editor, and old friend from 'Faith in the City' days, Ruth McCurry, has been a support over the years, including with this project. Without the heroic efforts of our office staff the book would not have been typed. They made space for Lyndsey Feilman to produce the script. To minister in the midst of Manchester is to engage with the amazing story of modernity. It is a privilege to be there, and particularly to share that journey with Vannie, my partner in life.

John Atherton
Feast of the Venerable Bede, 2000

Preface
Why Change?

Since the 1780s, fundamental change has become the norm for human living and environments. Beginning in north-west England, and cascading through Europe and North America into the rest of the world, industrial and urban processes have proceeded apace. They affect all life, from Chinese peasant to Amazonian rainforest.

Against that backcloth, the period we are living through, from the 1960s onwards, has been experiencing transformations which have 'probably changed human society more profoundly than any other period of comparable brevity' (Hobsbawm, 1994, p. 6). It is these processes which are the subject matter of this book.

How do we live effectively and purposefully with such change? Old certainties in politics, economics, social affairs and religion no longer convince. Developing Christian perspectives on these matters cannot be based on past experiences and insights, increasingly irrelevant to emerging processes. Yet much of Christian opinion is of this kind, exemplified by a speaker in the Church of England's General Synod debate on the ordination of women (itself key sign of these changes) asking: 'In this matter as in so much else in our great country, why cannot the status quo be the best way forward?' (Handy, p. 3). The answer is that in our world, the status quo no longer exists.

If we should no longer use old ways to engage new realities, how do we read the signs of these times and respond effectively to them? For it is inconceivable for a faith centring on a Christlike God not to do so.

It will certainly involve being global in our thinking and acting. In my own development, this book represents that change from a Western account of society's interaction with Christianity, to a recognition that 'the more these debates themselves become genuinely transnational the better' (Giddens, p. 155).

Within that global context, certain questions must be addressed, from the demands of a global economy and the challenge of a demographic explosion, with implications for the environment, to growing marginalization between and within nations.

The sheer scale of these questions in an increasingly integrated world demands large responses. There can be no strategic action without such accounts of how the world works. The task is to narrate them as fully and truthfully as possible, even if they are necessarily partial and subjective (see Appleby, p. 236). They will therefore not seek to explain everything, but will be major narratives, standing between the extremes of universal and grand narratives, and local fragmented ones. They will be substantial enough to cross 'local and contextual boundaries', and therefore able to engage global contexts and questions (Reader, 1997, p. 74). And such accounts, because there is no longer only one, require dialogue between and within them. Making serious sense of any one of the global questions requires at least that diversity in breadth and dialogue. Addressing them all, as now we must, makes any narrower approach inconceivable.

It is in relation to these large accounts of where we are and where we are going that Christian social thought and practice can and must locate itself. For religion is integrally linked to global contexts and questions as part both of the problem, as fundamentalism, and of solutions through commitments to justice, peace and loving relationships. It is recognition that any explanation of human affairs will have 'a theological dimension' (Boyle, p. 14). The task is to develop large theologies which connect in critical dialogue with the narratives demanded by global contexts and questions. There can therefore be no retreat from the Christian task of developing public theologies of global proportions.

Such theological accounts of what is happening to us should consequently be seen as contributions to wider tasks of engaging such contexts. They allow us to link 'the subject matter that is the secularity of its own time' to 'the characteristically Christian understanding of meaningful history', as the secular age of partnership and the theological age of reconciliation (Boyle, p. 304). Without such constructive interactions we will not survive gracefully on this planet.

The plan of the argument is almost a history of globalization processes from a Christian perspective, beginning in Chapter 1 with an exploration of the meaning of partnership and reconciliation for and through an understanding of public theology, God, Christ and the Church. It is in that focused sense, but by its very nature cascading through the thesis, that the exercise should be regarded as a 'fresh Christian apologetic' for our times (Carey, p. 20). It is a reminder that 'fragments' of Christian insights pervade the seemingly secular arguments, and are embodied in the major narratives of Christian traditions in Chapters 1 and 4 (Forrester). It is a reminder that we should no longer be writing essentially secular commentaries with theology tacked on as an afterthought.

Chapter 2 seeks to illuminate the dramatic changes of the last forty years first from a British and then from a global perspective. Britain is selected not simply because the author is British, but because globalization processes began and continue to unravel there. It presents an informative representative case study of global experiences, provided it is linked to wider realities in Europe, the United States and developing economies. It is recognition that the transcendent is incarnate in a particular time and place to cope with a post-modern, post-imperial, post-industrial, globalized, secularized, marketized planet by reaching out universally and yet remaining local and particular.

Chapters 3 and 4 interpret and evaluate these changes in the light of historical and contemporary processes from a global and British experience. The typology constructed for the previous two centuries of change develops into new frameworks for the emerging new age. It is that innovatory theme of partnership and reconciliation which is then elaborated and tested as practical divinity in the local, national and international contexts of Chapters 5, 6 and 7. As a reflective and practical exercise in public theology it therefore seeks to be 'a viable outline of the future which takes historical experiences into account, comes to grips with present social reality and at the same time transcends it in search of a (relatively) better world order' (Küng, p. xv).

1 A Public Theology for a Global Context

> Moving forward is no guarantee of success. Standing still offers the certainty of defeat. (Sassoon, p. 754)

> Is it possible that theology may have a modest but constructive and questioning contribution to make both to the theoretical discussions which undergird policy and to policy-making itself? (Forrester, p. 31)

Theft is an accelerating social disease in the West, part and parcel of growing divisions and marginalizations. Although locating problems in historical context never alleviates the victim's pain, it does put events in perspective. A sense of proportion is always an integral part of strategic responses to social problems. It is therefore worth noting that the English have always been thieving! The Venerable Bede, first great historian of the English people and Church, is buried in Durham Cathedral. He died in his monastery of St Paul's, Jarrow, in 735, but his bones were 'stolen' 300 years later, and taken to Durham by the cathedral's keeper of sacred relics. It is a salutary reminder that life does not change in some respects!

Looking out onto that great cathedral from the Department of Theology is a wondrous experience. Feeling envious may be human, but it is not attractive. Recently visiting the Department I did experience such ambition, but fortunately only fleetingly. Returning home, I realized that if I were based in that great medieval city, I would be like a fish out of water. For my pond is the centre of Manchester, its past, present and future, a story which is now the world's. My vocation is to show how natural it is for an understanding of God and his purposes for the world to be fully part of that context. This book reflects a journey to translate that understanding and conviction into a global context.

Connecting God to the contemporary world requires more than the help of a location like Manchester. It drives us deep into histories of urbanization and industrialization and their transformation as global processes. It confronts us with great global challenges, from environment to marginalization. Immersion in that world therefore means developing a familiarity with a variety of disciplines from economics and politics to history and literature, and with a variety of practical programmes and policies at all levels, from local to international.

It is an unfamiliar world to many in churches and theological departments. Yet absorption in the secular, in God's world and works, is one of the most exciting and creative of journeys. Indeed, for many, it is so enriching that to return to the words of much academic theology is to encounter alien territory, divorced from God's works and world which the contemporary global context so represents. I feel like a fish out of water again. Reinhold Niebuhr, that great theologian of public life, once described himself as 'a moralist who has strayed into theology' (*The Times* obituary, 3 June 1971). I find this comforting, for it is how I experience much theology.

Despite sharing Niebuhr's reticence, we must stray into theology because it is this book's purpose to establish connections between secular and theological in the contemporary arena on the basis that such a linkage has clearly historically been the case, and the emerging global context continues to require it. Developing this argument is consequently to contribute to the construction of a public theology for emerging global economy and challenges. In answering Forrester's question, it believes theology can and must make a 'modest but constructive and questioning contribution' to public debates and policies. Yet, learning from the importance of location in the midst of industrialization and urbanization, and from the interaction of theology and secular disciplines, then that theology will best make that contribution if it likewise undergoes a process of reformulation, as Sassoon observes. For not changing, 'standing still, offers the certainty of defeat'. The risk of moving forward, of changing to effect change, must be taken.

The construction of such a public theology is demanded by the context of public life and by the nature of Christian faith. On the one hand, the inexorable movement towards a global economy and its interaction with a series of dominating global challenges requires the development of a Christian faith sufficiently capacious to engage its nature and extent. The sheer size of the global economy, with its extraordinary growth since 1945, the astonishing demographic explosion and possibly irreversible environmental damage, surely demand a commensurate theological contribution. Similarly, analyses of the processes of economic growth, so decisive in the stories of modernization and accompanying marginalizations, require sensitivity to the plural, multifaceted, multicausal nature of the world we live in and its problems. The context, in other words, requires a public theology which is both capacious and plural.

On the other hand, Christian faith in itself demands participation in that emerging global context. God's word, communicated in and through the Scriptures, recounts public history powerfully as the very warp and woof of revelatory acts. God's works have always included both the whole natural order, so important today as environment, and the contributions of the human and its social constructs, as partners in co-creation. It is the interaction between word and works which takes us unequivocally into the public, and indeed every other, realm. It is a reciprocal action reflected in the relationship between secular and theological ages, from voluntarism and atonement in the nineteenth century to partnership and reconciliation in the twenty-first, and is elaborated in Chapter 4. Of course, there will always be other ways of expressing that connection; those selected in this argument have emerged out of recognized historical interpretations of stages in the development of modern societies. The attempt to take them forward through the present into the future acknowledges the dramatic changes of this generation as requiring a new understanding expressed as partnership and reconciliation. It is a development based on practical experience and reflective observation of contemporary secular and church life. That process in itself is of formative importance, in that engagement with the global reality of public life is profoundly a matter of praxis as the interaction of practice and theory. That is why theology must now be an exercise in practical divinity for the good of the world, of God's world, and that is developed with regard to the local, national and international in Chapters 5, 6 and 7.

Yet if a public theology for the global context is to make such a contribution, it is becoming clear that it is inadequate to simply stray into the realm of theology. It must be engaged as effectively as the secular, even if in profound interaction with it. In that sense, theology must be a disciplined reflection on the nature and destiny of life, with regard to an ultimate frame of reference, which for Christians implies beliefs about God and God's relationship to the world. That interaction between God's word and works in and through the contemporary context must be seen to work in the reciprocal relationship, both supportive and critical, between Christianity and the global context. Stout rightly argues: 'Serious conversation with theology will be greatly limited if the voice of theology is not recognizably theological . . . Conversation partners must remain distinctive enough to be identified, to be needed'. (Forrester, p. 31)

Yet it is not sufficient for the theological voice to be distinctive. The interrelationship between word and works, interacting with and through the context, as practical divinity, is even more important. Facing global economy and challenges has to be about praxis, about tangible practical consequences of that theological voice. It is about translating that complete set of interconnections into and through partnership and reconciliation operating in our contexts, discerningly interpreting and promoting what is going on, and should go on much more. It is what we will call reconciliation this side of the cross – for example, urging sub-Saharan African states to reconcile the disturbing imperatives of global markets with the needs of social cohesion and environment. It is how reconciliation the other side of the cross takes us into Christians, and others, sharing in the suffering of Christ as part of the process of the world's redemption. It is their combination as both sides of the cross which makes the Church a unique and indispensable part of our world's struggle for justice and peace. (It has, after all, been engaged in such struggles throughout its history, for example in the anti-slavery campaigns and now in the campaign against international debt.) What this book seeks to do is to help that contribution to be made more effectively as practical divinity, intentionally embodied in partnership and reconciliation. That is a public theology for today.

Yet even then it is not sufficient to identify ways in which theology interacts with the secular as discerning interpretation and praxis. That necessary task must now be reinforced by illustrating how fragments of Christian belief which illuminate and inform contemporary contexts are part of a more comprehensive and coherent Christian corpus or tradition of beliefs and practices. The task is to elaborate how such 'theological fragments come from a coherent view of reality and are related to one another', and how they are 'derived from a tradition which was and is nurtured in a community of shared faith' (Forrester, pp. 3, 201). Now the Christian fragments in the following argument are clearly identifiable. They include the use of stewardship or *oikonomia* and the orders of creation (Chapter 2), the secular and theological ages (Chapter 4), and the Christian insights into and practices of partnership and reconciliation (Chapters 5, 6 and 7).

The task now is to locate them in an elaborated Christian corpus. They can then be used to generate more fragments to promote more effective change; they can be resources for sustaining and informing Christian discipleship, and as part of an apologetic for the Christian contribution to necessary contemporary change. At the heart of this elaborated corpus, as a variety of contemporary theologians have acknowledged, from liberation theology to radical orthodoxy, are beliefs about God, Christ and the Church. It is these which we now need to address, yet following the principle of facing up to change through reformulation, including by responding to matters raised in the following argument. The latter will do so from the cautionary and exploratory perspective of a Christian social moralist straying into the realm of theology, but now confident that such theology will have to engage with such matters if it is to make an effective contribution to contemporary change.

DOCTRINES OF A CAPACIOUS GOD

In my Father's house are many rooms. (John 14.2)

Journeying from the origins of industrialization and urbanization around Manchester in the late eighteenth century to an emerging global economy and a series of great global challenges at the beginning of the twenty-first century is the greatest journey in history. It is full of extraordinary achievements and appalling problems, a bewildering plethora of insights, causes and strategies increasing in complexity and scale to the present global stage. Concepts of post-modern and post-industrial only capture part of these dimensions and profusions, informed as they are by competing forces of integration and fragmentation. Reflecting on them all drives us to an understanding of God commensurate with these realities because God is in and through and beyond them. So many understandings of God do not match up to that. They are too small. We are being driven inexorably to develop, worship and serve a God greater than all that, a truly roomy God, a truly capacious God.

A trinitarian God

It is not by chance that there lies at the centre of Christian traditions understandings of God as Trinity, as three Persons yet one God, as a social God. It is that ever-evolving understanding of God which is becoming more and more necessary and appropriate for the emerging global context we are now inhabiting. This conviction is reflected in the number of theologians now turning to a trinitarian God, from Moltmann and Leech to Hull and Meeks. Even the Church of England, not the most alert of bodies to contemporary change, has returned to the traditional use of Sundays after Trinity rather than Pentecost, to define that longest of seasons covering summer and autumn.

Two particular features of the trinitarian God, reciprocity and justice, interact powerfully with insights in the emerging context, including its interpretation as partnership and reconciliation. Reciprocity within God promotes the central human understanding of liking as a key element in love. Love in God, and therefore as example for Christian discipleship, has focused historically over-much on a transcendent view of love, through Christ, as sinless, heedless, self-sacrificial and sin-bearing, thereby distancing it from most loving human relationships. Some women theologians have sensitively argued that 'maybe the time has come to rehabilitate liking as not just respectable but excellent; as a central element in what we ought to mean when we talk about (Christian) love' (Oppenheimer, p. 94). Some partiality in love is proper acknowledgement that particular individuals matter, providing that this also involves an affective relationship with the Other. Such an understanding of reciprocity within and between people and groups is an important feature of effective partnerships.

On the other hand, a trinitarian God is always about righteousness as justice. Running through the Scriptures is a powerful social understanding of such justice focusing on the quality of relationships as obligation and responsibility. It certainly includes the contribution of contracts, as we shall see, but located in the deeper commitment to covenants. Again, as with reciprocity, justice reflects the very life of a social God, and is centred on the teaching, suffering and death of Christ, the second person of the Trinity. 'Ultimately, all that can be said by the Christian about justice rests on the doctrine of God, not simply as the God whose truthful love is directed towards us, but as the God whose very life is "justice", in the sense that Father, Son and Holy Spirit reflect back to each other perfectly and fully the reality that each one is, "give glory" to each other' (Williams, p. 210). Giving each his proper due lies at the heart of secular understandings of justice; that therefore takes us into, because it is also rooted in, giving glory to each within the Trinity, and by human beings to that God. That is why Bede ended his life giving glory to the Father, the Son and the Holy Spirit. From the first historian of the English people, it becomes a giving proper due to citizenship as English, European and now global, but all within an eternal dimension, a plurality of identities in and through the one identity. It takes us into the praxis of reconciliation itself.

It is through such understandings of God, and the human living illuminated and informed by them, that we are led deeper into a trinitarian God in ways which connect powerfully and decisively with what Christian discipleship and human living will need to become if we are to overcome the great global challenges.

First, there is the foundational understanding of God as knowable and yet unknowable. 'We shall learn to see God in the human world we have made for ourselves now, and not only in some past golden age,' yet we are also but 'the creatures of a wholly unknowable God . . . and . . . nothing we know in this world is ultimate' (Boyle, p. 93). It takes us into a God who is source of all form yet formless; source of thought yet beyond thought. It becomes glimpse of the timeless wholeness of all reality, the wisdom of God 'before' the creation of the world, into which we can now begin to enter (Shanks, p. 180). It is a journey through the rich multiplicity of the created order of the environment into an immeasurably rich multiplicity of God. It is about our participation in the One through the Other. For, in the words of the old Christmas collect, as Christ was 'made in the likeness of men, so we may be made partakers of the divine nature'. Again, the necessary struggle to hold such opposites together is the classic task of reconciliation, confirmation and extension of the historical task of the early Church Fathers with their attempts to reformulate our understanding of God as Trinity by trying to reconcile oneness and plurality.

The implications of such formulations are far-reaching for attempts to interpret and change our context. For we are bidden to recognize substantive intimations of the divine through particular historical acts and yet not to confine God within any one privileged area of existence. So the formative realities and insights emerging out of and challenging our world, such as the growing significance of women, black people and the environment, can be regarded as revelatory challenges in that they possess and exude a transformative power for the reformulation of theology through their shock qualities (Shanks, p. 23). Yet equally clearly there exists the historic Christian conviction that true knowledge also comes from a radical detachment even from the imagery of the Trinity. The consequence of that insight requires us never to confine God to one particular area of created existence, whether male or female, black or white. For Meister Eckhart, therefore, 'whoever seeks God in a specific way takes the way and leaves God behind' (Shanks, p. 183). Of course, this in no way negates the creative and formative contributions to our understandings of God and discipleship from feminist and black theologians. They stand, but like the contributions of male and white theologians, they can never tell the whole story about God, and when they presume to do so, they have failed quite decisively. In an equally creative and challenging way, the understanding of God as knowable and yet unknowable allows us to make strong but discerning linkages with the global issue of the environment. On the one hand it takes us through and beyond the personal, as three Persons of the Trinity. An undue emphasis on the person leads to that personalism which is associated with an unduly anthropomorphic view of the universe and the gross misuse of the created order. We can therefore 'be grateful for the divine governance, for all it sustains and makes possible without conceptually personalizing the Governor' (Gustafson, p. 271). This understanding of God as being itself is much more sensitive to renewed claims for recognition by the rest of God's creation. Yet on the other hand, these interpretations of the divine as beyond understanding also release us from an undue and romantic estimate of creation, and enable us to continue to pursue scientific and technological developments. We are required to negotiate between, to reconcile, the different narratives of science and technology, environment and theology.

Flowing through the interpretations of a reciprocal and paradoxical trinitarian God is an acknowledgement of the ongoing development of our understanding of God, of an ongoing process which is part of the nature of God itself. It is about Father begetting Son, and each of us, and the whole created order, 'without ceasing'. It is a process in the images of the Trinity, as 'confessional theology pushing urgently up against its limits', reflected in the processes of the natural order as evolution, and in such social constructs as economic growth. It therefore stands in sharp and decisive contrast to those images of divine and world which attempt to fix identities in static and unchanging forms. The challenge is to 'let God be God' and live with and in the 'self-unfolding of the absolute' (Shanks, pp. 184–5).

A dialogic God

I have come to regard the dialogic nature of God as one of the most seminal implications of a trinitarian God. As I have reflected on this developing argument, and been confronted by the multifaceted nature of modernization processes and the created order itself, time and time again I have been driven to acknowledge the importance of interdisciplinary work and practical collaboration. Faced with the increasing plurality of our world and with the unifying demands of the great challenges, I honestly cannot see ways forward for the human on this planet which do not take some account of partnerships and reconciliation. Of course, these reflections on dialogue could have been located in any other chapter, yet I am convinced that they belong most appropriately in deliberations on the nature of God itself.

God includes God as word, as linking divine and human through Christ. Thus 'God becomes the hope and guarantor of human communication' (Reader, 1994, p. 88). For the great Jewish philosopher and theologian Martin Buber, it is about the divine *I* encountering the human *Thou*, in such a tangible way that the *in-between* itself becomes a reality of substance. It is about the great concept of bridge builder, of Tillich's location of creative theology on the boundaries of life. It is an acknowledgement of the word translating powerfully into the seminal contemporary significance of communication technologies in a global economy. It is about affirming the 'discursive engagements which a world of cosmopolitan communication tends to enforce' (Reader, 1997, p. 16). Dialogue is an essential part of God as trinitarian God, and it is, and will be even more so, an indispensable part of human living in the emerging global context.

Five further features of this dialogic interpretation of God elaborate both our understanding of the divine reality and the human task today.

First, and most surprisingly for this increasingly secular world, a God in dialogue with itself, and therefore with the Other, points to the transcendent dimension of existence. Even for Habermas, the great exponent of communicative reason, religion is about 'intercourse with the extraordinary', indispensable source of ethical energy and inspiration (Reader, 1997, p. 161). However interpreted, whether as foundational or non-foundational transcendence, you cannot get rid of the Other, the symbol of transcendence, because it is critical for our understanding of God and spirituality, and for self-understanding as identity and non-identity. To remove either understanding increases the tendency to anarchy or totalitarianism. Yet God is not wholly other, as God is not wholly with us. The reconciling of the two, in and through discipleship, is a task of orthopraxis. It is as though, therefore, the function of transcendence in and through God is 'to keep us alert to . . . an inescapable dimension of existence' (Reader, 1997, p. 169).

Second, a dialogic God is for learning from encounters with others. The theology of F. D. Maurice, which so contributed to changing society in the nineteenth century and beyond, included entering into dialogue with a great variety of practical, religious and intellectual movements from Chartism and Socialism to Lutheranism and Unitarianism. He was a 'digger' into deeper truths through the recognition of the limitations of tradition revealed through engagement with other traditions. In a fragile and complex world, it is an encouragement to seek 'always the establishment of the widest possible basis for rational solidarity' or partnership (Shanks, p. 168). It is a recognition that our relationship with the Other is an indispensable part of self-knowledge, and consequently that despising the Other is likely to ensure no critical learning from the Other. 'The fear of the Other is perhaps the beginning of wisdom, as one is thereby compelled at least to pay serious heed to the relationship; but the fulfilment of wisdom must be in the development of a countervailing culture of "recognition", grounded not in any capacity for violent coercion or resistance, but solely in the intrinsic worth of the work each one does' (Shanks, p. 169). It therefore stands in sharp contrast to the fixing of truth into some rigidly abstract conceptual framework 'to the exclusion of that free play of ever-shifting meanings and associations by which a tradition properly unfolds' (Shanks, p. 177). It rejects, too, that undue restricting of our understandings of God and Christian ethics to the Church. For Hauerwas, Lindbeck and Milbank, 'There can be no autonomous reality for Christians, only the disciplined practices of the faithful within the confines of the church' (Reader, 1997, p. 69). Business ethics, natural law and common religion make no contribution to the development of faithful Christian social witness. It is to allow the absolutes from a Church the other side of the cross to determine life this side of the cross directly and absolutely. It excludes the necessary compromises essential for survival in society. There is no contact with a Church this side of the cross, the inevitable and necessary accompaniment to effective dialogue and partnership in this world. There is no practical divinity, with its advice from the Didache, one of the oldest Christian texts outside the New Testament: 'If you can shoulder the Lord's yoke in its entirety, then you will be perfect; but if that is too much for you, do as much as you can' (Shanks, p. 15).

Third, a dialogic God provokes and fosters the development of Christian character through particular virtues. For example, with its concern to relate to the Other, Christianity can be expressed as an ethic of unequivocal neighbourliness, of the recognition of the Other as neighbour, as Good Samaritan. As the virtue of generosity, it is 'a response to one's responsibility with regard to the sheer otherness of the Other; the Other as one's "neighbour" – whether fellow-citizen or not.' And that essentially 'transcommunal generosity' encompasses both Christians and non-Christians alike across locality, nation and beyond. It goes way beyond Karl Barth's restriction of dialogue to fellow members of the household of faith, and only coincidentally with the outside world. And, in doing so, you are all the more likely to have 'some sentiment of solidarity' with the people you are in dialogue with as fellow-citizens, and to have a more open frame of mind (Shanks, pp. 186, 189, 84). It is that generosity, too, which lies at the heart of the Christian contribution to justice. For then it leads to 'a more imaginative kind of reciprocity, a capacity to think of oneself in the other man's shoes, and see how the situation would look if roles were reversed . . . Reciprocity, then, points not only to consistent morality but to Golden Rule Morality' (Forrester, p. 232). It is such a generosity which then goes through and beyond that golden rule morality, to enact that generosity of God, which does not claim reciprocal rights, but gives without counting the cost, that has, in the end to inspire Jubilee 2000's campaign on international debt, and the altruistic nature of its claims.

Understanding God as the ultimate source and centre of all things also obliges Christians to practise the virtue of tolerance: 'God's transcendence beyond the human sphere becomes, then, the basis of principled tolerance' (Wogaman, p. 162). Our sinfulness and finitude inevitably means our insights are partial at best, and thereby require complementing and correcting by the insights of others. Dialogue, therefore, 'is not an optional extra for theism, but a religious imperative' (Markham, p. 184).

Fourth, facing great global challenges requires dialogue between the great religions of the world. In addition, the transition to a multiform political context and movement to sub-national autonomies is likely to continue the trend to more local conflicts, and the place of religions within them, ensuring that reconciliation 'today is such that it requires an interreligious effort' (Schreiter, p. vi). It is recognition that proper development of religious faith now includes learning from such dialogue: 'One enters dialogue both as a believer convinced of the claims of one religious tradition and as a human being open to the possibility that one has something to learn from representatives of another religious tradition' (Reader, 1997, pp. 152–3). It is acknowledgement of the old tradition of God's works, but now in contemporary form, that 'God has many saving projects' (Hull, p. 9). It is new acknowledgement that building religious tradition through dialogue with others is now a further stage in the process of self-understanding, including becoming 'more aware of the failings of their religious community' (Braybrooke, p. 19). As important, in our fractious context, including interreligious conflicts, it becomes essential part of developing 'a discipline for the healing of divisive memories' to build 'new bonds of solidarity' (Shanks, p. 4).

Dialogue between faiths, however tenuous, has been taking place for at least a century. However, only in this generation, and again quite reflective of a changing context, has such interfaith dialogue begun to be more widely acknowledged. The Second Vatican Council's Secretariat for Non-Christians transformed the Roman Catholic Church's attitude to other faiths, and around the same time the World Council of Churches established a similar organization. 'Many religious and denominational bodies now have agencies to encourage such dialogue' (Braybrooke, pp. 8–9). Of course, some are now arguing that such interfaith dialogue is used to promote religious pluralism by presupposing 'a timeless logos enjoying time-transcending encounters with an unchanging reality' (Reader, 1997, p. 140). It becomes a form of Western imperialism arbitrating between religions by downgrading the unique aspects of particular religions and merging them into a new grand narrative. Yet to then argue that differences preclude effective encounters between religions, even if that were true, invariably ends up with arguments for the survival of the strongest tradition. Given the global challenges we face, that cannot be allowed, never mind the proper argument that it cannot be the future for the necessary, and indeed inevitable, encounter between religions. It is like technology; apart from its rights and wrongs, once you have begun the journey, there is no going back. Yet listening to the criticisms of radical orthodox theologians and the insights of black theologians confirms the importance of self-identity, including that of religious traditions and communities. Our evolving understanding of partnership consequently acknowledges the significance of both identity and dialogue in this emerging global context. Interfaith dialogue is therefore not about promoting a melting pot, with differences fused into an invariably forced unity. The task is to be secure enough in one's personal and communal identity to be able to reach out to the Other without feeling unduly threatened. Yet equally that stretching out cannot be so extended as to become lost in the Other. Losing difference in such a way contradicts the different Persons in the dialogic God. The human path is likewise about preserving and promoting similarities and differences, including processes of global integration and fragmentation.

Promoting such interfaith dialogue inevitably means facing challenges from religions themselves, including continuing problems of religious extremism, and the misuse of religion for oppressive political and religious ends. A particular interfaith programme is being developed which will also engage such problems. However problematic, this search for a global ethic is of some significance because it links to various ethical endeavours to be encountered in the later survey of local, national and international programmes, and reflects part of the interfaith project. As such, it therefore does not seek to replace essential religious differences epitomized by the Talmud, the Sermon on the Mount, and the Qur'an, but rather points to a necessary minimum of common values, already affirmed by religions despite their dogmatic differences, and shared by non-believers. Küng, who has worked assiduously in this field, refers to it as 'the necessary agreement in fundamental, ethical standards which despite all differences of political, social or religious direction can serve as the smallest possible basis for human living and acting together' (p. 97). The contribution of interfaith movements to such valuable endeavours has come particularly through the Council of the Parliament of World Religions in 1993. Their recognition that what unites the world's faiths is greater than what divides is reminiscent of, and in continuity with, the ecumenical movement's promotion of a similar regulative principle through a series of conferences beginning at Edinburgh in 1910. Interacting with such a principle are two useful developments. One is the recognition that the golden rule is common to the great faiths. In the Christian tradition it is expressed as 'And as you wish what men would do to you, do so to them.' (Luke 6.31). From that, an InterAction Council of former Presidents and Prime Ministers developed four 'irrevocable directives' on which all religions could agree: the respect for all life (you shall not kill), deal honestly and fairly (you shall not steal), speak and act truthfully (you shall not lie), and respect and love one another (you shall not commit sexual immorality) (Küng, pp. 110–11). On the other hand, the elaboration of a global ethic is also reflected in the growing commitment to the universal importance of human rights. Although emerging powerfully in the West, other religions clearly do include ideas which support human rights, even if in very different frameworks. For Rabbi Borowitz, 'there is something about every human being which is identified with the absolute source of value in the universe'.

Pacem in Terris (1961), confirmed by Vatican 2 and by WCC teaching, supports those insights by declaring that 'any human society, if it is to be well ordered and productive, must lay down as a foundation this principle, namely, that every human being is a person, that is, his nature is endowed with intelligence and free will. Indeed, precisely because he is a person he has rights and obligations flowing directly and simultaneously from his very nature. And as these rights are universal and inviolable so they cannot in any way be surrendered.' All these understandings are linked to the Universal Declaration of Human Rights as the foundation for human rights law, with different interpretations in different religious traditions, yet equally with 'considerable agreement as to both the fundamental importance of human rights in the modern world and the content of human rights' (Braybrooke, pp. 11, 18, 19). It is precisely that dialogic theory and practice, rooted in our understanding of the divine and confirmed by human experience, which will need to inform and be reflected in all our approaches to the great global challenges. For engaging the divine and the human, 'there is both sameness and radical alterity, symmetry and asymmetry, identity and difference in my relation with "the Other" and above all in the ethical relation' (Reader, 1997, p. 148).

Such understandings of God, interacting with religion and life, are pointing increasingly to an evolving understanding of theology in general, and public theology in particular, as a 'colourful patchwork quilt, seamed into a whole' (Appleby, p. 116). They are not about fusing differences in a melting pot. Reflecting a capacious God, they represent 'an invocation of the kind of wisdom which comes from a close attention to the widest possible range of traditions' (Shanks, p. 175), and indeed sub-traditions. It is therefore not about a 'linear and single Christian doctrine, applicable at all times and in all places' (Reader, 1997, p. 137). It rather promotes public theology rooted in situations, using resources of traditions, to engage questions which people, structures and environment now encounter. In that it is truly enacting the biblical commitment to *oikonomia*, to the whole inhabited world. It is truly ecumenical. A dialogic capacious God demands no less.

A COSMIC CHRIST

> For in him all the fullness of God was pleased to dwell, and through him to reconcile to himself all things, whether on earth or in heaven, making peace by the blood of his cross. (Colossians 1.19–20)

In a global plural context, with a commitment to a dialogic God, why engage with Jesus Christ, the supreme symbol of division and conflict between Christianity and other faiths and the world?

First, in the development of this whole argument, the principle of incarnation will both provoke and inform it more than any other theological belief. Taking the contemporary context seriously as integral to the formation of belief and discipleship is a central reflection and requirement of an incarnational theology. Its greatest modern exponent, F. D. Maurice, said as much in his engagement with formidable political, social and economic issues in the earlier stages of industrialization and urbanization: 'No man I think will ever be of much use to his generation who does not apply himself mainly to the questions which are occupying those who belong to it' (F. D. Maurice). It is that embodiment of the divine in and through the secular which, in turn, will shape this whole argument through linking theological and secular ages, from atonement and voluntarism to reconciliation and partnership.

But there is a second, more personal reason why Christian reflection on the global context should be regarded as inadequate without serious elaboration of what Christ means in and for it. For over a generation, I stood in a theological tradition which has been described as 'social Christianity' or 'mainstream liberal' (Atherton, 1994, pp. 1–2) and was essentially linked to the age of incarnation and state. My journey has now gone beyond that, as travelling from the 1960s to the present will demonstrate and require. We have moved out of that great liberal age. And an important part of that change is an acknowledgement that we can no longer comment on contemporary secular affairs assuming their linkage with Christian beliefs will be self-evident. Increasingly, a more plural and secular society, the partial collapse of Churches in the West, and the pressure to develop personal and communal self-understanding, have combined to push Christians to acknowledge that 'dialogue implies interlocutors conscious of their own identity' (Rieger, p. 119). For Christians developing public theology that means paying serious attention to Christology, if it means anything. For what does Christianity literally mean? Theism or belief in God, and related doctrines of God, are not sufficient, 'for the world, now, is not just God's world, it is Christ's. And we are Christ's, whether we are artists or critics or anything else' (Boyle, p. 284).

In order to show what an engagement between contemporary context and public theology could mean for our understanding of Christ, five perspectives will be elaborated, again from the partial but now essential experience of one straying into the area of theology.

A distinctive and exclusive Christ?

Perhaps the sharpest question raised by the promotion of a dialogic God in an age of partnership and reconciliation relates to the traditional Christian commitment to the uniqueness and indispensability of Christ and particularly his saving death on the cross. It is a conviction which cuts across the dialogic principle, and fosters a strongly separated parochialism; it argues there is no alternative to explicit Christian faith. The implicit faith of a Virgil in pagan literature, or a Lear in Shakespeare, needs to be situated in a Christian perspective to make its human significance into a means of grace. It needs to be connected to the other side of the cross from which grace ultimately flows. Yet it can also be argued that poetry, and indeed history and economics, can speak of the grace of Christ without knowing it, if they incarnate divine meaning in appropriate material and relate it to meaningful history. For there is a common grace, mediated to the world through the orderings and structuring of life, which stands in its own right, as God's grace, yet which gains added value if linked to the saving works of God by Christians.

The contemporary proclamation of Christ as exclusive Word, with its unequivocal 'no' to culture, has owed much to the work of Karl Barth. Yet after years of a hard-line positivist Christology he too began to realize that 'this exclusivity does not correspond to God's purpose with human beings'. So then he rightly added that 'Christian exclusivity leads to intolerance'. It contradicts the very being of a dialogic God, and a commitment to Christ, the second person of the Trinity, simply cannot do that.

The same exclusive interpretation of Christ is developed through examination of the historic Christian claim that Christ is the only true Light of the World, reflected through the Scriptures, the Word of God. Yet in this increasingly and irreversibly plural world, millions regard Buddha as the Light, and millions regard Muhammad as embodying the Light. Can the one be reconciled with the other? Even Barth came to concede that 'there are also other lights alongside the one light; yet other words alongside the one Word of God, yet other truths alongside the truth of God'. It is a recognition that this 'compatibility corresponds to the spirit of Jesus Christ', in that Christ treated people of other faiths as human beings, whether Syro-Phoenician woman, Roman officer, or Samaritan (Küng, pp. 154–5). It is another way of acknowledging that Christ is a child of God thereby including all children in God, for 'when theologians claimed that Jesus was the *only* child of God for all humanity, not just *a* child of God embodying God's invitation to all, it paved the way for intolerance' (Rieger, p. 146). It is to reconcile both sides of the Cross, for in Christ the particular and the universal, the individual and the collective are brought together, each retaining its particular identity in an actively redemptive unity. It challenges us so to present Christ in this age that we do not let the particularity of the representation be obscured by the universality of what is represented, and equally we do not let the universal truth represented here about individuality be displaced by such an exclusive focus on the particularity of the representative individual who is the actual subject of the story (Shanks, p. 11). It is a rejection of those contemporary neo-orthodox or pluralist theologians who insist we choose between the reductive pluralism of a religious tradition or its irreducible particularities.

The mission of Christ

With such a Christ in such a God, is Christian mission still authentic or necessary? It is certainly necessary in the West if the Church is not to dwindle into insignificance. It is equally an authentic part of any discipleship of such a Christ, a sharing of understandings about the Christlike God, properly informed by them. So it continues to be testimony, but never conquest, thereby recognizing the legitimate right of other religions to exist and prosper. Acts rather than words, the way of the early Christians and the praxis of Gore, become the principal means of communicating this good news, so public theology as partnership and reconciliation moves to the centre of the missionary task. It is not about colonialism but embodying faith in and through the local context as inculturation. Laity not specialists become its foundation, and dialogue not confrontation its principal tool. Yet to announce the gospel like this as salvific dialogue presupposes respect for the Other; it does not imply renunciation of received faith, of Christ, because that very belief also includes proper engagement with the Other: 'To receive, not by one's own merit, but through the grace of God the truth of Jesus Christ in our lives does not invalidate our relationship with persons and other perspectives, but rather gives these relationships authenticity' (Rieger, p. 119). Such a Christ does not call us to 'pointless and exhausting competition with other religions' but to 'engage in the mission of God, which is to work for the coming of the Kingdom of God', and that is not about 'a triumphant ecclesiasticism but a renewed humanity' (Hull, p. 7).

Incarnation as oikonomia and kenosis

I have recently been struck by creative links between Christ, stewardship and sacrament which should inform our understanding of God and reconciliation. For the Orthodox Church, *oikonomia* or stewardship relates to God's economy which is focused on the incarnation. It is about God's home management, through *kenosis*, through God's self-emptying through Christ's death. It is about Christ's offering of the whole created order to God. The sacrament of holy communion therefore becomes participation in Christ's self-oblation. By offering bread and the wine, work of human hands and fruit of the earth, we receive Christ in turn. So the eucharist exemplifies the partnership between God and ourselves for our sustenance and the transformation of the world. And God's household, like ours, as *koinonia*, is structured round a table. So the dialogic trinitarian God becomes the model and means of managing our global household. And at the heart of that, as I now realize, is not simply the incarnational reality of divine embodiment in sacramental bread and wine, but also the means of our redemption, of our reconciliation, through the broken body and the spilt blood.

The glimpse of the kenotic understanding of Christ affirms the self-emptying and self-limitation of God through his embodiment in the secular realities of life on earth. It therefore acknowledges the growing need for that confidence of self-limitation required to avoid the catastrophes of global conflicts and challenges. It is a reminder that we can no longer use the cross to impose our beliefs on others, but can use it to promote partnership and reconciliation. It is a transformation of cross in the way Blackness has been: 'we must somehow confront and reconstruct the symbolism by which we have been wounded in order to be healed and become capable of healing others' (Rieger, p. 91).

The reformulation of Christ

There is a long tradition of using the inevitable interaction of faith and context to generate new understandings of Christ as contribution to change. From the classic credal formulations of the early Fathers, through Gore's incarnational theology, up to the efforts of such liberation theologians as Boff and Sobrino, reformulating our understanding of Christ has taken centre stage in any public theology. The '*Asian Faces of Jesus*' of R. S. Sugirtharajah represents well this contemporary endeavour: 'The christological enterprise is an ongoing task. Cultures and contexts are not static entities; they constantly change and throw up the warp and woof of political, social and religious strands in an ever-new fabric. As cultures evolve, as new contexts and experiences emerge, as new questions surface, so features and aspects of Jesus will continue to be discovered' (Reader, 1997, pp. 75–6). It is a programme powerfully engaged by Black theologians, too, including Britain's Robert Beckford. His *Jesus is Dread* is a reformulation of Christ, through the Rastafarian tradition of Black culture, thereby symbolizing a Black Christ of liberation. It represents a classic correlation of the revolutionary aspirations of the Black community in Dread culture, with the resistance of the Black Church, to produce a theology engaging with Black consciousness in Britain (Beckford, pp. 130–1). Beckford rightly recognizes the plural nature of Black culture and Church as important and he also sees the limits of such necessary christological reformulation. They are always time-bound and qualified by obvious deficiencies, in this case the male domination of such imaging. But that has always been the case for a Christ for our day, which is why each generation and context has to undertake the task afresh. A cosmic Christ includes such endeavours in an increasingly global context now reaching even beyond that in terms of environment and communication technology.

The praxis of reconciliation. The cross is the supreme symbol of reconciliation, for he is our peace. 'He has reconciled us to God in one body by the cross. We meet in his name and share his peace' (*Alternative Service Book*, para. 30). It is the engine of the multi-dimensional practice of reconciliation between people and God, people with each other and the whole created order. It is the epitome of praxis, the theory and practice of Christ in himself and the process in which we all participate. As such, that foundational praxis is sustained by its inherent characteristics, and resourced by an efficacy tried and tested throughout continuing history. For example, it acknowledges the empirical reality that all have sinned and fall short of the glory of God. A story is told about John Bradford, a Manchester reformer whose cruel death on 1 July 1555 is commemorated in our cathedral. On seeing criminals being taken for execution, he observed: 'There, but for the grace of God, goes John Bradford.' In that falling short all participate. Yet all then share in the costly gifted promise of forgiveness. Many have much to forgive in Church and society: 'Forgiveness cannot, if it is a virtue, be a matter of simply *ignoring* the serious wrong which the criminal has done, or pretending that it never happened: if forgiveness is to be consistent with a proper regard for the values which the criminal has flouted, as well as with a proper concern for the wrong that has been done, it must also be consistent with an attempt, perhaps through punishment, to bring him to recognise and repent that wrong.' If such reconciling of the sinner as a person or community is to be achieved, there must be a goal or *telos*, a reformed and reconstructed person in community. It is a costly discipline, for 'at the centre of the Christian understanding of justice there stands the cross, not a symbol but a historic deed in which the justice of God was manifested in his covenant of faithfulness right through to the point where the just died for the unjust' (Forrester, pp. 77, 78, 227). That is why such reconciliation is open to all and experienced by all at some point in their lives, yet achieved by few in anything like its fullness. That is why we are always living in the interim, living towards that final reconciliation the other side of the cross, yet sustained by its fragments this side of the cross. The task is to capitalize on them in the light of the *telos* of both sides of the cross.

That is the praxis of Christ's reconciliation, elaborated in practical details of living throughout Christian history. It should not therefore be surprising that non-governmental organizations are turning to their religious counterparts for help in the growing number of conflicts around the world. The practical stages in the process of such social reconciliation, moving from the genesis through the transformation and into the readjustment phase, will be described in Chapter 6. Complementing by inspiring and informing them, is the christological-based reconciliation process. For Schreiter, this has five features (pp. 14–19).

First, reconciliation is God's endeavour, initiating and completing in us reconciliation through Christ. It is about God working in and for us, and particularly, in conflict situations, through the lives of victims. If reconciliation depended on wrongdoers taking the initiative, it would rarely occur. The heart of reconciliation is therefore the restoration of damaged humanity: 'God begins with the victims, restoring to the victim the humanity which the wrongdoer has tried to wrest away or to destroy.'

Second, reconciliation is more spirituality than strategy. If reconciliation is principally God's work, then we are but 'ambassadors for Christ', with God working through us by the creation of spaces for the search for truth, justice and healing. Thus do spirituality and strategy interact with each other.

Third, experience of reconciliation makes both victim and wrongdoer 'a new creation' (2 Corinthians 5.17, 20); our humanity is given back to us. Yet that restoration is never a return to a former state; there can be no erasure of memory, no justice for the dead: 'it is a transformation of the experience that will be forever part of who we are'.

Fourth, the process of reconciliation creating new humanity is ultimately focused in the story of the passion, death and resurrection of Christ. It is in that 'master narrative' that our narratives of violence can find 'their form and their transformation in the story of what God has done in Christ'. These death and resurrection stories of God's healing and forgiving power can organize 'our chaotic and painful experience of violence into a narrative that will carry us, too, from death to life'.

Finally, the process of reconciliation will be fulfilled only through the complete consummation of the world by God in Christ. And that is not 'the inexorable unfolding of a preconceived scheme programmed to happen from the beginning' but involves our fallible agency and 'the coming together of a myriad of contingent events' as involving 'all things, whether on earth or in heaven, by making peace by the blood of his cross' (Colossians 1.20). It is in the end a truly cosmic Christ, yet he enfolds the heroic and the mundane. The amazing Nelson Mandela story has often been heard. Schreiter tells the story of a couple, pinning all their hopes on their only son, a young man committed to the active search for justice and social welfare. In his university vacation, he was killed in an accident. The parents were devastated. The cosmic Christ brought no comfort to them, even though they were faithful churchgoers. They simply shut themselves off, kept his room as it had always been, and frequently returned to the story of his death to see if it could have been prevented. Then one day it all changed. They suddenly remembered that he would never have wanted such a life for them. It was not what he would have done. Much of the burden was lifted from them. They began to live his kind of life, in terms of serving people and community. They still miss him terribly, but 'the story had been told from another perspective – and it made all the difference . . . In the reconciliation process, these are the moments of grace' (Schreiter, p.46).

It is that grace-given ability to locate our stories in that Story which gradually generates virtues and characters able to participate more effectively in reconciliation processes. Forgiveness is at the heart of them and takes us way beyond political and economic routines, decisively linking both sides of the cross in ordinary human endeavours. Forgiveness is essentially about not being controlled by the past, and deciding for the future. It represents the often unseen dramatic change in the balance of power as it passes from traumatic event to victim. In the practice of politics, it is about striving to undo the effects of the past, what Tutu called in South Africa 'the entail of the past'. It is certainly not 'reconciliation on any terms but takes form in the agreement to work together a political system which expresses the will to forgive' (Forrester, pp. 240, 241).

Almost invariably linked to forgiveness, in personal and social reconciliation processes, is the virtue of suffering. Moving beyond the passive state of suffering, in which so many of us remain bogged down, in christological reconciliation it enters into the Other's world, as Christ did. It becomes suffering *with*, and then 'in uniting our own suffering to Christ's, we become configured into his sufferings so that our suffering too might become redemptive'. Thus do the reconciled become the best leaders in the process of reconciliation. It is about seeking to transform the inchoate character of so much of our world, so powerfully impressed on us by the sheer intractability of the great global challenges. And that is the message of reconciliation, for 'when suffering is inchoate, it can threaten our very being. When it can be turned into redemptive suffering, that is, when it can be set in the context of a higher purpose, it can ennoble our humanity rather than debase it.' Facing up to globalization, facing up to change, ultimately requires, through all our endeavours, in whatever field and whatever level, such an achievable purposeful goal that is both partially present and distantly inviting. I believe that is what partnership and reconciliation are about – the Church, in terms of spirituality and strategy, working 'with all people of good will to bring about the healing and transformation' which the global context so clearly requires (Schreiter, pp. 71–2, 80, 130). It is about locating our global journey in the cosmic Christ.

A TRULY ECUMENICAL CHURCH

> All this is from God, who through Christ reconciled us to himself and gave
> us the ministry of reconciliation. (2 Corinthians 5.18)

Growing benefits of industrialization and urbanization are inextricably
bound up with growing problems affecting people, structures and environment. Given their historic commitment to the vulnerable, to those on the
receiving end of decisions, it was to be only expected that sooner or later
Christians would become involved in struggles to change society for the
better. It is an impressive story within and between nations, from F. D.
Maurice and Washington Gladden in the nineteenth century to Desmond
Tutu and Martin Luther King in the later twentieth century. And it is a continuing story. It is equally not surprising the effort required to address such
agendas led many Christians to become over-absorbed in their heroic task. At
best they took the Church for granted, at worst they regarded it as major
liability.

In my early years at the William Temple Foundation, a small institute
for the development of Christian social thought and practice, I well recall
David Jenkins arguing that we certainly address the problems of modern
advanced economies but equally that we likewise took the Church seriously as institution. That was wise advice. Much contemporary theological debate has revived that concern in new ways appropriate to the new
context. In the midst of an increasingly plural and secular society, they
rightly argue that the Church is preeminently about the formation of our
identity through its traditions and existence as a community of faith.
Much of the analysis and programmes in this book have taken those arguments to heart but only within much wider concerns. For the Church is
certainly an essential contributor to the process of partnership and reconciliation. Yet in order for it to be effective in this way, it will itself have to
undergo change, to be reformulated in and through contemporary change.
A divine institution embodied in the realities of worldly existence as part
of the processes of redemption will always reflect the dialogue between
God and world, not least because it is embodied in the nature of God itself.
Involvement in promoting partnership and reconciliation will likewise
confirm that plural nature of the Church, envisioning it as truly ecumenical, a Church to and for the whole inhabited world. So a Church promoting
partnerships in today's world will be both dialogic and global.

As a dialogic Church it will be a genuinely 'open Church' (Shanks, p. 90) to
itself and the world. It will not suppress differences or conflicts, but will seek
to reconcile them, and if that fails, it will resort to conflict resolution measures
(Forrester, pp. 185–6). An open dialogic Church will embrace a variety of traditions and sub-traditions. It will therefore recognize intolerance for what it
is, a sin-bearing aberration of the human spirit and structures, but will not

resort to exclusion. For a dialogic Church, that would be a contradiction in terms. And that dialogic nature will clearly extend beyond itself to engage with the Other, both as matter of foundational principle and because, since it is subject to sin and finitude like any other institution, it will need to learn from the Other. Only a Church at ease with itself can develop its traditions like this, changing in order to address change. Like the nation state, pressured by globalization, it will learn to accept constructively such limits on sovereignty.

As a global Church, it will promote its international character and organizations, since 'no account of human political life can possibly ignore the supranational economic and institutional order' (Boyle, p. 146), but also because of its credal basis in catholicity and its international development through denominational transnational bodies like the Anglican communion, and international institutions like the World Council of Churches. Yet because of commitment to the principle of subsidiarity, the strength of its international developments will depend substantially on maintaining strong expressions as national and local Churches. The Church is therefore 'an irresistible symbol of a world order that is not purely subjective or functional but can relate the global and the local so as to make realism still possible' (Boyle, p. 281). In this context, the continued absence of the Roman Catholic Church from membership of the WCC is particularly short-sighted. Interestingly, in terms of reflecting contemporary trends of plurality and cohesion, the Anglican communion's reconciling of local and national with international through a confederal model is instructive. The Porvoo Agreement between the Anglican Churches of Britain and the Nordic and Baltic Lutheran Churches represents a similar institutional expression to encourage partnership between different Churches based on recognizing each other's ministries and sacraments.

Implicit in all these developments should be renewed recognition of the seminal importance of the ecumenical movement. Its remarkable growth in the twentieth century represented for William Temple, one of its principal architects, 'the great new fact of our era' (Iremonger, p. 387). Rapid globalization has reinforced that prophetic judgement. Yet these more recent trends reinforce the need for a radical reformulation of the WCC, like the UN, if it is to sustain and increase the commitment to and credibility of such global institutions and their engagement with global realities. The growing convergences between a protestantizing Roman Catholicism and a catholicizing Protestantism is a powerful acknowledgement that learning from encounter with the Other is an indispensable experience, whether as Churches or as world. As important, now, is the extension of these concerns to other faiths as the need to promote a much wider ecumene: 'In a global society Christians are invited to take shared responsibility with those of other faiths for peace, justice, the preservation of creation and a renewed ethic. The fate of the earth is the concern of all human beings, regardless of the religion or world-view to which they adhere' (Küng, p. 156).

Such a positive but critical engagement with the contemporary context, in the form of a dialogic and global Church, invariably involves avoiding temptations presented by other ecclesiological models. For commitment to a capacious God, embracing all as creator, redeemer and sustainer, means that we also are committed to a global society which includes all men and women. And that, of course, means that the Church also must be inclusive. When it is faced with the challenge of global marginalization, there is no time to argue for the Church to become the Church of the poor, to narrow it down at the precise moment in history when the foundational need is for a breadth and diversity of understanding, for a Church which proclaims reconciliation for all by itself being a sacrament of reconciliation of all. Similarly, promoting the Church as small discipleship groups or faith communities reflects a body committed to the loyal few, not the indifferent many on the margins. The drive for the unsullied purity of doctrine and life ignores the reality of the Church and Christian discipleship as a profoundly interim existence, this side of the cross, and the nature of organizational development from sects to denominations. The empirical Church is quite different from such creative fantasies. As with misleading searches for socialist purity and the rejection of the compromising nature of social democratic parties, we need to be reminded that 'when all is said and done, these parties are the only Left that is left' (Sassoon, p. 777). In the end the Church, as it is, is all that we have. A like judgement should be made on those who argue that such a distinctively different Church should embody, in institutional form and lifestyle, an economy at total variance with the global economy and traditional models and processes of political economy. For these advocates, 'if the church does not manifest an alternative economy in space and time, it is not a candidate for serving God's redemption of the World' (Rieger, p. 47). There is no interaction of God's word and works here, no learning from the Other as in other disciplines. It is the embodiment of pure word in the economic order, irrespective of what we know about economies and economic processes. It is certainly not about partnership and reconciliation, and most of all, it will not work. It is an impractical divinity.

A Church promoting partnerships also becomes *a Church embodying reconciliation*. It will therefore be a Church providing space for reconciliation, a safe location for meetings between different groups in society concerned to recognize moral and spiritual concerns in their deliberations. It can become a place of safety for victims to explore wounds, to be listened to, build trust, recover meaning and begin to generate hope again. For the Black Churches 'the worshipping tradition ensures that the Black Church is one of the only safe places where Black identities are celebrated and perpetuated. For many, the Church is a place of affirmation and empowerment' in the midst of great change and hostility (Beckford, p. 26). The

Church is therefore pre-eminently a place of and for worship, which can still provide means for public expression of deep communal and personal emotions. Symbolizing ultimate meaning and compassion made the cathedral in the heart of Manchester the natural location for the civic community to gather the week after the IRA bomb devastated the commercial and shopping centre of the city in 1996. Great movements like the World Wide Fund for Nature still seek religious legitimation for their necessary endeavours on global environmental matters. The historic gathering of the world's main religions in Assisi, home of St Francis, in 1986, provided that opportunity. Finally, above all the Church is a place committed to a Christlike God whose worship, through the eucharist, is a continual re-enactment of the very processes of divine and therefore human reconciliation. It will consequently continue to sustain an ecclesiological self-understanding which 'takes seriously the need to affirm and empower all who enter the church doors' (Beckford, p. 39). The active pursuit of a more just social order is intimate part of the processes of reconciliation in terms of rebuilding shattered communities and preventing the recurrence of conflict.

A Church embodying reconciliation will also promote *universal reconciliation* through a fully ecumenical solidarity. The great model of the Church as a body of diverse and interrelating parts, dependent on proper recognition and participation of the weakest, demonstrates how a global society should operate, and how reconciliation is an indispensable part of it (1 Corinthians 12.22), for it includes the departed and future generations as well as the living, dead victims as well as surviving friends. The Church offers such a possibility because 'it is based upon a faith which is embodied in an actual community which encompasses past and future generations as well as people of today' (Forrester, p. 192). The Church therefore points to a universality of the broadest and most capacious kind, a truly ecumenical Church and universe.

Offering the possibility of a future is perhaps one of the most important contributions the Church can make at this time. Faced by seemingly intractable global challenges, the Church can live in hope precisely because it knows it is living in the interim, this side of the cross. Its worship, and particularly its eucharist, reflects its calling to be 'a kind of anticipation of the life and the justice of the City of God'. Some, like Milbank and Hauerwas, argue that this means the Church should be an asylum. Yet involvement in partnership and reconciliation require that Church to be involved in wider global processes of the search for justice and peace. And it is supported in that task because it is itself finite and sinful, 'a defective church' in a 'deformed world, full of sin and suffering, injustice and oppression' (Forrester, pp. 244, 245). It is precisely that recognition, and the forgiveness it experiences through the grace of God in Christ, that enable the Church to be a place of hope through what has been achieved and experienced and through what is yet to come. It enables the Church to become intentionally involved in the whole process of reconciliation, including partnerships. For Hull, writing in terms of the educational task today, including the relationship between Christianity and other faiths in the global arena, 'neither Christian faith nor Christian identity are unchanging, but are in a mutual relationship with culture and history. The principal task of Christian education today is to enable Christian men and women, boys and girls, to grow into this dynamic mutuality through processes of faith development and critical exploration, so that the mission of God in Jesus may reach its fulfilment for the good of all humanity' (Hull, p. 13). And that is sustained by a trinitarian and dialogic God and a truly ecumenical Church.

Part 1
Facing up to Change:
Making Sense of How We've Got
Here and Where We're Going

I was recently asked to talk about how the Church organized its mission to society in the region. We met in the local pub. As I looked into the men's faces, I decided to talk about something quite different which engaged their lives more directly. You see they had all lived through the generation spanning the 1960s to the present, the most revolutionary experienced by the human race. So I went through the changes in work, family life, politics, culture and religion, and their eyes begin to see the significance of what they had and were now experiencing.

For commentators like Eric Hobsbawm, the collapse of the Soviet Union has been interpreted as the end of the 'short twentieth century' (which began with the First World War). Yet given the 'extraordinary, unprecedented, fundamental' changes transforming this generation from the 1960s, it may well be that 1989 marks the end of the first act of an emerging new era (Hobsbawm, 1994, p. 256).

How do we make sense of these changes, complexities and upheavals through which we are now living? For without 'naming' these processes, as the writers of the book of Genesis recognized, we cannot begin to influence them. We need, in other words, to develop frameworks of meaning to gain a cumulative perspective on the world in order to evaluate it, and then locate and make our contributions to it.

The task of developing such frameworks is recognized by Pope John Paul II: 'models that are real and truly effective can only arise within the framework of different historical situations, through the efforts of all those who responsibly confront concrete problems in all their social, economic, political and cultural aspects, as these interact with one another' (John Paul II, para. 43). That is what I am going to attempt, by setting out frameworks which relate to what is going on in our world, and yet also reflect fragments of Christian insights and values generated by the public theology elaborated in Chapter 1. And, of course, the complexity of our world and the speed and extent of change will require a series of interpretive frameworks, each with its sub-framework, both secular and theological. We will all have to cultivate the skills and spiritualities of working with a variety of analyses and insights in order to portray, however fleetingly and inadequately, the profusion of forces now characterizing our world.

Christianity has long recognized that we are deeply affected by engagement with such a world. It believes God was thus affected by embodiment in Christ through living on earth. Yet through being influenced we can influence. Christ's redemption of the world is token and promise of that change. As an exercise in interpretation, Chapters 2, 3 and 4 are therefore the next stage in the necessarily interactive process of changing the world and theology.

2 Changing Britain in a Changing World

Peter Green was one of my predecessors as Canon Theologian of Manchester Cathedral. Once described as 'the greatest parish priest in England' (Sheen, p. 119), he died in 1961, after 50 years of dedicated ministry in inner-city Salford. He had lived successfully through the upheavals of two world wars and the decline of traditional manufacturing industries and working class communities. Yet at the end of the 1950s, sufficient of both remained to give clear and tangible sense of continuity with the past. That sense of security through gradual change was confirmed by a Church still holding its own in terms of attendances at services and membership. Yet in retrospect, Peter Green died on the edge of a series of changes which transformed for ever the traditional contexts of a modern urban industrial society. By the 1990s, in only a generation, the continuities which had sustained Green's ministry and his generation's lives and livelihoods had gone for ever.

It is not surprising that commentators have defined the period from the sixties to the nineties by the preposition 'after' using terms such as post-industrial, post-imperial, post-structural and post-modern. They all recognize the death of Peter Green's world, but 'without implying any consensus or indeed certainty about the nature of life after death' (Hobsbawm, 1994, p. 288). That understandable uncertainty is questioned by arguments here rehearsed that there is growing awareness of issues to be faced with demanding urgency, and they are affecting us all, because of their increasingly global nature. These transformations are daily brought home to clergy through their pastoral experience. Ask how many babies they are baptizing, and whether they are all from married couples, and compare that to the situation 30 years ago, and they then know what you mean by living with great change.

Exploring the signs of globalization, particularly its more economic dimensions, is a great turn-off. It is too complex and technical, too remote from our particular experiences and locations. We must therefore begin by identifying key changes encountered by people in a particular place in this historic generation from the 1960s to the present, and then locate them in global contexts. Britain is chosen as that location because it was the first nation to begin that journey of modernization in the late eighteenth century, and exhibits signs of a society continuing to experience the symptoms of change described by the prefix 'post'. Although still an advanced or developed economy, its experiences of change speak to nations which have not yet achieved a similar stage of economic growth. I recently showed a man from sub-Saharan Africa round Manchester, sharing with him problems and challenges of a society moving from an industrial to post-industrial situation. Astonishingly, he had no difficulty in identifying with our situation, because there were so many points at which it resonated with his experience. Yet I should not have been surprised. Living in a global society will mean that convergences across cultures, nations and stages of economic growth will become more evident. So although contemporary change will be examined from a British perspective, there will be continual reference to equivalent experiences in other nations, including the United States. The latter may well be further along a particular path of globalization processes, which, among other things, have global pretensions as a neoliberal global free market society and world. A critical conversation with it will be of mutual benefit.

Identifying and interpreting these changes which Britain has undergone since the 1960s requires assistance from interpretive tools or frameworks of meaning. The Reformed tradition's understanding of the orders of creation lend themselves to that task (Preston, 1987, pp. 49–51). Essentially, they recognize that we are influenced as people by certain great structures or orders of life in which we find ourselves. They mould us, before we mould them, so we are conditioned but not determined by them. They are used here in the sense of those orders which influence, for good or bad, our personal and social living in the economy, politics, family, culture and religion.

Each is broadly interpreted in and through contemporary experiences. It is in that flexible spirit that a sixth is added, relating to the processes of marginalization, because though not a traditional order of creation, it is sufficiently structured and influential on people, communities and nations to be a related framework of interpretation. It links to those global processes of marginalization which have proved to be so decisive for human living and environment. All the orders overlap and interact with each other.

THE ECONOMIC ORDER: FROM MILLS, MINES AND FACTORIES TO OUT-OF-TOWN SHOPPING MALLS

In 1959, two years before Peter Green's death, Harold Macmillan won the British general election for the Conservative Party with the slogan 'You've never had it so good'. He was right. The British, like all other developed economies, was deep into an astonishing period of economic growth and material prosperity. Between 1955 and 1960, the economies of the OECD countries as a whole grew by 3.3% a year. Even between 1973 and 1989, Britain's GDP growth averaged 2% a year. From the 1980s to the early 1990s the US economy grew by more than a third, creating 38 million jobs since the early

1970s. Yet despite these successes Britain's economic growth, although 'at the top in terms of her *own* historical record', was consistently at the bottom of the growth league table. By 1995, the US was also experiencing relative economic decline. But 'what all these countries shared was a consumption boom' (Sassoon, p. 194). Against the backcloth of economic growth, three features illustrate the radical nature of changing economic life in this generation, the movement to a consumption-oriented society, the feminization of work, and the fragmentation of identity.

Take the first, the transition from industrial to post-industrial economy and society, represented by the ending of the dominance of large factories and an over-inflated state employment system. The former is dramatically illustrated by the collapse of the textile, shipbuilding and mining industries in Britain, for a century the dominant employers, informing a whole class and structure of urban living. The latter rose to a peak between the 1940s and 1970s, reaching 40% employed in the state sector in Britain. In the US, after the Vietnam war, the number of school employees overtook those in defence. From the 1970s, that harbour of mass secure employment was consistently eroded. It represented the ending of a large factory-state based working class (what are sometimes called Fordist workers or the Fordist phase of modern capitalism, of mass production systems and employment) and its replacement by smaller and more flexible production systems and employment.

More significantly, these physical environmental signs of the decline of an industrial society were reflected in major changes in the labour force itself, as it moved from a more manufacturing, or secondary sector, workforce to a more service-oriented, or tertiary sector, one. In 1960, 34% of the economically active population was employed in manufacturing in Britain, falling to 18% in 1992–93. In the north-west of England, the centre of manufacturing, the numbers fell from 1,155,000 in 1971 to 482,000 in 1997, whereas service sector employment rose from 1,332,000 to 1,799,000. These trends have been experienced in most advanced economies.

The decline of an industrial society is only half of the story. Economic prosperity, as the engine of change, has provoked the transition from an industrial to post-industrial society, from a production-oriented to more consumption-oriented one. Emerging in the 1950s, but then accelerating through our generation, it has generated a consumer society characterized by growing standardization of consumer taste and transnational corporation activities, and the complementary rise of individual choice. For the first time in history, people have the power to choose and purchase an ever-growing number of goods and services. Although sloganized as the American way of life, it represents a broader and more complex series of changes, including linkages to the rise of more permissive societies, lifestyles and cultures. It is certainly revolutionary. The fact that the Soviet Union's command economy was incapable of responding to the transition to a more service- and consumer-oriented economy was its undoing. Those who cling to old dreams and systems, whether communism, socialism or the churches, were taken so much by surprise by all these changes of modernity, that it is perhaps not surprising that they have suffered collapse or dramatic losses. 'Mass consumption is a revolutionary force.' Socialism could not beat it, nor could more conservative and dogmatic churches. Choices in sex, money and goods in Catholic Ireland, Spain and Italy are now similar to those in other developed, secularized economies. As for communism in 1989, 'history had come to an end' (Sassoon, pp. 606, 642).

A clergyman retired after 25 years service in a suburban parish. He observed how, when he arrived, people stayed in bed or went to church on a Sunday. Now, they go shopping, watch a football match, visit a DIY store or gardening centre, go away for the weekend, stay in bed or attend church. That is what it means to move from an industrial to post-industrial society.

Take the second sign of economic change, the feminization of the labour force, represented by the growing proportion of women and part-time jobs in the service sector, and the decline of full-time male manual jobs in manufacturing. Together they have generated a historic change in our experience and understanding of work from patterns set in the nineteenth century until the 1960s. Industrialization separated the place of employment from the household, with women being confined to the role of household manager, and men as breadwinners. In 1911, only 10% of British women had a recognized occupation, a position roughly replicated in the US and Western Europe (Hobsbawm, 1987, pp. 199–200). Until the 1950s, paid employment continued to be male as the norm, linked to mass production systems in great factories, and to the welfare state, a division of labour made explicit by Beveridge: 'In any measure of social policy in which regard is had to facts, the great majority of married women must be regarded as occupied on work which is vital though unpaid, without which their husbands could not do their paid work and without which the nation could not continue' (Sassoon, p. 193).

The rise of women in the workforce, particularly married women, transformed the situation. By the end of the 1990s, women constituted almost half the British labour force, supported by equal-opportunities legislation. In the United States in 1940, less than 14% of the female population represented married women at work. By 1980, the figure was over 50%. In the newly industrialized countries of South East Asia, women dominate the manufacturing sector, because they are paid less than men, and in Singapore 23% of engineering students are women.

The rise of women in the workforce connects to the other major change, the decline of full-time (male) manufacturing work and the rise of part-time, principally female, work, particularly in the service sector. In Britain, between 1951 and 1991, the number of full-time male workers dropped from 15 million to nearly 13 million, but the number of part-time male workers rose from virtually none to 1.5 million. Female full-time employment remained stable at around 6 million, but the number of female part-time workers rose dramatically from three-quarters of a million to just over 5 million. In Germany, part-time work was the fastest growing sector of the labour market at over 40%, and overwhelmingly female. It is a story of the re-entry of women into the world of production, and the entry of men into the world of supermarkets and consumption, essentially a feminization of the workforce. The consequences of such transformations are even greater, affecting our understanding of work itself. For the growing significance of part-time work generates a different view of work as a less defining activity of life. It leads to increasingly plural experiences of work within the labour market, and beyond, encompassing the unpaid work of women now linked to their paid role. 'The labour market tends to a point where no single form of work is dominant.'

The third sign of economic change is the changing role of work as definition of identity, relating to changes in employment and its connections to people's communities and organizations. The full employment policies and achievements of the post-war golden era gave way to the growth of unemployment on a major scale after the 1970s, rising to 11% in the European Union in 1993, with most commentators arguing that full employment was unlikely to return in the foreseeable future. When this is linked to dramatic transformations of the labour market, with the decline of full-time male manual work and rise of part-time female service sector work, the likelihood of a comprehensive impact on human associations becomes possible. That is precisely what has occurred. Take the classic expression of male manual working class organizations, the trade union. Across much of the Western world, it has experienced decline, dropping from over 50% of the workforce in the 1960s in Britain, to under 40%. In France, membership dropped from 22% in 1970, to 9% in 1990 (Sassoon, pp. 654–65). It adds up to the end of class alone as provider of identity. In this much more plural labour market and economy, we slip in and out of identities. In one day, we can be parent, consumer, teacher, citizen, patient, Christian. We each belong to a variety of identities and communities. The working class, or the forms of work or organizations with which it was associated, is no longer the sole definition of identity. A changing economy has many deep-seated implications, not least because it is so obviously connected to changes in all the other orders of creation.

THE POLITICAL ORDER: FROM BUTSKELLISM TO BLATCHERISM

The sixties to the nineties span a period of decisive political change in Western economies which can be characterized as the movement from more state- to more market-oriented societies. Since this was clearly linked to economic change, it reverberated across other societies. Britain and the United

States illustrate the nature and extent of the changes in a particularly focused and representative way, including the development of more plural political movements.

The early years up to the 1970s formed part of that golden age of economic growth following the end of the Second World War. It was connected in Britain to a world of secure jobs, large companies, low unemployment, relatively closed national economies and strong communities and families. It was an age of a strong interventionist corporate state, big national and local government having working alliances with large corporations and trade unions. It can be described as a moderated socialism of a welfare state, joining government management of the economy on Keynesian lines, and a burgeoning welfare state based on a generous view of entitlements. Through accelerating high personal direct taxation, welfare expenditure as income maintenance became an increasingly large part of public expenditure, and more and more people were employed by the state.

Developments in the United States paralleled the social democratic politics of Western Europe. The sixties experienced Rooseveltian reformist governments, enlarging the New Deal moderating of capitalism through income supplements and medical care for senior citizens, followed by Johnson's Great Society project to eliminate poverty by state interventionist policies. For one critic, it represented 'the Social Assistance State' displacing the 'little platoons' of voluntary bodies (Novak, p. 10). In the United States and Britain, it was an age of prosperity, of Galbraith's '*The Affluent Society*' (1958), of a consensus beyond ideologies as described in Daniel Bell's *The End of Ideology* (1960). It was what we call in Britain 'Butskellism', a corporate welfare state consensus based on a convergence between the left of the Conservative Party led by Butler, and the right of the Labour Party led by Gaitskell.

By the 1980s that consensus lay 'dead in the water, or awaits that fate' (Field, p. 11). 'The original post-war deal between labour and capital or, rather, between social democrats and conservatives, a deal which underpinned West European capitalism, was at an end' (Sassoon, p. 533). Out of those ashes arose a new consensus based on the displacement of state regulation by the free market. Distrust of the market was replaced by distrust of the state, particularly in the United States. This rise of market societies, especially as neoliberalism in the 1980s, can be characterized as the running of society as an adjunct to the market, rather than an economy embedded in social realities. It was spearheaded by the Thatcher revolution in Britain in 1979, as part of what became a bigger movement, affecting the United States, New Zealand, Australia and Canada.

Essentially, the changes replaced the Keynes–Beveridge consensus of the golden age with a market-oriented society based on a strong but controlled central state, reduced significantly in size. This was achieved through massive privatization programmes, and the replacement of a state-managed economy promoting full employment by the focus on low inflation, the erosion of the local state, the United States model of a flexible mobile low paid labour market, the greater control of public expenditure, and the reduction of personal direct taxation. The latter particularly became a central campaigning issue because of the eighties' view that people were 'taxed to death and molly-coddled into the grave' (Sassoon, p. 448). More significantly, it connected to the growing autonomy of individuals demanding consumer government. The old entitlement welfare state was increasingly unsustainable in an unremittingly competitive global economy, not simply because of spiralling costs but also because of the growing demand for greater individual choice in education, health care and pensions.

For Britain, it represented a much needed modernization of the economy, a coming to terms with post-imperialism through membership of the European Union, the beginnings of a 'genuinely modern European state at last' – 'the modern centrally directed form of society' (Boyle, p. 25). For the United States, the move to free-market neoliberalism was even starker, with a more deregulated and flexible low paid economy, and the dismantling of much of the welfare bureaucracy and taxes, climaxing in the 1996 Welfare Reform Act, with its project of breaking the cycle of dependency by providing only a minimum safety net for temporary misfortune.

The challenge facing both societies, reflecting a wider global predicament, was how to reconcile tradition and modernity, the deregulated free market economy with social cohesion, and all in the context of economic globalization. What you could not do was 'to escape the integrationist course set by the irreversible growth of global interdependence' (Sassoon, p. 343). Yet so much of economic globalization is charged with weakening traditional social institutions on which the market economy has depended, whether religion, family or other communal associations of civil society. This emerging consensus, and its new struggles to reconcile market and wider social purposes, can be called Blatcherism, symbolizing the convergence between Thatcher and Blair, and the latter's attempt to develop consensus into a 'Third Way', supported by Clinton.

The potentially more broadly based consensus of the nineties is also an indication of a more varied and fragmented political scene. For the seventies onwards have also experienced the rise, for example, of identity politics and new social movements. The former is particularly evident in the United States, based on such concerns as ethnicity, nationalism, and religious fundamentalism. It has been characterized as 'militantly nostalgic movements seeking to recover a hypothetical past age of unproblematic order and society' (Hobsbawm, 1994, p. 342). It has interesting resonances with strands in nationalist movements in Scotland, Wales, the Basque country and Belgium, and even more disturbing links to religious fundamentalist movements in

Islamic societies, tribal conflicts in Africa, and the maelstrom of what was once Yugoslavia.

The latter, new social movements, often appear as single issue campaigns around such concerns as peace, the environment, feminism, the disabled, ethnic minorities, self-help groups and, on the right of the political spectrum, against abortion and crime. Unlike dominant traditional political movements, they are not class-based and cross the left-right spectrum. Many of their concerns (particularly environmental, peace and gender issues) have been accepted by mainstream political parties; the Green Party persists as an independent force, epitomizing these pluralities and developments. In many ways, it can be argued that the Greens are 'more in tune with the rapidly developing post-Fordist Zeitgeist than the traditional parties of Left or Right' (Sassoon, pp. 676–7). That may also be reflected in the growing disenchantment of citizens with those parties, including the disturbing trend to lower turn-outs in elections. Less than 25% voted in elections to the European Parliament in Britain, and only a fraction more for the local elections in 1999.

THE ORDER OF THE FAMILY: FROM MARRIAGE TO LIVING TOGETHER

Changes in family life and personal relationships are as much examples of the fundamental transformations of this generation as those in any other sector. Indeed, because they are so intimate and integral to human living, major changes here cause greater disturbances, even though there are significant continuities of relationships through fundamental change.

Statistical profiles of radical transformations in family life become more astonishing when contained within one generation. Take marriage, traditional bedrock of society and personal relationships in social policy and Christian discipleship. In 1971, there were 459,000 marriages in the United Kingdom, but only 349,000 in 1991, and a growing proportion of these were second marriages, from 15% to 30%, and more and more were conducted outside church; in 1951, only 4% of marriages took place in a Registry Office, rising to 51% in 1979.

Divorces rose from 90,000 in 1971 to 175,000 in 1992, against a wider backcloth, in England and Wales, of 1 divorce for every 58 weddings in 1938, to a ratio of 1:2.2 in the 1980s. It was a rate only exceeded in the United States, but also an increasing occurrence in Catholic societies like Belgium, France and the Netherlands, where the divorce rate tripled between 1970 and 1989. 'Clearly something unusual was happening to Western marriage', not least the preference of a growing number of couples for cohabitation. In the 1950s, only 1% of British women cohabited with their husband before marriage. By the early 1980s, it had risen to 21%, and continues to grow.

Linked to these changes were three other developments. There was a dramatic increase in lone parent families, doubling between 1971 and 1992 to 1.4 million, representing one in five families with children, with 2.2 million dependent children. By 1991, 58% of black families in the United States were headed by single women. Children born outside marriage also showed a remarkable increase, from 6% in Britain in 1961, to 31% in 1992, and still rising, a trend occurring across the Western world, even in Catholic countries. Essentially, the classic Western model of the nuclear family, a married couple with children, was in patent retreat. In the United States, such families dropped from 44% of households to 29% (1960–80), and the same pattern is repeated in Sweden, Canada, Germany, the Netherlands and Britain.

To begin to understand these changes, two other developments are particularly informative. On the one hand, there has been a significant rise in people living alone, from 6% of households in Britain between 1900 and 1930, to over 25% in 1991, rising to half the households in some larger Western cities. On the other hand, the crisis in traditional family living was also linked to 'quite dramatic changes in the public standards governing sexual behaviour, partnership and procreation' (Hobsbawm, 1994, p. 322). Liberalization for heterosexuals, especially women, also affected homosexuals and other cultural sexual dissidence. Most Western societies have decriminalized homosexuality. Explaining these changes has not surprisingly generated heated arguments. More conservative American and British commentators have identified a correlation between high welfare expenditure, levels of divorce and children born out of wedlock. Yet this overlooks more complex issues in the changing roles of men and women in more global societies. Some have suggested that the trend to more deregulated markets has increased the pressures on families so as to provoke more marriage and family breakdowns. They point to the minimal size of the welfare state in the United States, and its greater espousal of a deregulated and mobile labour market, as more likely causes of the highest family and relationship breakdown figures in the world. Beyond these interpretations, it may well be more useful to connect these changes to the global growth in prosperity, individual choice and the privatizing of lives, and the erosion of absolute moral norms.

Yet through all these changes, the quality of human relationships has persisted. For the trend from covenantal relationships for all time to more ephemeral contractual relationships should not be regarded as signifying the absence of a serious loving and faithful commitment within relationships. Cohabitation within and between sexes, one-parent families, and remarriage as serial monogamy should be regarded as different rather than diminished relationships. For the contract culture is generating changing forms of obligations and rights, without which contractual relationships cannot be sustained. Better faithful contract than unfaithful covenant, particularly in a context of change and upheaval.

Transformations in family life have been related to equally significant developments in the place of women and young people in society. The sixties witnessed the rise, or re-emergence, of feminist movements throughout Western societies and beyond. As 'the very width of the new consciousness of femaleness' (Hobsbawm, 1994, p. 312), it was linked to the major entry of women into the labour market, supported by equal-opportunities legislation, making women less dependent on men and the household role. This still left them, of course, with the continuing problem of how to reconcile job with marriage and family. It can be argued too, that the rise of the consumer society liberated women more than men, contributing to the fact that women now 'expected more and acted accordingly' (Sassoon, p. 434). They were enabled to do so partly because of the movement of women into higher education, from around 15% in 1945 to around 50% in the 1990s in most Western societies, and partly because of the liberalizing of reproductive customs and systems. The availability of birth control, linked to a growing acceptance of sexuality as a rich human experience to be enjoyed and not just endured, combined to reinforce the changing role and nature of women in society, as part of wider demands for personal autonomy and freedom. Later feminism built on these developments by recognizing gender difference as well as equality, acknowledging the role of affirmative action as a temporary measure in order to be consistent with the primary commitment to equality. Such innovations challenged men as well as women, requiring radical changes of both, but particularly men with their increasingly uncertain role in family, relationships and employment. Any debate on the role of women in Church and society which does not connect to these transformations should be recognized as inherently defective.

The growing significance of young people should be regarded in a similar way to that of women. Demographic changes are ensuring that in the majority South, young people are becoming the dominant force in the population. This trend is confirmed and exacerbated by the rise of a youth culture, influenced by the United States, but spreading those 'marks of "modern" youth . . . in every country', particularly in terms of fashions, music, sex and drugs. Their rise as independent social agents, particularly through purchasing power, is transforming the relationship between generations, as it has between men and women. It also separates societies from their past traditions and histories when over half the population has no memory stretching back before 1960 (Hobsbawm, 1994, p. 327).

The journey, in other words, in this order of creation, is quite immense, from marriage, with the superiority of husband over wife, parents over children, senior over junior, to a plurality and greater equality of relationships, genders and ages.

THE CULTURAL ORDER: THE POST-MODERN JOURNEY FROM GRAND NARRATIVES TO PAST TIMES

Travelling from the 1960s is about more than travelling through material changes in standards of living, organizations, work and politics. Change on such a scale not surprisingly connects to changes in the way we understand life. It represents a transition from regarding the universe as ordered, harmonious, and so revealed by science and empirical proof, to scepticism with regard to the objectivity of knowledge as therefore universally accessible. It is a move from understandings of life as grand narratives which claim to explain all matters, to a plurality of competing interpretations, none of which can claim priority. It raises in profound ways, and across more and more fields of experience, issues of truth and relativism, and it is increasingly referred to as post-modernism.

We should not be surprised that this challenge to ways of interpreting reality has occurred in this generation, marked as it is by trends from more monochrome to more plural experiences. We have seen, for example, how we have moved from domination of the labour market and understanding of work by full-time male manual work, in huge plants and heavily managed, to a much greater diversity in the labour market and organizations and the rise of a more individual portfolio approach to work. The consequent erosion of class as alone providing identity, means that more and more people slip into and out of a number of identities each day. Family life, too, has undergone a transition from marriage for life to serial monogamy and a much greater variety of structured relationships between and within the sexes. Instead of one TV channel in the early 1950s, there is now a bewildering explosion of technologies and choice, with hundreds of channels accessed by pressing a button.

The arrival of large numbers of immigrants in Britain from the 1950s is the most tangible sign of these changes. Britain, and particularly its cities, now include significant ethnic minorities, mostly from the New Commonwealth and Pakistan. By 1991 they constituted 13% of Manchester's population, an indication that Britain was now irreversibly a truly and richly multicultural society. It is a phenomenon represented in most West European nations, but especially in the United States, home of Black nationalist and Black consciousness movements in the 1960s. Yet even that expression of multiculturalism is changing, and dramatically so. By 2050, Hispanic Americans are likely to be the dominant group in the population.

Given these pressures for the break-up of single universal understandings of our experiences, what are the main features of post-modernism? Arising in the 1960s in the arts, and particularly in architecture as an unstructured style, it spread to other disciplines including philosophy, history, literature and theology, especially in the 1980s, and principally through the influence of such French intellectuals as Derrida, Foucault and Lyotard. North American academic communities were particularly influenced by it. One commentator has characterized it as 'not so much a "movement" as a denial of any pre-established criteria of judgement and value . . . or indeed of the possibility of such judgements'. Across all these fields, it had 'in common an essential scepticism about the existence of an objective reality, and/or the possibility of arriving at an agreed understanding of it by rational means' (Hobsbawm, 1994, pp. 516–17). It therefore rejected world views, grand narratives or meta-narratives, for claiming too much, and settled for a plurality of incommensurable realities, a profound relativism. There was no reality out there, objectively and scientifically verifiable, demanding the commitment of all reasonable people. Not surprisingly, post-modernism challenged all those big ideas which constituted modernity, including technology and science and the world they have transformed. In such a plural context of a bewildering profusion of choices, people are pushed back to rethink the nature of self-understanding, to the consideration of our identity in order not to be overwhelmed by it. To put it in a nutshell, whenever students ask 'What's post-modernism?', I tell them to go to the shop 'Past Times' with each section dedicated to goods exemplifying a particular period in British history. Do you want to be Victorian today? Then take a piece from that shelf. Medieval tomorrow? Purchase an example from that section. Or Saxon on the next day? Different roles, different perspectives, none superior to the others, existing only through your choice and enjoyment. That's post-modernism.

Interestingly there is a growing debate over whether we are in the midst of post-modernism or a new, radicalized stage of modernity. These arguments allow us to recognize that we do live in a more fragmented world, in a plurality of experiences and interpretations of the world, with a variety of social and ethical systems. Yet to rely on that perspective alone is foolish, 'when the unity and boundedness of our planetary existence has become concrete, and more visible, than at any previous time in the history of the human race' (Boyle, p. 151). Never have we been so part of a single system, a global economy with its worldwide, integrated, financial, information, trading, manufacturing, and communication systems. The need, therefore, continues to be to find ways of relating across different cultures, religions, interpretations, experiences, and histories, even when these persisting endeavours break down, as in Kosovo. It is to recognize the reduced confidence people have in science, religion and managerialism. Yet it is also to acknowledge that we cannot manage without their insights and competencies, without some trust in abstract systems and experts in order for the world to continue. So we accept that the hegemonic claims of grand narratives are now unhelpful, yet we are prepared to develop provisional working frameworks but not with the great nineteenth-century historian Ranke's belief that historical narratives mirror exactly past reality as it actually was. For rejecting the grand or meta-narrative is not to reject the narrative form, and its ability to give us traces or fragments, and so partial accounts of past or present. It is to accept the usefulness of diverse narratives whilst rejecting the relativism of incommensurable pluralities. It leads to more broad and inclusive constructions of our experiences by listening to a growing chorus of voices as an indispensable contribution to making sense of our world, as well as recognizing globalization processes. And that broad, complex, pluralistic understanding of ourselves as well as our world will help us make more sense of our lives. For our growing awareness of what is going on, say in family life, will allow us to decide more effectively what kind of relationship to pursue. Giddens called this 'reflexivity', the need to adapt to change, to know ourselves so we can cope better, to use new ways of relating to each other, including through new technologies. 'In the individualized society the individual must therefore learn, on pain of permanent disadvantage, to conceive of himself or herself as the centre of action, as the planning office with respect to his/her own biography, abilities, orientations, relationships and so on' (Reader, 1997, p. 129).

THE RELIGIOUS ORDER: DECLINING CHURCHES AND PERSISTING RELIGION

Only the most blinkered would expect the Churches to remain untouched by such comprehensive change. Globalization, new technologies and unfettered markets have a long history of eroding traditional values, cultures and authority structures, including religions. Western Churches have been particularly damaged by such developments, certainly in Britain, and in this remarkable generation. Yet the picture, as we have seen in every other sphere of life, is more complex than that. The emergence of Black Churches, new religious movements and other faiths, and the stubborn persistence of common religion, contribute to the growing plurality of the religious scene rather than to its demise.

The effects of contemporary change have been marked by the major decline of official mainstream Churches in the West. The British experience is representative of these and wider developments. What the statistics of membership and attendance reveal is a remarkable decline in Church effectiveness in the midst of post-industrial and post-modern society. What is particularly interesting is that the decline affects every mainstream denomination, including the Roman Catholic Church. It is easier to begin with the established Church of England, whose attendances were reduced by 50% between 1960 and 1985 (Hastings, p. 603). If that is astonishing, figures for the diocese of Manchester, at the heart of historic industrialization and urbanization processes, are more calamitous, for church attendance in this diocese decreased by two thirds in only thirty years (Atherton, 1997, p. 58). Free Churches experienced similar decline, and the Roman Catholics in England and Wales now suffered the same fate as other denominations.

Between 1964 and 1976, infant baptisms dropped from 137,000 to 70,000, and in the diocese of Westminster attendance at mass dropped from 49% in 1968 to 32% in 1978. More importantly it was the same story virtually throughout the Western world. Attendance at mass in Quebec dropped from 80% to 20% in the 1960s. The widespread practice of birth control, abortion and divorce has persistently eroded the authority and attractiveness of the Roman Catholic Church in such traditional Catholic countries as Italy, Spain, Poland and now Ireland. Even in the United States, still 'a country of widespread, intense and often fundamentalist religiosity,' with 42% still attending Church services weekly, there have been 'massive losses suffered by mainstream Protestantism' (Gray, 1998, p. 126; Rieger, pp. 48, 154).

Against such a backcloth, it is not surprising some argue that the attempt to broaden and revive the flagging ecumenical movement in Britain, by involving the Roman Catholic Church for the first time in the new ecumenical organization, Churches Together, in 1990, reflects the demand for collaboration in the face of major decline. This new ecumenical consensus, remarkable as it is with the arrival of the Roman Catholics, makes too easily for uniformity and bureaucratic centralization. It 'could appear to conform so neatly with the take-over economy of post-industrial capitalism' (Hastings, p. 621). It is the opposite of that 'popular ecumenism' of evangelical Nonconformity and Anglicanism in the late eighteenth- and early nineteenth-century period of dynamic religious growth (Gilbert, p. 58).

Interestingly this generation also experienced religious newness. On the one hand, Britain lived through the arrival and growth of Black Churches, particularly in inner city communities. Unwelcomed by mainstream denominations, they reflected commitment to primacy of congregations over buildings and denominational networks, as in early Methodism. Indeed, they replaced them in many inner city areas. Again, it is important to recognize the diversity of Black Churches and Christians. There is not one Black Church. The links of Black Churches, especially Black Pentecostalism, are particularly with African religion and Black Pentecostalism in the United States. They represented Black resistance to white racism, through communal worship and Bible study, developing early signs of a Black political and indigenous theology.

On the other hand, the 1960s onwards also witnessed the arrival of other faith communities, particularly from India, Pakistan and Bangladesh. Between 1980 and 1995, the Hindu population of Britain remained virtually the same, at 400,000, but the Muslim population grew from 600,000 to 1,100,000, particularly concentrated in the inner cities. There are now more Muslims than Methodists in Britain, reflecting the involvement of Britain 'in an increasingly interconnected and mobile world' (Davie, p. 64). It symbolizes the movement from the historic challenge of intra-faith relationships between Christian denominations through the emerging ecumenical movement, to the new more global challenge of inter-faith relationships, between the great religions inhabiting this planet.

It is worth pausing to reflect on why Churches have declined so dramatically. Pre-eminently, they have shared in a crisis of the relevance of long-established patterns of thought and associations in a period of intense change. The transition from industrial to post-industrial and from modern to post-modern society has been, and continues to be, rapid and turbulent, affecting all Western societies and Churches. Any account of industrialization and urbanization will record that modernization processes have often been at best disruptive of traditional religions, and at worst hostile to them. Adjusting to an increasingly secular and plural environment has been profoundly difficult for the Churches. The drastic decline suffered in the late twentieth century can be seen as the cumulative effect of such long-term changes, accentuated by rapid and intense change in this generation which has radically affected all social, political, economic, cultural and moral traditions.

The Churches cannot remain aloof from such change. The problem is that even some of their more enlightened virtuous responses may have compounded their decline, so complex is the task of reformulating tradition in response to major change. Take the Church of England. Its periodic bursts of necessary reform may have improved its organizational effectiveness and increased its self-governing ability, vis-à-vis the state, yet the unforeseen cost has been the separation of the Church from the common life of people and society. 'There looks to be an almost inexorable law that every effective measure of Anglican pastoral reform also contributes to a narrowing in the Church's sphere of influence, as well as undermining just those institutions and observances which have hitherto provided some sort of bridge to the poorer classes' (Hastings, p. 445). Making the eucharist effectively the only service, producing synodical government which excludes the common people from participation, and moving to national and diocesan centralized self-government, represent a profound narrowing of the character of the supposedly national Church. It erodes the federal character of the Anglican ethos, and puts power in the hands of essentially unaccountable mediocre bureaucracies, narrowly elected élites, and at best an average managerialist episcopacy. The classic resort to shared ministry and training programmes can appear to spread more jobs among fewer people, but essentially in running the Church. It confirms the judgement that the periodic attempts to reform the Church appear to be linked to their failure to achieve much, particularly in terms of halting, never mind reversing, decline. It is as though the Church has never understood what has been happening to society, and therefore to the Church, since 1750. Maybe the dramatic decline in this generation is the heavy price exacted for that failure.

Once again, that is not the whole story. Alongside such decline is the remarkable survival of common religion (as private choice) and civil religion (as the function of religion in society), despite all the gloomy and false prognostications of those who argued for the imminent secularization of society. Some 71% of the British people still believe in God, even though only 15% go to church; a remarkable 70% of Americans still believe in the devil, against 33% in Britain, and 20% in France. Such high levels of belief and low levels of practice are described as the phenomenon of believing not belonging. As privatized religion, it is the most prevalent form of religiosity in Britain and Western Europe in the late twentieth century. In a more consumption-oriented society, it reflects a 'pick and mix' approach to religious belief, drifting further away from traditional Christian orthodoxies, and linking with the rise of New Age movements, and the outburst of interest in spirituality of a wider and diverse kind. It suggests that religious life is mutating rather than disappearing. Yet even this wider penumbra of believing not belonging is eroding, particularly in the younger generation. Maybe the most important issue arising from this situation is whether the dramatic declining membership of the Churches is falling below a level which will threaten the effectiveness, extent and survival of common and then civil religion. The other side to this problem is 'How far can the present structures of religious life in this country maintain themselves if increasing numbers of people in British society prefer a passive rather than an active relationship to these structures?' (Davie, p. 107).

A Sixth Order? Growing Marginalization and Disorder within Nations

Change on the scale experienced since the 1960s is invariably accompanied by turbulence, disorder and social divisions. Globalization processes are associated with growing polarization *between* nations. Britain's experience, shared with developing as well as developed economies, indicates that accelerating divisions are also occurring *within* nations. Disturbingly, Britain appears to be following the United States in terms of increasing poverty and inequalities, and the accompanying social disturbances controlled by increasing committals to penal institutions. If the global economy follows the neoliberal route advocated by many Americans, these disturbing consequences are likely to become more widespread.

Take the growth of poverty itself: although 'essentially a contested concept . . . nevertheless it is still a problem', in that however it is defined, it is invariably rising, particularly since the late 1970s (Forrester, pp. 86–7). So, between 1979 and 1992/3, the numbers in Britain with below 50% of average incomes rose from 5 million (9% of the total) to 14.4 million (25%) including 1 in 3 children. The poorest 10% have seen their real incomes actually decline. Now, one third of the population live in households drawing at least one major means-tested welfare benefit. In 1987, over a third of Manchester's entire population was dependent on Supplementary Benefits.

Developments in the United States followed similar but more extreme trends, achieving the highest poverty rate in 30 years. Of developed economies, it has the highest percentage of poor people (persons in families with adjusted incomes less than half the median) at 16.6%, with Britain at 11.7%, and Germany 4%. More than half of the poor in the United States are lone parents (mostly women), representing the increasing feminization of poverty. There are now 15 million children living in poverty, with the rate among young families in the mid-1980s standing at 39.5%, as against 23% in Britain, and 18.8% in Germany. Half of black children under six years old live below the poverty line. The United States has the worst record of major industrialized countries with regard to child mortality, life expectancy and visits to doctors. Yet it leads in politicians who talk most about family values. Advanced economies increasingly share in that shame. In 1998, 100 million lived below the official poverty line in North America, Europe, Japan and Australia, and nearly 30 million were homeless.

The problem of poverty is only made worse when it is part of accelerating inequalities. In Britain, the gap between highest and lowest paid is greater than for 50 years, but that situation is rendered more intolerable by the fact that the poorest 10% have seen their real incomes decline. In terms of those in households with below 50% of the average income, their real incomes (after housing costs) fell by 17% between 1979 and 1992/3; those on the average income saw theirs increase by 38%, and the top by 62%. Such growing divisions are part of wider processes, stretching beyond Thatcherism. Even under the socialist President Mitterrand, the rich got consistently richer, and the poor poorer.

Once again, these trends are magnified in the United States, the only advanced economy in which productivity was rising whilst the income of the majority (80%) was stagnating or falling. 'Such a growth in economic inequality is historically unprecedented.' The average weekly earnings of 80% of rank and file working Americans, adjusted for inflation, fell by 18% between 1973 and 1995. At the same time, between 1979 and 1989, the real annual pay of company chief executives rose by 19% (two-thirds after tax) (Gray, 1998; Sassoon; P. Kennedy, 1993). In 1990, such chief executives received 150 times the average worker's salary. In Japan the figure was 16 times, and in Germany 21. America's inequalities in the distribution of income and wealth now moved it out of the Western experience, and put it alongside Brazil and the Philippines. How long will civilized people put up with that? For 'what thoughtful rich people call the problem of poverty, thoughtful poor people call with equal justice the problem of riches' (Tawney, 1979, p. 112).

The emergence of an underclass, however contested a concept, symbolizes the new turbulences of this generation. It is 'as difficult to define as it is easy to recognise when confronted with it' (Field, p. 17), yet it takes us directly into many of the changes we have described, from the collapse of male manual worker jobs and full employment to the fragmentation of the old working class, from the rise of means-tested welfare benefits and their erosion of the habits of working, saving and honesty to the alarming growth of workless households from 6.5% (1975) to 19.1% (1994). It is therefore important to question Murray's argument that it is the product of the moral hazards of a universal welfare state, because America, with the poorest welfare system, has the biggest underclass, whereas the Europeans, with the largest welfare systems, have a much smaller underclass. Rather, it would be wiser to examine globalization processes too, and regard it as 'a textbook example of the manufacture of poverty by the neo-liberal state' (Gray, 1998, p. 42). It is certainly incubated in a culture of welfare dependency, yet that culture is also informed by deregulated labour markets and neoliberal welfare reforms. The United States, New Zealand and Britain, all with substantial underclasses, exemplify this creation of post-industrial poverty in global, deregulated free markets.

What is much less open to dispute is that the underclass is marginalized from effective participation in mainstream economic, social and political life and concentrated into 'settlements of the marginal, the socially problematic and welfare-dependent' (Hobsbawm, 1994, p. 309), what Galbraith has called 'centres of terror and despair', in the great industrial cities of America (and Britain), 'Hobbesian jungles' where 'wild, adolescent males, now increasingly armed' cause a 'universal fear' (Sassoon, p. 764). Yet at exactly the same time, the trend is also towards the growth of walled, 'gated and proprietary' ghettos of the wealthy, now over 10% of the population.

It should not be surprising that such 'a divided society, in which an anxious majority is wedged between an underclass that has no hope and an overclass that denies any civic obligations' (Gray, 1998, p. 111), should be associated with poverty, inequalities and social divisions, and that these should be reflected in such dislocatory indices as growing crime and imprisonment. Serious crimes in England and Wales rose from 1.6 million (1970) to 5.6 million (1992). Prison populations reveal a similar scale of increase, by over a third between 1992 and 1995, to well over 50,000. By 1999, 65,600 were incarcerated in England and Wales.

If these trends are disturbing, they are as nothing compared to the United States, a world capital for crime and incarceration. In 1993, the male murder rate was 12.4 per 100,000, compared with 1.6 for the European Union, and 0.9 for Japan. With regard to rape figures, these were 1.5 per 100,000 in Japan in 1994, and 42.8 in the United States; in the case of robbery, 1.75 cases per 100,000 in Japan, and 255.8 in the United States. Murders of children are particularly common in the United States. Nearly 75% of all such murders in the industrialized world are in the US. There are more people murdered in New

York than the Calcutta slums. Not surprisingly, these dreadful figures, a scandalous challenge to the so-called freedom to carry a gun, are reflected in the incarceration tendency of the United States. Over a million and a half of US citizens are in prison, massively more than any other advanced civilized society (four times the Canadian rate, five times the British, fourteen times the Japanese). The Californian jail population of 150,000 has grown eight times since the early 1970s, with black people seven times more likely to be imprisoned. Many suggest these trends cannot be separated from wider processes, including the free market, which are eroding the bonds of family and community; gatekeepers such as park keepers and bus conductors are being discontinued for cost-competitive reasons. All that are left as effective agents of social control are the police, lawyers and prison. In other words, 'crime of the kind that afflicts Britain and much of the post-industrial world reflects an altogether deeper malaise' (Gray, 1998, p. 31). The transition from a rehabilitative model of social justice and progressive change to a justice model where the punishment supposedly fits the crime, is another indication of these changes which reflect a society seeking to preserve a social ordering which is being undermined by wider, more global economic and social changes. They are generating, in America and now Britain, 'policies for managing the danger and policing the divisions created by a certain kind of social organization – and for preserving the political arrangements which lie at its centre' (Forrester, p. 70).

IS THAT ENOUGH? WHAT ABOUT GLOBALIZATION AND UNANSWERED QUESTIONS?

Most of the food we eat, the cars we drive and the televisions we watch are produced in different parts of the world by transnational corporations. The pensions more will rely on are based on shares traded across world stock markets 24 hours a day. Behind routine yet revolutionary experiences lie fundamental changes relating to the globalization of economic life. These in turn link to global issues of unprecedented population growth, environmental threats, and the marginalization of nations from the global economy. These great unanswered questions increasingly inform our global context.

Faced with all that, reflections on the biblical Greek word *oikonomia*, stewardship, and its two meanings illuminate and challenge these contextual processes.

First, it means managing the household by providing basic resources for sustaining all its members. From this meaning of *oikonomia* our word 'economics' is derived, but reflecting the earlier, broader concept of political economy, relating to the whole process of creating and distributing wealth.

The second meaning refers to the whole inhabited order, the ecumenical, way beyond the narrower meaning of relations between Christian denominations.

The emerging global economy. Despite the scepticism of some scholars (Gray, 1998, p. 64), the most striking development in economic life since 1945 has been the rapid globalization of economic activities, centred on market economies, 'that process through which markets and production in different countries become increasingly dependent on one another, because of the dynamic of trade in goods and services, and the movement in capital and technology' (Küng, p. 160). We all now inhabit such an increasingly integrated world economy, as well as the multiple disconnected world of postmodernism.

Essentially, globalization resulted from interactions between transnational corporations and nation states (Dicken), the latter operating increasingly in the great regional trading blocs of the European Union, the North American Free Trade Agreement, and the New Industrialized Countries of South East Asia; they control 77% of world exports and 62% of world manufactures.

Three aspects of globalization warrant particular attention. First, growing world trade, from 0.37 trillion US$ in 1950 to 3.5 trillion in 1990, accelerated particularly by the reduction of tariffs on trade, and promoted by the General Agreement on Tariffs and Trade and now the World Trade Organization (Finn, p. 17).

Second, growing world manufacturing output, from 567 in 1953 to 3041 in 1980 (base figure of 100 in 1900). Service sector growth was even greater. All in all, 'the global economy grew more since 1945 than in all world history prior to World War Two' (P. Kennedy, 1993, p. 48).

Third, the spectacular, disturbing growth of international capital markets, with the deregulation of world money markets and the high-speed electronic transfer systems ensuring global financial flows act as one. Daily foreign exchange movements amount to over $1 trillion, as against $1 billion in 1970, with 90% unrelated to trade or investments, and reflecting dramatic rises in speculation in currencies and other financial instruments. They constitute major challenges to national and international stability.

Technological improvements in transport and communications have supported globalization processes. Information technology and the integration of computers and telecommunications are at the centre of this emerging stage of the global economy's history. Such creative technological breakthroughs and their capitalization have been called the 'Genesis' factor (Landes, 1969, p. 284). As much research and development is now occurring in a year as the aggregate of all R&D up to the 1960s, and concentrated now, for example, in such areas as biotechnology and robotics. The consequences could be awesome. If biotechnology replaces land for food production, and robotics displace labour, what will that mean for human living on this planet, never mind for economics' traditional focus on the factors of production of land, labour and capital?

The demographic explosion. At the beginning of urbanization in 1798, Parson Malthus wrote *An Essay on the Principle of Population*, addressing the central problem of the relationship between increasing populations and the resources needed to sustain them, particularly if the former outran the latter. For the balance could only be restored by natural disaster or war, or by restraint of family size. He was right to be disturbed, because Europe was experiencing dramatic population explosions which have accelerated globally ever since. What should give us sleepless nights is the return of Malthus' spectre of famine, disease and war as world population increases beyond resources and the environment for supporting it. We are experiencing demographic explosions unparalleled in human history. Take the figures:

- in 1825, it had taken all human history to reach one billion people;
- in 1925, it rose to two billion;
- in 1976, to four billion;
- in 1999, to six billion; and
- it is likely to reach 8.5 billion by 2025.

These dramatic figures have far-reaching implications.

First, the population explosion is occurring in the poor South, with over 50% of people likely to be under fifteen years old in many countries, in contrast to the greying Northerly populations.

Second, world population is moving from rural to urban locations, so that by 2025, over 57% will live in cities. Many in the South will be 'centres of poverty and social collapse', overwhelmed by the concentration of people (P. Kennedy, 1993, p. 26). For the first time since the Stone Age, peasants will be a minority population.

Third, extraordinary population imbalance between North and South, with resources in the North and population growth without resources in the South, will result in:

- unrest in the South, with unstable societies, with a majority of young people with unrealizable expectations;
- migrations from South to North: ' "people now, even if they are very poor, know how people live in other parts of the world," and will attempt to get there, by land, sea or air';
- inordinate pressure on resources and environment to deliver food, education and health care which 'cannot be sustained with our current patterns and levels of consumption';
- a change in the balance of power, for will those Western values of democracy, market economy, human rights, and liberal social culture, maintain their position in the world if it is increasingly peopled by

societies which 'did not experience the rational, scientific and liberal assumptions of the Enlightenment'? (P. Kennedy, 1993, pp. 45, 36, 46).

Threatening creation. Our planet is enclosed by a 'thin film of life . . . entire and interconnected' (P. Kennedy, 1993, p. 96), and consequently is a closed system thermodynamically, profoundly interrelated, with a self-sustaining cycle of life. Damage done to any parts affects all. Natural impairments have occurred throughout earth history, but since the industrial revolution, and especially since 1945, the extent of damage has been so great as to be cumulatively different. Between 1950 and 1990, world population doubled and economic activity quadrupled, putting enormous pressure on the environment. The North bears most responsibility for this situation, yet developing economies are increasingly contributing to it. Between 1950 and 1990, the world lost:

* 20% of tropical rain forests, including 75% of the biggest, in South America;
* 20% of the topsoil from its croplands through overgrazing and soil erosion;
* vast numbers of species, with 50% from the richest South American rain forests.

All this has occurred in a generation and, given population projections, worse may come, with pressures from greenhouse effects of global warming, and depletion of ozone in the earth's atmosphere (P. Kennedy, 1993, p. 98; Hobsbawm, 1994, p. 569). The challenge is how to change lifestyles and short-term political visions in the North, and improve standards of living for the poorest nations without making large areas of the world uninhabitable.

Marginalization in the global economy: 'the greatest single problem and danger facing the world of the Third Millennium' (Landes, 1998, p. xx). Trends to a global integrated economy are clear and irreversible. Yet they have been accompanied by increasing marginalization between nations, as well as within them.

Once again, changes since 1945 have been decisive. Conceptually, the collapse of command economies in 1989 ended the usefulness of the division into First, Second and Third Worlds. Even by 1970, the Third World was 'demonstrably no longer a single entity', encompassing Papua New Guinea and the oil rich countries (Hobsbawm, 1994, p. 361). Empirically, too, the difference between rich and poor nations has accelerated dramatically since the 1970s, particularly in terms of international debt.

These disturbing trends are reflected in the characteristics and causes of globalization. For example, the share of the least developed countries in investment fell from 4% to 1% between 1980 and 1990. 'Businessmen know to go elsewhere.'

Similar patterns occurred in the share of the poorest nations in world trade, overdependent on price vulnerable primary commodities; it has fallen by 50% in the last 25 years.

It all ensures that the gap between the richest and poorest 20% grew, between 1960 and 1990, from a ratio of 30:1 to 60:1. Movements to global integration are not simply about progress: 'clocks go backward as well as forward' in our world (Landes, 1998, p. 507).

Inevitably, processes of dramatic change are accompanied by such divisions, and these invariably link to great turbulence, from civil wars to the massive displacement of people, with 27 million refugees in Africa alone.

The cumulative effect of trends to a global economy and growing inequalities represent 'a large part of the world . . . dropping out of the world economy' (Hobsbawm, 1994, p. 424). It is a rejection of the biblical stewardship principle of *oikonomia*, of household and economy including the whole inhabited world.

Now it is within these processes of marginalization that the issue of international debt is prominent, particularly in the poorest nations of sub-Saharan Africa, 'the Third World's Third World' (P. Kennedy, 1993, p. 211), the only region where poverty is expected to increase in the next 10 years. With a population of 450 million, doubling every 22 years, its GDP was less than Belgium's with 11 million. Its share of world manufacturing trade, a key modernization indicator, fell from 0.4% in 1965 to 0.2% in 1986. It has experienced a marked increase in signs of decay, from crumbling infrastructures to disintegrating communications. It is an area of profound political instability, and its investment in human resources is totally inadequate. All Africa has only 53 scientists and engineers per million of population, compared to Europe's 1,632 and the United States 2,685.

It is these marginalized nations which are also sinking beneath the burden of unpayable debt. The whole of sub-Saharan Africa now owes more than it produces. It is the servicing of that debt which now absorbs more than their investment in education and health care. Uganda, suffering an AIDS pandemic, spends $2.50 per person on health care (an AIDS test costs $2), yet pays out $30 per person in debt repayments. It means that the poorest in Africa transfer $10 billion in debt repayments to rich world creditors.

In all those ways, the scale of the poorest nations' debt confirms and accentuates the paradox of globalization and marginalization. It reduces the poorest to abject poverty, yet ensures that the already inadequate resources of these countries are drained away to the wealthiest nations. It becomes a stark account of marginalization, poverty and injustice, a supreme challenge of and to globalization.

3 Changing World: Oneness Through Multiplicity

The causes of the wealth and poverty of nations – the grand object of all enquiries in Political Economy. (Thomas Malthus, 1817)

Occasionally, a few words say it all. The title of a great biography of John Wesley by Henry Rack, *Reasonable Enthusiast*, does precisely that; it summarizes key, often contradictory, features of a person's life; it captures attention through words which gain power because they reflect complex realities as well as provoke the imagination. So it is with Malthus' few words, written to the economist Ricardo, in 1817. They summarize the historic task facing civilized people. Yet, as always, the more we probe into a great life or issue, the more we realize that there is 'more to it than meets the eye'. We encounter a multiplicity of strands underlying and informing the simple features to which an argument or interpretation can be reduced. The nature of our emerging global context will make uncovering and facing up to those complexities an indispensable obligation, if, for example, we are to reduce the growing marginalization between and within nations. Responding effectively to contemporary change by a better understanding of it will therefore mean probing into the economic nature of globalization processes, particularly through their histories, yet it will also involve enquiring into complementary political processes. We will then observe how, on the one hand, economic integration is built on immense variety, and on the other hand, how bipolar politics have developed into multipolar practices. These progressions in themselves will challenge any idea that humanity has somehow arrived at its destination, or can do so. Fukuyama's thesis that we have reached 'The End of History' has to be set in that critical context, as have the often millenarian utopian dreams of liberation theology. Handling coherences in and through multiplicities will be shown to affect even our ways of understanding and structuring the universe. Through all these perspectives on our context, this chapter will therefore draw out important themes for our argument. It will do so by reflecting on what has happened and is happening in our world. It will seek, in other words, to discern the signs of the times through exploring trends which have been revealed in our analysis and the development of Malthus' commitment to enquire into 'the causes of the wealth and poverty of nations'. Responding to such change will mean, as it always has in the last 200 years, 'altering one's own social priorities, educational system, patterns of consumption and saving, even basic beliefs, about the relationship between the individual and society' (P. Kennedy, 1993, p. 17).

ECONOMIC GLOBALIZATION AND GROWTH AS INTEGRATION, DIFFERENTIATION AND MARGINALIZATION

The dominant feature of our world today, the globalization of economic activities, is the story of the growing integration of trade, manufacturing, services and finance. It is a long, complex series of stories, beginning in the late eighteenth century in Britain, and exhibiting a number of characteristics. Examining them reveals, for example, movement from economic activities confined initially to European localities, to their practice on a global scale, increasingly in an integrated form, yet including great variety within these forms. A brief enquiry into economic growth, the main engine of industrialization and urbanization, will also reveal its multicausal nature. As the decisive factor behind the winners and losers in our world, it leads naturally into a reflection on marginalization processes, but again revealing its complex nature. It is as though whichever perspective on economic globalization we explore uncovers differentiation in relation to integration.

From Eurocentric to polycentric

Take the turbulent transformation of economic activities from local and closed to universal and open neighbourhoods, in the movement from European to global context. The industrial revolution began in Britain and north-west Europe, and was 'almost inconceivable in any form other than the triumph of a bourgeois-liberal capitalism' (Hobsbawm, 1962, p. 14). A variety of factors contributed to the emergence of modernity in this location, including economic and technological advances, supportive political institutions, intellectual liberty, and the interaction of climate, geography and social structures. Yet processes which began this momentous series of changes inevitably drove the revolution worldwide. Without wider and wider markets it could not thrive. Between 1780 and 1840, the international trade of the West increased threefold. That has been the trend ever since, but now on a global scale, transforming the globe 'from a geographical expression into a constant operational reality' (Hobsbawm, 1975, p. 63). Yet that globalization is not simply a universalizing theme. It is about movement from Eurocentric to polycentric world, with increasing participation by Japan, South East Asia, China, and Latin America in the global economy. From now on history becomes world history but as profusion of narratives and sub-narratives. 'The inexorable growth of a world market does not advance a universal civilization.

It makes the interpenetration of cultures an irreversible global condition' (Gray, 1998, p. 193).

The transition from local to world economy is even more powerfully demonstrated through communication revolutions, beginning with road and canal improvements, through rail across continents, steamers reducing to days journeys which had taken months if not years, submarine cables under the oceans, and the internal combustion engine and aeroplane, to space travel and instantaneous communications across the world and beyond through telecommunications, all forging the globe into a single economy. It is a remarkable journey from people living, making, growing, trading and dying in the village in which they were born, to the late 1980s when Spain welcomed over 54 million foreign tourists a year. In the eighteenth century, travellers from London could reach Leith, Scotland, more quickly by sea than they could villages in Norfolk by road. Yet only one hundred years later, the advent of the electric telegraph meant that in 1871 the result of the Derby horse race in England was known in Calcutta, India, in five minutes (Hobsbawm, 1975, pp. 55, 76). It all generated a world economy as single interlocking complex. Yet global functions of modern communication technologies have also given access and support to individuals, their concerns and cultures. The Internet and digital TV are about diffusion as well as integration, about a geographically smaller yet more diverse world.

The complexity of economic growth

Economic growth is now essential for human survival. Despite historic and undoubted problems, without it the demographic explosion will become a demographic catastrophe, a Black Death of the twenty-first century, involving not millions but billions. If we do not use increasingly productive technologies to generate higher incomes, we shall stay poor. Economic growth is a complex reality; it certainly has an elegant coherence, yet only through the intricacies of a variety of interconnections. Because they are so decisive for human living, some understanding of them will contribute to reordering our understanding in ways which are already occurring and must continue to occur. Reflection will reveal both cause and effect – realities which have multiple causes, yet conforming to certain basic rules which therefore stand in critical judgement on worthy but misguided projects for tackling economic problems. That will therefore lead us into considering how we begin to face up to the marginalization of nations.

Economic growth is about both cause and effect. Between the 1950s and the 1990s the unparalleled increase in trade and growth was linked to the liberalization of trade by, for example, the reduction or removal of tariffs. Yet equally, that economic growth also generated the liberalization of trade. Similarly, the rise of large populations, with increasing incomes, developed into the growing demands of mass consumption which led to introducing mass production as a feasible and profitable system. Yet equally, that system also generated habits of mass consumption, illustrating the synergy of economic growth processes: 'we are dealing at the very least with something that is effect as well as cause'. Our approach to understanding economic processes must, from now on, like history, abhor 'simple cause and effect'. 'Certainly in the economic sphere, significant changes are almost invariably the resultant of a mutually sustaining conjuncture of factors, so that most variables are at once both cause and effect, independent and dependent' (Landes, 1969, p. 513). Yet it is even more complex and intricate, for linkages between cause and effect move backwards and forwards.

Take the central role played by technological advance in the processes of economic growth. We have observed how clusters of innovations have continued to lead to new stages of the industrial revolution. Initially, in the textile industry, human skills were replaced by machines, and animate by inanimate power. Those operations led, through an intricate history of changes, adaptation and diffusion, to contemporary breakthroughs in information technology and robotics. Technological innovations stimulate investment, with change being built into the system itself.

Take the much abused car, an invention which played a critical role similar to rail in economic growth, through, for example, the assembly line and its dependence on interchangeable parts and precision engineering, and the consequent reduction in costs, making the car accessible to ordinary people, to mass markets. In 1908, the model T Ford sold at $1,000, and in 1924, $300. By 1926, 15 million had been sold. In Britain, in 1905, registered cars numbered 32,000, and by 1938, 3,422,000. In the United States, 79,000 in 1905, rising to 29,443,000 in 1938. Their manufacture involved the production of steel, components and fuel; it provided work for mechanics and other services, and prompted capital investment in roads and bridges, and new developments in metallurgy, chemicals, and engineering. No wonder an eminent contemporary economic historian has judged that 'no other product yielded such a rich harvest of forward and backward linkages' (Landes, 1969, p. 443). Both technology and economic growth are continually changing. They are not self-exhausting processes, heading to new points of rest. They are characterized by recurring long waves of growth, pause, and more growth.

Economic growth is also a multicausal reality. The emergence of the industrial revolution in Britain was associated with widening the domestic market through improving incomes and extension into foreign markets; increasing specialization of productive functions, particularly in textiles and engineering; the growing division of labour, and a series of technological innovations. These factors in turn reflected the importance, on the one hand, of such institutional and material arrangements as government actively supportive of enterprise and trading, protection and promotion of private property, a domestic market unrestricted by local tariff systems, and the availability of coal, iron, power, and wool. On the other hand, it also reflected the growing significance of such human elements as entrepreneurial initiative and scientific knowledge. In other words, cultural factors are of immense importance in the history and contemporary development of economic growth, yet material and institutional factors also play an indispensable part. 'Economic analysis cherishes the illusion that one good reason should be enough, but the determinants of complex processes are invariably plural and interrelated. Monocausal explanations will not work' (Landes, 1998, p. 517).

Despite complexities economic growth generates cohesion, including certain rules, though there is no one path to economic growth. One such rule would be that to enjoy more later, requires first savings or capital accumulations for investment. Another would be that growth is most rapid when resources are allocated to areas of highest return. Both are painful rules; for example, directing resources to certain areas takes them away from other areas, which may then decline and gradually disappear. Thus when resources were transferred to mechanized weaving in factories, handloom weaving was displaced and eventually destroyed, with all the pain and upheaval that caused. Schumpeter referred to it as the creative destruction feature of capitalism. If these basic rules are ignored, the cost to people and communities is ultimately greater. So, in more authoritarian societies, resources are allocated on ideological grounds, whether nationalist, political or religious. The laws of supply and demand are ignored. And the role of ideology tends to increase with the backwardness of a society. It is such lessons of economic growth which should lead us to avoid the single answers of more ideologically based systems, to avoid simple universal remedies for complex problems. We are being driven to recognize (maybe reluctantly, because many harbour a sneaking admiration for them) that 'all proposals of panaceas are in a class with millenarian dreams' (Landes, 1998, p. xx). There is no evidence from history to suggest such diversions will engage effectively the questions we have identified in our global context. This judgement relates to three important but defective alternatives.

First, the argument for an ideologically controlled economy often relates to the restriction of growth for non-economic purposes. Medieval guilds were collective monopolies based on rural economies, and consequently dominated by a profound sense of the limited nature of resources in land or customs. It was essentially a zero-sum game, you gain I lose, so you cannot expand by taking on more apprentices than allocated, or by charging lower prices than your competitors. The moral order therefore took priority over the commercial. If you worked conscientiously, you were entitled to a living, never mind what the market or consumers wanted or deserved. One reason why the industrial revolution occurred in England and not Italy is that for generations, if not centuries, English merchants had moved their production increasingly from the guild-controlled towns to the countryside, through a system of out-workers. Systems regulated by non-economic criteria, however noble, do not produce the growth necessary to meet the basic needs of growing populations, never mind increasingly varied needs. It is the way of some fundamentalist religions, like some branches of Islam and the environmental movement, of political religions like communism, and those new developments in Christianity, like radical orthodoxy, which essentially seek to return to a medieval system (Long).

Second, linked to these arguments are earlier but equally deceptive views of one of the founding political economists, Thomas Malthus. Early signs of a historic and dramatic rise in population in Britain were already evident in 1798. Malthus' concern was that the demographic rate of increase would far outstrip the ability to resource it, in terms of food, clothing and housing. That problem of scarcity developed into the central problem of economics. In one major way, he was right. The world was on course for a startling unbroken rise in population. But his other premise was profoundly inaccurate, because it failed to allow for the 'built-in upward spiral of economic growth and technological advance' (P. Kennedy, 1993, p. 9), which produced more and more goods and services required to sustain the growing population. In nineteenth-century Britain, population increased fourfold but national product fourteenfold. In other words, 'both the economy and knowledge were growing fast enough to generate a continuing flow of investment and technological innovation, a flow that lifted beyond visible limits the ceiling of Malthus' positive checks'. That trend in economic growth has continued, and will continue, not least because of the dynamic nature of modern technological change. To hold that back, or try to reverse it, as some argue, will mean the return of Malthus' nightmare. Even more, it is to ignore the human drive for knowledge, with all its dangers, described in the story of Adam and Eve's expulsion from the garden because they ate of the fruit of the tree of knowledge. What we need to remember about that narrative is that they retained the knowledge in their expulsion. 'In sum, the myths warn us that the wrestling and exploitation of knowledge are perilous acts, but that man must know and will know, and once knowing, will not forget' (Landes, 1969, pp. 41, 555). Dr Johnson was right: 'all the business of the world is to be done in a new way' (Landes, 1998, p. 192).

The final defective analysis of economic processes relates to the argument that economic growth is generated by a rich centre or core exploiting outer surrounding markets. As the dependency theory, originating in the early twentieth century through the work of Lenin and Hobson, it has been used to explain the relationship between First and Third Worlds as primarily and disturbingly one of dependency manufactured by the rich capitalist nations for their benefit and therefore for the disadvantage of the poorer nations. It is an argument particularly promoted in Latin America and the West by liberation theology (Northcott). However, by focusing on one explanation, which clearly possesses some legitimacy, it overlooks the complex mosaic of reasons why some nations are rich and some are poor, why South America has had such sluggish growth and North America has grown so quickly. Because of that analytical deficiency, one commentator wryly noted that 'Latin America's most successful export' is the dependency theory. That is 'bad for effort and morale. By fostering a morbid propensity to find fault with everyone but oneself, they promote economic impotence. Even if they were true, it would be better to stow them' (Landes, 1998, p. 328). The problem with the dependency theory is that at the height of imperialist expansion in the late nineteenth and early twentieth centuries, which provoked and inspired the theory, it was not even accurate as a monocausal explanation of economic growth. Between 1876 and 1914, eleven million square miles were annexed by colonial powers. Yet even in 1914, the industrial powers were still each others' best customers by far. And that is still the case, with most trade occurring within and between the three great regional blocs and transnational corporations.

Taking account of the complex nature of economic growth does not simply challenge the accuracy and therefore value of alternative panaceas. It also reminds us that the concern for a different order is itself rooted in profoundly empirical reality, the marginalization of peoples and nations from the processes of globalization and economic growth. That interaction is the great paradox: 'the Industrial Revolution brought the world closer together, made it smaller and more homogenous. But the same revolution fragmented the globe by estranging winners and losers. It begat multiple worlds' (Landes, 1998, p. 195). Even that polarizing of rich and poor worlds, First and Third, no longer conveys the complex plural nature of global marginalization. Addressing the problem is therefore likely to involve taking seriously lessons we are beginning to learn from reflecting on stories of economic growth.

Divisions between economic winners and losers can be traced back into the history of industrialization. Even from the mid-nineteenth century, divisions were clear, substantial and widening. We were dealing 'not so much with a single world, as with two sectors combined together in one global system: the developing and the lagging, the dominant and the dependent, the rich and the poor.' By 1880, the per capita income of the developed world was twice the Third World's, having been reasonably close only 200 years before (1:1.8). By 1913 the gap had trebled, and by 1970 it was over seven times as large (Hobsbawm, 1987, pp. 15–16).

The argument that the problem of the poor nations is caused by oppressive policies of the rich, although ignoring the complexity of marginalization processes, does rightly acknowledge that, among other things, 'the two phenomena are not unconnected with each other' (Hobsbawm, 1962, p. 220). But that recognition has to be put alongside wider understandings of the complexity of economic growth itself. Even the concept of Third (poor) World no longer matches the plural character of these divisions. For the Third World includes such varied performances as the astonishing growth of the South East Asian economies, the very mixed fortunes of South America, and the regression of Burma and most of Africa, a 'diversity of outcomes' revealing that 'colonization in itself . . . does not dictate failure'.

All these accounts reinforce the obligation to learn from the analysis of economic growth in order to address more effectively the processes of marginalization. For example, the multicausal nature of economic growth includes contributions of technology, capital, equipment, company formation, banking systems, communications, attitudes, education, skills, institutions, views of property and law, civil service, and work ethic. Increasing productive outcomes and incomes, so that population growth begins to be moderated, relies on combinations of such factors. If you don't pass through an industrial revolution, then poverty accompanies increasing populations. The task is to break the vicious circle by moving into a pattern of self-sustaining economic growth. The South East Asian nations have done that through a cluster of policies and practices, including education, savings, political stability, commitment to exports, and cultural attitudes. Sub-Saharan Africa has not done so, and is poor. Yet even oil rich Middle Eastern nations cannot compete with the South East Asian ones. The former are under authoritarian regimes which subordinate economics to politics. They have not promoted informed and capable workforces; new technologies and ideas are often mistrusted because they are Western, Christian or heretical; the contributions of knowledge and women are neglected. For example, the support and resourcing of the status and role of women is increasingly acknowledged as 'the best clue to a nation's growth and development potential'. Cultural factors are just as effective in promoting economic growth as more material factors. It is confirmation that, both for people and for nations, 'at bottom, no empowerment is so effective as self-empowerment' (Landes, 1998, pp. 433, 413, 523) – provided it is part of a whole series of other cultural and material factors.

THE POLITICS OF GLOBALIZATION: FROM BIPOLAR TO MULTIPOLAR

Much attention has rightly been devoted to an examination of the world's economic life. Yet we need to remember that modernity begins with two revolutions: the industrial in Britain in the late eighteenth century, and the political in France in 1789. They are a testament to the historic importance of the political as well as economic order of creation, and they are an intimate part of the contemporary thesis, to be examined shortly, that we have reached the end of history. That journey has a profoundly political character in the twentieth century, focused on domination of the world by the struggle between two great powers or empires. The historic change symbolized by the collapse in 1989 of one of those empires, the Soviet Union, signalled the transition from that bipolar world to a multipolar one. Living with that is just as disturbing and challenging as, but very different from, previous struggles.

The 'short twentieth century' was overshadowed by 'a duel between the forces of two rival social systems' (Hobsbawm, 1994, p. 56), between capitalism and socialism, liberal democracy and communism, the United States and the Soviet Union and their satellite states. The conflict prophesied at the height of British world domination by de Tocqueville in 1835 as 'marked out by the will of Heaven to sway the destinies of half the globe' had arrived (Tocqueville, p. 452). In doing so, it evolved through two stages: the coming of a bipolar world, from 1900 to 1950, and then the Cold War, from 1943 to 1989. It was the latter which saw 'the division of the globe, or a large part of it, into two zones of influence, negotiated in 1944–5', an uneasy balance of power conveying a certain important stability.

The two opposing empires are of continuing significance, despite the collapse of one in 1989. Capitalism is the dominant exclusive influence on globalization after 1989, while socialism remains the paradigm of alternative dreams, providing an object lesson in the strengths but more importantly the limitations of countermovements. Much attention in our argument has been directed to the global market economy focused on the United States, the principal engine of globalization. In 1945, it possessed 50% of world manufacturing production and shipping, and, despite suffering relative economic decline since then, it remains the major world economic force. Yet a bipolar world rightly requires proper recognition of the other dominant force in world politics for most of this century, not least because it inspired, and continues to inspire, radical Christian traditions from Christian Socialism to liberation theology.

The Soviet Union erupted on the world through the Russian revolution of 1917, but particularly after 1945, as the 'historically predestined alternative to bourgeois and capitalist society' (Hobsbawm, 1994, pp. 169, 7). At its height, it included a sixth of the world's land surface and one third of its population, spreading through Central and Eastern Europe, Yugoslavia, China, North Korea, Cambodia and Third World countries attracted by the opportunity offered by decolonialization to promote planned economies. The sheer extent of that empire generated much of its power and distinctiveness, crossing continents, nations and religions in ways which dwarfed the French Revolution. Most significantly, it incorporated and addressed First and Third World aspirations for liberation through alternative models to capitalism. 'The crucial fact that Russia straddled the worlds of the conquerors and the victims, the advanced and the backward, gave its revolution a vast potential resonance in both' (Hobsbawm, 1987, p. 300).

As really existing socialism, as actualized dream, for those nations and for

many others, it was characterized by control of political, economic and cultural life by a single party, rigid restraint of movement, and isolation from the
capitalist world commercially (two thirds of its trade was internal in the
1960s) and through the Cold War. Yet its achievements were breathtaking in
literacy, education, health, housing, pensions and the economy, although the
fundamental defects of the latter became more and more apparent from the
late 1970s. Despite Stalinism's appalling inhumanity, it gave the world an
alternative route to modernization through coercive central state planning. It
offered a way of engaging change through change. That was its attraction for
Third World and theologians: 'Nobody else within sight offered both to
interpret the world and to change it, or looked better able to do so.' It was a
profoundly apocalyptic vision, but actualized through industrialization and
urbanization, the central forces of modernity, offering 'the hope of the millennium the guarantee of science and historic inevitability'. Yet therein lay its
downfall, for a one-party political system, with a central planned economy
and culture subordinated to the party, was an imposed unitary panacea con-
tradicting the trends to complexity and plurality which characterize modern
economic growth. 'In regimes where politics was so obviously in control,
no sharp line between political and economic development can be drawn'
(Hobsbawm, 1994, pp. 75, 72, 397). The pretensions of an aggrandizing hegemonic politics are as dangerous for the contemporary human project as
neoliberal free market economics. It is a lesson of equal importance for
attempts to reimpose theology on the world as queen of the sciences, or politi-
cize it as liberation theology.

So there are the two empires of capitalism and socialist alternative, the
embodiment of bipolar politics in the twentieth century. Reflecting on that
relationship reveals characteristics which only gain in significance when con-
trasted with the multipolar world of today. As the binary opposites of capitalism and communism, they portray a Manichaean politics of good against evil,
reminiscent of previous religious wars. They suggest that bipolar classification of Enlightenment, achieved by two of its successor regimes, into civilized
against barbarian, the West versus the rest, the clash of civilizations evoked in
Samuel Huntington's thesis. Even for the liberal John F. Kennedy in 1960,
'the enemy is the communist system itself . . . implacable, insatiable, unceas-
ing in its drive for world domination . . . This is not a struggle for supremacy
of arms alone. It is also a struggle for supremacy between two conflicting ideologies: freedom under God versus ruthless, godless tyranny.'

Yet the conflict was also a Cold War for forty years; it did achieve a balance
of power between two opposing interests and not just between two hard ideologies. It was never simply a life–or–death struggle, but increasingly 'the politics of mutual intransigence' which do not imply 'the daily danger of war'
(Hobsbawm, 1994, p. 231). It therefore confirms, but now politically, the
growing irrelevance of zero–sum interpretations, where gain by one can only

be at the other's expense, particularly as the politics of total victory or defeat. After the total war of 1939–45, nuclear weapons on a mass scale removed that option for any project assuming the survival of the human race. The multipolar world of the late twentieth century confirmed and extended that extension of balance of power to interests, and movement away from zero-sum interpretations.

By 1989, the replacement of bipolar by multipolar politics was finally accomplished with the fall of the Soviet empire. Within less than five years, only North Korea and Cuba had command economies. It was the end of a process of erosion, to which a variety of factors contributed. The collapse of command economies because of inherent structural deficiencies, particularly economic and political, was highlighted and exacerbated by growing contact with the West from the late 1970s. It was a formative example of the achievement of change by communication or dialogue between systems. However, 1989 did not simply bring to an end the first great experiment in 'actually existing socialism', but also the socialist project itself as a realistic alternative to capitalism. As early as 1979, the leader of the Italian Communist Party, Enrico Berlinguer, acknowledged that 'we must accept that the phase of socialist development which began with the October Revolution has exhausted its driving force' (Sassoon, p. 730). Although it eventually collapsed, moderate Eurocommunism, and current reformulations of socialism as social democracy, represent important attempts to create new radical movements out of the ashes of the old. Other contributors to the erosion of the Soviet system and development of multipolar politics included heroic policies of détente, the Ostpolitik promoted by Brandt in West Germany. The rise of the non-aligned movement, led by India, Yugoslavia and Egypt and other Third World states, also played its part in the growing 'political fragmentation of the globe'. The relative economic decline of the United States, her defeat in Vietnam and the rise of the European Union were also linked to the gradual 'fissuring of the bipolar world' (P. Kennedy, 1989, pp. 505, 509).

What emerged finally and decisively after 1989 was therefore a profoundly plural polycentric world, with global economic power distributed between the United States, Japan and South East Asia, China, and the European Union. In such a complex world, no one superpower could rule alone. In 1994, Singapore defied the United States' request to cancel the penalty of six strokes of the cane for Michael Fay, an American citizen, for using graffiti to deface a public place. Under strong pressure, including an appeal by President Clinton, they reduced it to four strokes! It is in this sense that global politics is now as much concerned with balancing interests as well as power within and between major interest blocs. The old politics of North against South, West against East, rich against poor, no longer capture the complexities of a multiplicity of economic and political forms, religions and cultures. The search for solutions out of the old dichotomies of left or right, of capitalism or communism, as mutually exclusive positions, seems almost irrelevant.

The transition from bipolar to multipolar does not mean the removal of turbulence. The possible ending of zero-sum politics and conflicts, and of the security of the Cold War, has produced a more messy world characterized by local wars and conflicts. The proliferation of nuclear weapons has added to that new global uncertainty. With the collapse of the only feasible alternative to the global market economy, some have expressed a very different anxiety with regard to the threat of 'the world's last great Enlightenment regime, the United States' (Gray, 1998, p. 2), to impose a neoliberal free market on the global economy. Yet the waning of American power is more likely to confirm the emerging multipolar situation with its demand for new ways of holding together a wide variety of understandings, rather than the simple reconciling of opposites. That is the principal lesson of political globalization.

The Global Market Economy as the End of History?

The ways in which the two great systems of communism and capitalism responded to change in the late 1980s provide a paradigm for facing up to the contemporary context. Among other things, the latter explodes the provocative theory that the triumph of liberal democratic capitalism is the end of history, that command economies, with their systemic inflexibilities, ceased to exist, whereas the more dynamic market economies did not simply survive, but dominated the global economy. For Fukuyama, that victory was 'the triumph of the Western idea', the end of the ideological conflict of the Cold War. The dominance of a liberal democratic capitalism now became the 'project of a universal civilization in what is likely to be its final form' (Gray, 1998, pp. 120, 3), the grand narrative of a global free market economy. All that could happen in the future would be simply variations on that one theme. It was the ultimate synthesis, with no more antitheses. It was 'the end of history'. Yet those very processes of global economic growth, including centrally as the market economy, demonstrate the profound inadequacy of that thesis. For they reflect the continuing need for change and what that means for the invariably changing nature of capitalism. They confirm the need to persist with history as continuing narratives of change.

Writing the obituary of capitalism has been a persisting endeavour. The theologian V. A. Demant, after the landslide victory of the Labour Party in Britain in 1945 and the triumphant spread of communism in the world, proceeded to write *Religion and the Decline of Capitalism*. In 1979, after twenty-five years of the fastest economic growth in history, R. H. Preston had to revisit the issue, with his *Religion and the Persistence of Capitalism*. And so the rumours of the imminent demise of capitalism have continued through the Stock Exchange crisis of 1987 to the South East Asian turmoil of 1997. That death has not occurred has been due significantly to capitalism's ability to adapt to change. So the Keynesian reforms of the 1930s and 1940s helped to overcome the endemic unemployment of the interwar years. Effective responses to 'system-endangering' crises exhibit this dynamic character of the market economy, driven by the engine of economic growth itself (Hobsbawm, 1994, p. 87). It is as though recurrent crises in capitalism and in the wider context are 'mechanisms which enable capitalism to restructure itself' (Sassoon, p. 592). What is not clear is whether it can similarly respond to the global challenges of population, environment, financial turmoil and marginalization. Their sheer scale illustrates two problems for the global market economy. On the one hand, the tradition of orderly change in advanced economies could be threatened. After the revolutions of 1848, 'there was to be no general social revolution . . . in the "advanced" countries of the world' (Hobsbawm, 1975, p. 14). The 'ending' of history in 1989 did not bring peace but local wars, the return of old conflicts based on ethnicity, religion, economics and territory, yet these were in more marginal and underdeveloped nations. The risk is that the size of the problems could now overwhelm the advanced economies, given the intimacy of globalization, and generate revolutionary change.

On the other hand, great contemporary challenges only reinforce the inherent inadequacies of the free market, that it cannot deal effectively with every problem in life, and that when it tries to do so, the consequences can be extremely damaging to human and environmental well-being. Historically, spaces left by the market economy have been filled by traditional and socialist countermovements. Their contemporary persistence, for example as religious fundamentalism, is powerful reminder of their tenacity. Even the death of 'actually existing socialism' in 1989 may not necessarily be the end of the socialist dream. We cannot tell what will be the verdict of posterity. Their replacement by New Social Movements from the 1960s only confirms the continuing presence of the great gaps in the capitalist project which others have filled. Women, peace, racism, poverty and environment, the great concerns of the New Social Movements, are hardly modest omissions! They certainly suggest that the end of history has not been achieved at all as long as such changes are generated from outside the market economy. They underline the profound changes experienced in this generation, but even more so, their continuing nature. That in itself will surely provoke great change within and beyond the economic system.

There are other ways in which capitalism is so plural and changing as once again to question the usefulness of referring to it as an endgame of any kind. That kind of thinking ignores the increasingly complex and plural nature of market economies in the global context. The triumph of capitalism in 1989 was about transition not from bipolar to univocal political economy, but to a multicentre one, including the three great regional trading blocs. With their very different forms of capitalism, they move from the more deregulated free market economy of the United States, through the more social market economies of the European Union, to the strong state-directed market economies of South East Asia. As long as more advanced economies require broader, looser organization, with far less ideological control, (Sassoon, pp. 326, 643), there are likely to be various ways of working a market economy. Global convergence does not represent the end of national striving and therefore difference. It will continue to result in the relative rise and decline of national economies, from the British in the earlier part of the twentieth century to the United States in the later part. 'The history of the rise and fall of the Great Powers has in no way come to a full stop' (P. Kennedy, 1989, p. xxiii).

It is important to recognize, too, that capitalism and economic growth are continuing processes. In Kondratiev's persuasive theory, long waves of technological and economic change and growth do not stop at the end of the twentieth century. They will continue, and be associated with wider changes affecting every area of life, from economics as the free market to politics as liberal democracy. The dynamics of capitalism and economic growth deny the usefulness of the zero-sum understanding of life. They are not, as a whole, 'subject to a ceiling of diminishing returns; innovation is not a self-exhausting process; the era of radical change we now experience is not headed toward a "new point of rest" ' (Landes, 1969, p. 536).

Finally, even the linking of liberal democracy and global capitalism as the end of history, by Michael Novak as well as Fukuyama, has itself been subject to serious criticism. Capitalism is not necessarily about a particular end stage, but is rather essentially a mode of production subject to political regulation. 'Modern capitalism has no purpose except to keep the show going' (Robinson, p. 143). It is therefore impossible 'to deduce a particular political regime from the requirements of capitalist accumulation' (Sassoon, p. 642). We are confronted, rather, by a variety of models, economic and political, from South East Asia and China to the United States. Indeed, democracy itself has had a very volatile history in the twentieth century, to the extent that some argue that democracy and the free market are not allies but rivals. That is a sharper recognition that we cannot accept the self-sufficiency of the free market, that the free market cannot run all, even if we cannot operate without it. Without the challenges to the market economy, it is not sufficient. And that is to confirm the role of morality and therefore religion at least as a part of these challenges. 'If, however, it is utopian to ignore the element of power, it is an unreal kind of realism which ignores the elements of morality in any world order. Just as within the state, every government, though it needs power as a basis of its authority, also needs the moral basis of the consent of the governed, so an international order cannot be based on power alone, for the simple reason that mankind will in the long run always revolt against naked power. Any international order presupposes a substantial amount of general consent'

(Carr, pp. 235–6). It requires collaboration. Morality, in other words, cannot be collapsed into underwriting a particular system of political economy, the free market. It will always also be an integral part of the challenge to existing systems. The end of history is not the end of morality. The stories are rather about a continuing interaction, of market and challenges, of politics and economics, of morality and 'realities'. And, as we have observed from our reflections on economic growth, it is about more than the clash of binary opposites. It is about the holding together of a variety of concerns including 'economic efficiency, social justice, and individual liberty' (Preston, 1983, p. 47, quoting Keynes). It is part of a new theological paradigm. And that is way beyond any idea of the end of history, because it is about an inherently evolving breadth and plurality. It is to reject its essential parochialism in a global economy full of diversity: 'To think that history would end because a conflict between ephemeral Enlightenment ideologies had come to a close exhibits a parochialism that is hard to credit' (Gray, 1998, pp. 120–1).

CHANGING WAYS OF UNDERSTANDING WORLD AND UNIVERSE

Science has played a central part in the emergence of the modern world, and particularly globalization processes. It will continue to do so, on an accelerating scale. Yet the scientific community itself has undergone radical change in the very ways it understands the universe. Most interestingly, these resonate with recurring characteristics emerging from reflecting on economic growth and the politics of globalization. It is a story of scientific communities learning to live with contradictions and our inability to express coherence in a single perspective. Since the early twentieth century, scientists have been coming to terms with fundamental changes in the ways we understand our world. For three centuries, the perspective of Newtonian physics dominated the fields of engineering, architecture, technology and economics, central skills in the construction of urban-industrial societies. This world-view was based on the tested assumption that objects could be observed, that they were unambiguously one thing or another, and phenomena were linked as cause and effect. Discoveries by Einstein, Planck and Heisenberg revolutionized the way we apprehend the universe, snapping links 'between the findings of scientists and the reality based on, or imaginable by sense experience; and ... between science and the sort of logic based on, or imaginable by common sense'. What emerged was subject to regularities and predictable, but in very different ways than before, for example, as probabilistic rather than deterministic causality. So beyond certain points, classical physical concepts such as position or velocity do not apply, and other concepts are required. Opposing theories of light and atoms were developed which could not be synthesized but had to be given proper recognition. Even more bewildering, Heisenberg's uncertainty principle acknowledged that the very process of observing a phenomenon changed it. Contemporary chaos theory again severed the links between causality and predictability. It was not that events were therefore fortuitous, but that 'the effects which followed specifiable causes could not be predicted'. Chains of events are explainable after the fact, but results cannot be predicted from the outset. In other words 'the ball-game was new. The old rules no longer held good'. Understandings could not be encompassed in one model, but had to include a variety of perspectives, of different ways of perceiving reality in order to grasp its totality. 'The only way of seizing reality was by reporting it in different ways, and putting them together to complement each other.' In terms of the economics and politics of globalization, it confirms the importance and relevance of understandings which recognize the multicausal and multifocal nature of change, of change as both cause and effect, as beyond the simple dichotomies of insider versus outsider perspectives, centre versus periphery, bad ways against good. It is about understandings that include that 'exhaustive overlay of different descriptions that incorporate apparently contradictory notions' (Hobsbawm, 1994, pp. 534, 542, 539). It is about changing understandings as part of the process of changing worlds.

4 Changing the World: From Voluntarism and Atonement to Partnership and Reconciliation

The centre of Manchester, the first city of modernity, 'the shock city' of the early industrial revolution (Briggs, 1982a, p. 96), is one of the best places on earth for gaining insights into change. Walking round the ancient Collegiate Church (now a cathedral) is to walk through stories of how the modern world emerged and where it is going. It is to traverse the pre-modern age, stepping over the medieval bridge spanning the great Hanging Ditch, and linking church and early township, probably of Saxon origin. It is to journey across sites of early mills of the first industrial revolution, corn and produce exchanges and their contribution to capital formation, and the accompanying squalor of early urbanization observed by Engels in his *Condition of the Working Class in England*. It is to pass Chetham's Library, where Marx and Engels developed ideas central to the formation of great counter-movements to industrial capitalism. Just across the road is one of the headquarters of the modern co-operative movement, another pillar of the labour movement. And then, looming over them all is the new Marks and Spencer's store, the biggest in the world, and the great Arena for mass leisure productions of a global kind, from the Spice Girls and Tina Turner to ice hockey and basketball: the new cathedrals of a post-industrial and post-modern world.

How do you make sense of that? How do you interpret but also influence it for the good? And particularly in this generation which has experienced change on a greater scale and more rapidly than ever before. That was a question addressed by a university adult education course in the Cathedral several years ago. If contemporary changes have been so decisive then surely that requires new ways of illuminating and informing them? The most tried and tested route was to resort to an exploration of the last two centuries of change, to look for patterns in former periods which fed into the present. It might then be possible to confirm whether the present age did represent such a break with the past as to warrant new interpretive symbols and if so what? It was to try to take 'a grasp of those future possibilities which the past has made available to the present' (MacIntyre, p. 223).

This journey of exploration took place initially in the north-west of England, yet spreads like industrialization and urbanization to Western Europe, the United States and then the rest of the world. It represents an explosion engulfing other experiences and stories, with important resonances between them. It is these which we will proceed to explore in the light of their origins but substantiated by these wider understandings.

What soon became clear was the breadth and complexity of that task. For we are addressing a 'total web of interconnected political, economic, social and religious factors', entailing consideration of 'corporate religious and philosophical trends, folklore and folk religion; and the connection between these and the main concurrent political, economic and social developments; as well as their comparison with contrasting situations elsewhere' (Hylson-Smith, p. 271). In other words, surveying these two centuries of momentous change required the use of a number of interpretive frameworks from a variety of disciplines, including economics, economic political and ecclesiastical history, and Christian social thought and practice. Interestingly, a vertical schema following each of these disciplines revealed horizontal resonances across historical periods and stages in the development of a complex of complementary understandings. For example, the age of evangelical Nonconformity in ecclesiastical history, linked to economic history's early industrial period, the emergence of classical economics and the age of voluntary activity in a free market, and all resonated with the age of atonement in Christian social thought. These will form our first age of voluntarism and atonement. By the late nineteenth century, and through most of the twentieth century, the problems generated by industrialization and urbanization required increasingly the attentions of a strong interventionist state. It is this age of the state which was paralleled by the theological age of incarnation. The series of changes which appear to herald the end of that age, occurring in the generation from the 1960s to the present, could be seen, it will be argued, to lead to the growing demand for partnerships and its resonance with the emerging age of reconciliation. And that of course will mean a continuing demand for new understandings to engage with and through the changing contexts as they emerge in the twenty-first century and beyond. Like Kondratiev's long waves of economic growth, there is no end of these processes. But the distant future is not our concern here.

In constructing a typology or classification of social phenomena, a number of issues have to be addressed. For example, because of the scale and complexity of the material, developing such a typology is always to some extent arbitrary. There are always alternative plausibility structures. An important test is whether it has worked in the past, and whether it can be shown to work in the present and immediate future. Testing against previous experience will be the task of the rest of this chapter. Testing the model against practice today and tomorrow will be the aim of the rest of the book. Yet even if that should demonstrate the usefulness of the typology, it will still only provide working frameworks, essentially provisional, never claiming the title of a grand or meta-narrative but, at most, one among a variety of major narratives. It will always be under judgement:

> Our little systems have their day;
> They have their day and cease to be:
> They are but broken lights of thee,
> And thou, O Lord, art more than they.
>
> (Tennyson, 'In Memoriam A. H. H.')

Clearly, too, such typologies are never tidy. There is always overlap between different ages, and regulatory principles of the previous ages always continue to exercise influence, even though no longer dominant: 'real-life demarcation lines are never clear-cut or all-encompassing'. So the age of voluntarism, as business and societies operating in a free market with minimum state intervention, has experienced a significant revival since the late 1970s, albeit in modified form.

Why link theological and secular typologies? As an exponent of Christian social thought and practice, my starting point is a theological typology, but always recognizing the intimate relationship between theological movements and their changing contexts. Like a recent masterly study of a political movement, theological history is 'inseparable from the history of the economic and social structures which shape it and against which it strives' (Sassoon, pp. 22, xxv). Both histories have to be engaged, and what better way than recognizing the relationship between theological and secular types in particular periods of history? It is acknowledgement too of the importance of theology and religion in understanding the emergence of urban-industrial societies. There has been a tendency, among historians, political scientists and philosophers, to ignore the contribution of religious opinions and organizations as we get closer to the present. That is just bad history, as we will see. Atonement and incarnational theology exercised considerable influence on the construction of modern societies in Britain and the West. Thomas Malthus played a seminal part in the development of early political economy, later acclaimed by J. M. Keynes, and continues to do so, given the decisive demographic problem in today's global context. Yet he was only following a long tradition, including the much earlier moderating impact of Ambrose and Augustine's atonement theologies on the harsh penal policies and philosophies of their day (Gorringe; Forrester). More and more commentators are now recognizing the growing contemporary significance of religion in the United States and developing economies, from Luther King to Mandela and Khomeini. Religion has to be taken very seriously as a 'real universal phenomenon' (Küng, p. 120).

This does not, however, underplay the contribution of secular factors to historic and contemporary change, but neither does it unduly restrict parts played by religion and theology. It is to acknowledge, with other recent theological commentators, that much in liberal social Christianity has given undue weight to secular factors in processes of change, and underestimated and underused the particular resources of Christianity for effecting change. That led one important theologian in that tradition to assert recently that 'all the advances in understanding seem attributable to the secular disciplines' (Preston, 1981, pp. 83–7). This argument is rather about the interaction between theology and secular disciplines and contexts. It is to acknowledge that inhabiting the emerging global context, and facing immense global questions, will require a public theology, as in the previous two hundred years, and again rooted in the particularities of Christian beliefs, traditions and communities. Such a public theology will therefore seek to encourage biblical understandings of life to be 'critically related to the contemporary debate among social philosophers, political scientists,' economists, and so on. It will, in other words, powerfully emerge out of 'the particularities of Christian faith while addressing issues of public significance' (Forrester, pp. 56, 33). In a plural society clarity about identities, while rightly interacting with other identities, is indispensable for achieving continuing influence on the plural complexities of globalization processes and questions. That is what the age of reconciliation and partnership will seek to establish on the authority of an examination of the previous ages of atonement and voluntarism, and incarnation and state.

The Age of Voluntarism and Atonement

The changing context has always played a decisive part in the formation of Christian beliefs and organizations, and never more so than in the last two hundred years of the most dramatic and continuing changes in the history of humankind. The industrialization of British society in the later eighteenth century heralded those transformations. Certain aspects of that revolution and context were particularly relevant to processes of change. The explosion of inventions in textile manufactures, from Kay's flying shuttle for weaving (1738), to Samuel Crompton's spinning mule (1779), which combined features of Hargreaves' spinning jenny (c.1764) and Arkwright's water frame (1769), gradually became focused in great mills, symbols of new industrial organizations, the concentration of people and resources in bigger and bigger units, controlled by the timing of machines not nature. It represented the great breakthrough in productivity, with repercussions across the whole of society and human living. There were similar supportive changes in the field of political economy. The publication of Adam Smith's *Inquiry into the Nature and Causes of the Wealth of Nations* in 1776, emphasized the essential role of the free market as the most effective and efficient way to produce and distribute wealth. Conversely, it rejected the role of strong interventionist government in the economy. Eventually these views and economics developed into the full-blown laissez-faire understanding of the free market, particularly as propagated by the Manchester School in the 1850s, and linked powerfully to the liberal promotion of free trade. This classical economics, consolidated by Ricardo in 1817, and then by John S. Mill by 1850, emphasized competition between producers in a free open market as the most efficient way to produce goods and services to sustain the greatly increasing population. It was therefore an age of entrepreneurs and private companies, as integral parts of these processes. And it spread like wildfire. By 1808, even Brazil had a chair in political economy, and Argentine in 1823, symbols of liberal advance. In the political context, the growth of nation states was not the growth of large government. The state was regarded as a dyke against sin, not active intervener in promoting a good society. It was there to protect and encourage trade and industry by letting it be, by laissez-faire, by enforcing law and order against trade unions and theft and civil unrest. Such policy likewise reflected commitment to enterprise through a free market and minimal government. The notorious Poor Law Amendment Act of 1834 epitomized such philosophy and practice. Through its carrot and stick approach, determined to pay benefits less than the lowest wage, and concentrate the destitute in punitive workhouses, the task was to encourage individual self-help in a free competitive market as the way to improve life. It represented a decisive break with traditional societies, the move from status to contract, from estates to classes. The benefits were enormous in terms of the creation of wealth, and the costs were enormous in terms of the destruction of familiar life-styles, and their replacement by initially appalling conditions in the new industrial cities and urban communities. De Tocqueville again summarized that profound ambiguity at the heart of the industrial revolution, when he commented on Manchester that 'from this filthy sewer pure gold flows' (Hobsbawm, 1962, p. 42).

It is that context which can be described as the age of voluntarism and atonement, beginning in the late eighteenth century and continuing toward the end of the nineteenth-century; by 1914, that 'liberal world system and nineteenth-century bourgeois society' had collapsed (Hobsbawm, 1987, p. 334). Although they will be considered separately, they represent two sides of the same coin, their interaction being of equal significance.

The age of voluntarism is the time of entrepreneurs and companies, voluntary organizations and societies, operating in a free market, unimpeded by a strong interventionist state. Because individuals and individualism were such a central feature of this age, the story of Robert Owen provides a symbol and commentary on some of its principal characteristics. His statue stands outside the Co-operative headquarters, two hundred yards from Manchester

Cathedral, but it is the early, pre-co-operative Owen that best tells this story. Arriving in Manchester as a young man in 1789, the ex-draper's assistant could begin his amazing manufacturing career with a borrowed £100. By 1809 he had become so successful that he could buy out his partners in the New Lanark Mills in central Scotland 'for £84,000 in cash' (Hobsbawm, 1962, p. 52). He was not the most prosperous by a long way, yet he epitomizes free voluntaristic enterprise, for he represents the self-made, self-confident men who built the industrial revolution. Owing little to birth, family or higher education, they projected a spirit of dynamism and achievement in stark contrast to the traditional hierarchical societies of the past, a spirit sharpened and augmented in the United States by criticism of its colonial past. Their intellectual certainty was provided by Samuel Smiles and his classic *Self-Help*, the Bible of the Victorian entrepreneur.

Energy, hard work, shrewdness and greed did not translate unduly into wasteful habits of conspicuous consumption. 'An economy based on profit-making private enterprise' (Hobsbawm, 1987, p. 173) had been built on the personal motivations of entrepreneurs, and that included savings and profits ploughed back into the enterprise for further growth. The rise of Robert Owen's business embodies these virtues and aspirations. In this revolution a supportive context was equally decisive. For a free market was conducive to voluntary effort, and that involved a minimalist view of the role of government, a rejection of the preceding mercantilist state with its privileges, monopolies, subsidies and import restrictions. It is highly doubtful whether economic change could have been achieved in any other way: 'no superior authority could have effected an industrial revolution so rapidly and efficiently as the impersonal market' (Landes, 1969, p. 549). Government was too ignorant, perverse in its judgements, and inconsistent in action. That is still a problem experienced in most underdeveloped economies.

Owen's purchase of the New Lanark Mills (now a post-industrial and post-modern world heritage and leisure centre) was also a recognition of the growing importance of industrial organization. The 1850s and 1860s saw the passing of various Company Acts, removing restrictions on corporate endeavour and liabilities, as companies and joint-stock enterprises, in an increasingly risky and competitive world. Equivalent company formations occurred in the rest of Europe and the United States.

What Owen's story did not exemplify was particularly important and central to the age of voluntarism. His growing interest in co-operation and socialism, and his rejection of organized religion and dogmas, separated him from two key features of the period. On the one hand, entrepreneurial activity was increasingly connected to free-market practices and theories, to 'the absolute faith in economic liberalism and (conversely) the rejection of non-economic activities' which socialism and co-operation so often represented (Hobsbawm, 1962, p. 232). On the other hand, the spiritual certainty of the early exponents of self-help was provided particularly by evangelical Non-conformity. Indeed, free market and Christian beliefs were readily combined by people and culture. So laissez-faire was underwritten by Christian convictions like Burke's, that the laws of commerce are the laws of nature and therefore the laws of God, and by theological comment, like the Congregational journal in 1846, expressing the view that 'Economical truth is no less divine than astronomical truth. The laws which govern the phenomenon of production and exchange are as truly laws of God as those which govern day and night' (Winch, p. 213; Cocks, p. 35).

The age of voluntarism was not simply about economic activities. The freedom which spawned entrepreneurs also promoted a vast array of organizations and societies, what we would now call voluntary bodies and constituting civil society. It was as though 'Only liberty and competition – in both the political and economic realms – could accommodate the needs and nature of the self-willed individuals who formed civil society' (Appleby, p. 122). They covered a wide spectrum of activities, from trade unions to friendly societies, from music to sport, from learned organizations like the Manchester Statistical Society (1833) to a whole host of religious bodies, including the Church Missionary Society (1799), the British and Foreign Bible Society (1804), and the Lord's Day Observance Society (1831). They soon tapped into the aspirations of the working classes, with their concern for improvement through self-help, thrift, and their necessary inclinations to mutuality. By 1821, Lancashire had the highest proportion of friendly society members to total population, an astonishing 17%. By 1863, Germany had 1,000 self-improvement associations. By then, too, in the United States, local meetings and voluntary associations had begun to play a formative role in the development of the constitution and nation.

The Royton Temperance Seminary splendidly exemplifies them all. Founded in 1843, near Manchester, membership was restricted to mostly young male cotton operatives 'who had taken the pledge of abstinence, refused to gamble and were of good character'. Within only 20 years they had produced 'five master cotton spinners, one clergyman, two managers of cotton mills in Russia . . . [and] "many others had attained respectable positions as managers, overlookers, head mechanics, certified school masters, or had become respectable shop keepers" ' (Hobsbawm, 1962, p. 247). That the majority of the working classes did not participate in such societies or succeed in life does not detract from the scale and achievements of voluntarism. As the basis of civil society, they stood between the individual, government and business, providing mutual support in times of need, and that collective self-confidence essential for survival and growth in an urban-industrial society. As schools of democracy, where participative skills were acquired and then practised in wider fields, they played a formative part in developing modern democracies in the West. 'In a market economy, dependent upon voluntary efforts, the cultural element is critical, because it is through explicit social values that people are given the personal ambition and essential knowledge to keep the system going' (Appleby, p. 120).

It is precisely at the recurring point of 'social values' and 'the cultural element', stretching across economic and voluntary activities, that the link between the age of voluntarism and atonement is particularly apparent. Magisterially elaborated by the Cambridge historian Boyd-Hilton, who served as a boy in St Anne's, a daughter church of Manchester Cathedral, the age of atonement relates to that evangelical character of the nineteenth century, centring on the sin and conversion of the individual, and regarding life on earth as a journey through a vale of tears to an eternal destiny, a testing place for faith and conduct producing characters imbued with what has become known as the protestant work ethic. It was a clear, decisive, conviction faith with immense social consequences.

The growth of evangelical Nonconformity began in the mid-eighteenth century, particularly in Britain, and particularly through the enterprise of John Wesley and the Methodists, although it soon spread to the Congregational, Baptist and Presbyterian Churches, and to the Church of England itself. Their impact on a hostile novel urban-industrial society was astonishing in its spread and extent. Wesleyan Methodist membership in England grew from 22,410 in 1767 to 77,402 in 1796 and 285,000 in 1851. The USA was particularly affected by the evangelical movement, experiencing mass conversions on a major scale, so that by 1850 nearly 75% of all churches were Baptist, Methodist or Presbyterian (Gilbert, p. 31).

The evangelical atonement-based gospel profoundly affected individuals but also society, though often unintentionally. It was a conversionist Christianity in theology and purposes, summarized as what God does for us through Christ's atoning death (Romans 1.16–17), and then what God does in us as the fruits of the Spirit (Galatians 5.22–6). Its beliefs therefore centred on a strong conviction of the importance of the individual in its relationship to God, and therefore on responsibility for its life to God. So it began by recognizing that all are born and live in sin. William Wilberforce declared: 'We should not go too far if we were to assert that [the corruption of human nature] lies at the very root of all true Religion, and still more, that it is eminently the basis and ground-work of Christianity' (Vidler, p. 39). It is from that that we are forgiven but only through God's gracious gift of Jesus Christ's atoning death on the cross. From our acceptance of that, flows those gifts of the Spirit transforming our lives.

With such beliefs, evangelical Nonconformity engaged urban society with a vigour and effectiveness never since experienced, other than in the growing churches of developing economies today. Using an itinerant, non-professional ministry, normally lay, preaching that simple gospel, unencumbered by ancient buildings, and separated from the established orderings of society, they generated a strong sense of religious community with a clear distinct identity. Through leaders like Wilberforce, Venn and Simeon, and John Bird Sumner in Manchester, it soon made deep inroads into the established Church of England.

Not surprisingly, such beliefs and organizations are linked to values in society. The enterprising in business and self-help organizations might have found their intellectual support in Samuel Smiles, but they equally owed their spiritual certainty to evangelical Nonconformity. For some interpreters, such 'pietistic protestantism' was 'rigid, self-righteous, unintellectual, obsessed with puritan morality to the point where hypocrisy was its automatic companion' (Hobsbawm, 1962, p. 230). Yet although this rigid creed lacked intellectual depth, it did promote practical skills and endeavours which produced the industrial revolution, and therefore fed the scholars. For Samuel Smiles, 'the experience to be gathered from books, though often valuable, is but of the nature of *learning*: whereas the experience gained from actual life is of the nature of *wisdom*; and a small store of the latter is worth vastly more than any stock of the former' (Smiles, pp. 35a–60). In other words, evangelical Nonconformity's influence on individuals, and then society, did have a perverse side to it, yet it also contained seeds for affecting change for the better, in terms of promoting enterprise but also through the self-help mutuality of working class organizations. What provided support for the separated lifestyles and communities of evangelicalism, intentionally or unintentionally also provided support for the changing of society. It was as though 'the social character of the new sects militated against their theological withdrawal from the world' (Hobsbawm, 1962, p. 277), and thereby contributed to those organizations campaigning for change, from Anti-Corn Law League to anti-slavery movement.

In the profound interaction between faith, values and society, the key contribution of the age of atonement is located. It represented the congruence of faith, business and voluntary endeavours as a set of values governing conduct, a worldly asceticism. The promotion of character, so significant in theological debate today, emanated from evangelical faith and community as honesty, diligence, conscience and therefore dissent, and the value of time over pleasure. The connections between early industrialization, its culture and organizations, and the religious spirit located in, although wider than, evangelicalism, were profound, both stultifying and liberating. It was an essentially interactive, two-way relationship. It was as though secular change 'reinforced the evangelical preference for voluntary, face-to-face action' showing 'a distaste for state intervention' and emphasized 'above all the key necessity for preaching the gospel' (Wolffe, p. 45). It is the first case study of modernity in terms of the argument for changing theology and society.

What was the story most loved by evangelicals, epitomizing the age of both atonement and voluntarism? The parable of the talents (Luke 19.11–27), expounded in his biblical commentaries by John Bird Sumner, first evangelical Bishop of Chester (1828 – the diocese then included Manchester) and then Archbishop of Canterbury (1848). These were written to help clergy and lay visitors promote a Bible-based family life. Interestingly, Sumner had been an important contributor to early Christian political economy, with Malthus, Whately and Copleston. Again, the connection between economic change and Christian convictions. Listen to Sumner's words on that parable of the talents and you will hear how profound and substantial that link was: 'And it is the nature of that state of moral trial in which we are placed on earth, that every man, in every rank, shall have the power to improve or to abuse his talents of fortune, his talents of authority, his talents of grace, his talents of education' (Sumner, p. 345). That is the age of atonement and voluntarism.

THE AGE OF THE STATE AND INCARNATION

Towards the end of the nineteenth century, the age of voluntarism in a dominant laissez-faire era began to wither away. The concentration of resources in bigger and bigger units was increasingly inimical to philosophies and policies of non-intervention in the operations of the free market. It was a period heralding the arrival of great corporations and mass media, and of explosive population increases, accompanied by the struggle for democracy and labour movements. It witnessed the rise of collectivism and the consequent waning of individualism. There would be no going back to that earlier age of voluntarism, despite romantic protestations of neoliberals and conservatives in the 1980s and beyond. The age of the state, the symbol of that new collectivism, had made sure of that.

The emergence of giant national firms or corporations was integral to the development of mature industrial capitalism, particularly in the United States. Led by 'robber barons' presiding over feudal empires, they became a direct challenge to the Jeffersonian tradition of minimalist government. Their rapid transformation into huge cartels, trusts and monopolies, representing what the great Baptist preacher-theologian Rauschenbusch regarded as the core of anti-democratic power, exacerbated even further that threat to voluntarism. Yet the forces challenging these trends were increasingly more pervasive, even if linked to the emergence of larger and larger corporations. On the one hand, it was the age of mass markets, of the development of large-scale consumerism, connected to the development of mass production systems, of the huge assembly lines of great manufacturing industries. Integrally part of these progressions was the arrival of mass cultures aided and abetted by technological innovations. It was the age of mass entertainment, from newspapers and magazines, to radio, cinema, television and videos: 'The plebeian arts were about to conquer the world, both in their own version of arts-and-crafts and by means of high technology. This conquest constitutes the most important development in twentieth century culture' (Hobsbawm, 1987, p. 236). Mass markets and mass media were both uneasy bedfellows of mature industrial capitalism, as capable of promoting criticism and discontent as affirmation and complacency.

On the other hand, at the heart of the issue of size was Malthus's continuing 'geometrical' increase in population, concentrated in great industrial cities and towns, often dominated by large companies and industries, from textiles in Dundee or Lowell to chemicals in Widnes or Ludwigshafen. Mass populations, increasingly educated and prosperous under mature industrial capitalism, demanded more say over lives now regularly affected by affairs outside the household. The pressure led inexorably to the mass vote, to the extension of democracy in late nineteenth-century Europe, reaching its climax of universal suffrage in advanced economies immediately after the Second World War, in Britain somewhat earlier in 1928, in France 1945, Italy 1946 and Belgium 1948. Implications of these extensions were widespread, requiring political parties to obtain wider support if to be electorally successful, thereby pushing government into deeper social reforms and the management of economic affairs. Life from now on was about 'an increasingly wide electorate dominated by the common people'.

Closely associated with these developments was the rise of mass working class organizations. Appalling conditions in the workplace and urban communities for a majority of the population, the inevitable accompaniment of industrialization, not surprisingly generated a variety of protest or countermovements. Arising particularly in the late nineteenth century, they were firmly and substantially embedded in European and North American societies as 'structured collective action', nationally organized. As trade unions, the co-operative movement and social democratic parties, they attracted increasing numbers of supporters in the West. One million people even voted for the socialist candidate in the 1912 American presidential elections. But that was a momentary lapse in that politically conservative nation! In Third World countries, these movements were absent, not least because industrialization had not as yet had a significant impact on them.

The cumulative affect of all these foundational changes was what the great lawyer Dicey saw as the disturbing rise of the age of 'collectivism' and its displacement of the valued individual and voluntary enterprise (Hobsbawm, 1987, pp. 236, 116, 87, 125, 54; Yeo). That transformation reached its climax in the twentieth century in the form of the dramatic eruption onto the world stage of state socialism, of the great communist command economies of the Soviet Union and China. It was in the latter that Chairman Mao embodied the darkest end result of that process: 'the individual's total self-abnegation and total immersion in the collectivity [are] ultimate goods . . . a kind of collective mysticism' (Hobsbawm, 1994, p. 467).

Taking to extremes a legitimate and necessary development should not detract from the achievements which the modern state represents. As the nation state and nationalism of the late nineteenth and early twentieth centuries, the age of the state was significantly a product of the French Revolution, but also, and increasingly, of the industrial revolution, of mass populations and organizations. It was not therefore a natural and spontaneous development, but a human and social construct. And it was the growth of 'the state which makes the nation, and not the nation the state' (Hobsbawm, 1987, p. 148), imposing national uniformity through education, employment, and local government policies. It was this state's growing domination of more and more areas of life in advanced economies in the twentieth century which epitomized best the transition from the age of voluntarism and free market. The symbols of that transfer of power were there for all to see in the great public buildings, the libraries, art galleries, and schools, but particularly in the town halls, 'those gigantic and monumental buildings whose purpose was to testify to the wealth and splendour of the age in general and the city in particular'. In 1858, Leeds Town Hall was built at the gigantic cost of £122,000, 1% of the total income tax yield for Britain (Hobsbawm, 1975, p. 329). And so it was across the land, from town to town. Less obvious, but more important, was the proportion of the workforce employed through national and local governments, rising threefold in Britain between 1891 and 1911, to 10–13% in the European Union in the 1970s. By then, state activities touched virtually every part of a citizen's life.

It was the 'short twentieth century', however, which saw the modern state reach its apogee and particularly through two World Wars and the intervening years, which 'multiplied the occasions when it became essential for governments to govern'. This related particularly to economic and social affairs. The partial collapse of capitalism in the late 1920s and early 1930s provoked economists, led by J. M. Keynes, 'to finding a way of saving capitalism from itself', essentially through 'an economy managed and controlled by the state' turning such economies into 'mixed public-private economies'. Management through accounting by companies was now replicated by the state, with the rise of national statistics measuring production and income becoming available for the first time in history. Through the Bretton Woods Agreement, the cornerstone of the international system, that national management of economies evolved onto an international plane. Cumulatively, it meant rejection of reliance on the free market alone, and its replacement by a belief in 'the active management and planning of the economy by the state' (Hobsbawm, 1994, pp. 140, 333–4, 176) based on the new assumption that 'the hand of the state is indispensable in good times as well as bad; that, indeed, only the state can assure continued economic growth in an atmosphere of social harmony; further, that the economy, like any other aspect of national life, should serve the state, rather than the reverse' (Landes, 1969, p. 399). It was the age of planning, based on the New Deal in the United States, Keynes' work in Britain, and the Soviet Union's Five Year Plans, beginning in 1929, blossoming into the planning of post-war reconstruction in 1945. An astonishing change of ethos and practice. Even Averell Harriman, a US statesman of 'ironclad capitalist credentials', accepted in 1946 that 'people in this country are no longer scared of such words as "planning" . . . people have accepted the fact that government has got to plan as well as individuals in this country' (Hobsbawm, 1994, p. 273).

Accompanying these changes, at the heart of industrialization, to more state managed markets, was growing state intervention in social policy matters, epitomized by the welfare state in Western Europe, and its equivalents, though on a much reduced scale, in the United States. Building on earlier achievements by Bismarck in Germany in the 1880s and Lloyd George in Britain in the 1900s, post-war reconstruction greatly accelerated trends to state welfarism. Again, all marking clearly the transition from voluntarism, with the state taking over functions performed by churches and voluntary bodies in strategic fields like education and welfare. The difference was that the state extended these supportive and interventionist measures to a degree undreamt of by voluntary philanthropy, providing cradle to grave support for citizens. Given the turbulence created by market collapse in the interwar years, and the fear and anxiety this caused, post-war reconstruction focused on providing protection for citizens from the worst consequences of economic instability. In doing so, it widened 'the consensus and the legitimacy of the modern state' (Sassoon, p. 145). Current and future turmoil in global markets reinforces the need for such reformulation of the welfare and economic functions of the contemporary state, if capitalism is to retain that authority.

It was the combination of the economic and social managing of market economies in the international system of reconstruction that led to the golden age of growth from 1945 to 1975, and its culmination in the corporate state, the most symbolic representation of the hard core of the age of the state. The corporate state focused the collaboration of government, trade unions and big business into governing institutions: 'the arrangement was triangular, with governments, formally or informally, presiding over the institutionalized negotiations between capital and labour' (Hobsbawm, 1994, p. 282). It addressed such issues as inflation, income polices and labour market restrictions, through the joint managing of such creations as the National Economic Development Council. The fact that up to 60% of a West European nation's economic product was consumed or distributed by public authorities made this role extremely likely and feasible. Such corporatism was evident particularly in West European states, from Scandinavia, West Germany, Britain and the Benelux countries to Austria, but it was also present to a lesser extent in the United States, with the Great Society programme of the 1960s. The corporate state, like the command economies, represented the end of the line of the age of the state. And both terminated in the late twentieth century. Their achievements as well as failings should be recognized, with the corporate welfare state, particularly through interventionist policies, constituting a necessary legacy of value.

The age of incarnation embodies the transition from the age of atonement, regarding life on earth as journeying through a vale of tears to an eternal home, to regarding life on earth as a calling to transform God's world for the better. In that process of change, the incarnate Christ is both model and means. In that process, Christian social reformers increasingly embraced the state as principal means for achieving progressive change, thereby linking the age of state and incarnation.

The formative influence on the emergence and development of a tradition of incarnational theology and social involvement was undoubtedly F. D. Maurice, founder of Christian socialism, particularly in its more social reformist mode. From its origin in the mid-nineteenth century, through the major contributions of Charles Gore and B. F. Westcott at the turn of the century, and then into the seminal work of William Temple and R. H. Tawney, that tradition persisted and evolved almost as an apostolic succession, and continues into the present through R. H. Preston and Duncan Forrester, and emerging younger theologians like Markham, Graham and Sedgwick. The United States witnessed the emergence of an equivalent tradition, beginning with the early social gospel fathers like Washington Gladden and then Walter Rauschenbusch, through the critical interpretations of Reinhold Niebuhr, and into the later and recent contributions of John Bennett, J. P. Wogaman, and Charles Murray.

The process of incarnate faith being embodied in society inevitably placed increasing emphasis on interpreting and engaging contemporary contexts. Since they were recognized as essentially and profoundly changing contexts, faith was transformed through promoting the transformation of society. That interaction between faith and context, embedded in the act of incarnation, was initially and most clearly expressed by Maurice in his commitment both to Christianize society and to socialize Christianity. In terms of influencing the reformulation of faith in the light of, and as contribution to, that interaction, the work of Gore in the collection of essays *Lux Mundi* in 1889, interpreted incarnational theology as liberal Catholicism, using current developments in evolutionary thinking, biblical and historical criticism and philosophical idealism. The progressive orthodoxy of Gladden and Rauschenbusch, making greater use of sociology, illustrated a parallel reconstruction of faith in the United States. Both were about the reformulation of faith for and through more effective social engagement, not its erosion through accommodation to the context.

The other side of the coin of this interactive incarnationalism was the strategic intent of changing society for the good, the better to realize God's purposes in and for the world. Maurice, Kingsley and Ludlow's attempts to Christianize socialism through co-operatives, trade unions and pamphleteering undoubtedly contributed, with movements like Primitive Methodism, to eroding the chasm between Christianity and socialism, so evident on the European continent. Rauschenbusch's heroic *Christianizing the Social Order* (1912) powerfully went beyond semi-Christian areas of family, education and politics to address pagan areas like business and economy, providing inspiration for such later Christian social reformers as Martin Luther King and Gustavo Gutiérrez. Linked to that broad tradition of Christian social involvement, the Roman Catholic John Ryan's influence on the struggle for a statutory minimum wage in the United States was of equal importance.

In terms of Christian beliefs, incarnational theology embodied a number of central convictions clearly and firmly based on Christian tradition, but in themselves, and through the process of interaction with society, having formative social consequences. At the heart of the new tradition was belief in God's intervention in the world through the life, death and resurrection of Jesus Christ. Powerfully dependent on the Johannine tradition, it emphasized the incarnation as God reclaiming his own, as fundamental affirmation of the world, now embodied in the Trinity through the humanity of Christ. It was William Temple who produced the classic expression of this interpretation in his *Readings in St John's Gospel*. Interestingly, these were formulated partly on Blackpool beach, in the Manchester diocesan missions to working class folk who descended on that great leisure facility every summer for their 'Wakes week' holiday. The Christ, coming into his own, in and through the great working masses; the rise of the social welfare state as the means for transforming their lot; and the age of incarnation and state – it is all there.

Linked to the belief in incarnation was recognition of the fundamental goodness of God's creation, including the human made in God's likeness. Sin was clearly, tangibly and powerfully present, but that was not, for Maurice, the fundamental fact of the divine constitution of humankind. And that was a fundamental departure from the evangelical age of atonement.

Similarly at the heart of the tradition, and developed particularly by Rauschenbusch and the Brotherhood of the Kingdom in the 1890s in the United States, was commitment to the Kingdom of God, and encouragement of its presence on earth, including through social reform and state action. Bishop David Jenkins recently referred to that same tradition by arguing for the Christian task as promoting the already visible signs of the Kingdom in and through the contemporary context (Jenkins). The early Christian social reformers expressed this conviction and concern in a more simple and effective formula, that the Fatherhood of God required the brotherhood of man.

Finally, the tradition recognized God as immanent, as with and among us, in and through his world, in and through Christ. It was therefore profoundly affirmative of the world, including discoveries in science, like evolution, in sociology and politics. A powerful progressive, gradualist and evolutionary commitment to change flowed from this belief. It represented, once again, a decisive break with the age of atonement. That development and difference was particularly exemplified in growing commitment to sacramental theology as interaction of spiritual and material, including through the masses, social- ism and state. It linked back into Kingdom and incarnation beliefs, and Johannine tradition. When I was a young curate in Aberdeen, the mass always ended with the great incarnational gospel reading from John 1.1–14, ending with: 'And the Word was made flesh, and dwelt among us'. And then you went out and embodied that faith in Labour Party meetings and CND demonstrations.

The Church also played a central role in the age of incarnation and its the- ology, becoming vehicle for God's transforming of the world. It therefore moves from being support for reaction to agent of social change and better- ment. It was a move from the 'squarson', the alliance of parson and squire, including parsons as repressive justices of the peace, to great campaigning socialist parsons like F. Donaldson, leading the unemployed march to London in 1905, and arguing that 'Christianity is the religion of which social- ism is the practice', including using the state to provide employment (Bryant, p. 115). In particular, it developed into a variety of Christian social reform and socialist groups, and came to dominate the official Churches' thinking on social affairs, through bodies like the Board for Social Responsibility and the Justice and Peace Commissions in England, and the great Church reports like *Faith in the City* (1985), *The Common Good* (1996), *Unemployment and the Future of Work* (1998) in England, and, in the United States, *Economic Justice for All* (1986). Thus had Maurice's strategy of socializing the Church, as an agent of social change, come to fruition. The ecclesiological emphasis on sac- ramental living and socialism can also be linked to the growing embodiment of churches in local living in mass society, as cradle to grave service, providing educational, leisure and social welfare facilities. In stable dense urban com- munities surrounding mills and factories, working class life was profoundly influenced by the churches' calendar, moving from Christmas through Lent to Easter, to Whit Walks, Sunday School sermons, summer treats and camps, to harvest festivals; it was a rich social life, exemplifying the strong tangible mixture of sacred and secular.

The linkage between ages of state and incarnation become more evident the more the ages are reflected on. But they came to a head in two particular ways. Dicey's recognition of the emergence of an age of collectivism replacing his beloved individualism, as state replacing voluntarism, points to the importance of the values of co-operation, community, and fellowship and the rejection of the values of individualism and competition. For B. F. Westcott, first President of the Christian Social Union, 'Individualism and Socialism correspond with opposite views of humanity. Individualism regards humanity as made up of disconnected or warring atoms; Socialism regards it as an organic whole, a vital unity formed by the combination of contributory members mutually interdependent' (Atherton, 1994, p. 81). It is the age of incarnation's contribution to formative social and personal values, in the same mode as the protestant work ethic's role linking voluntarism and atonement, but as profound contradiction to it. But the most obvious and tangible connecting of state and incarnation was represented by William Temple, great exponent of incarnational theology and yet also the person who named the Welfare State, epitome of the age of the state. His classic *Christianity and Social Order* was published alongside Beveridge's great report on the Welfare State in 1942, the one underwriting the other; the one influencing the other in formation and practice; two sides of the same coin. And there you have it, the age of incarnation and state.

Again, not surprisingly, the story from the Christian Gospels most used by incarnationalists was the parable of the good Samaritan (Luke 10.29–37), the great narrative of love in action, of what it means to embody love in society. My father, a trade unionist out of the Primitive Methodist tradition, interpreted and developed that parable true to that age of incarnation and state. From that story he argued for state intervention in society, making the road from Jerusalem to Jericho safe for travellers, having a health service to bind up the wounds of those who fell by the wayside, being tough on crime but equally on causes of crime through better management of the economy, full employment, and the tackling of poverty and marginalization. It all fits, doesn't it?

THE AGE OF PARTNERSHIP AND RECONCILIATION

As a generation of changes affecting all areas of life, and on a global stage for the first time in history, the 1960s to the 1990s was an era of turbulence and upheaval, like the 1780s and 1880s before it. These dates signalled the transition to the ages of voluntarism and atonement, and then state and incarnation. It is not therefore surprising that our generation's greatly changing context should project a strong sense of the eroding of one age and the need to discern signs of its replacement. Then it can be named and its implications for the changing context developed. The outlines of that task can now be attempted, and its more detailed consequences for society and theology elaborated in the remaining chapters.

Reflecting on the period running from the 1960s into the more immediate future has revealed clear indications of irrevocable transitions in every walk of life. In economies, movement from industrial to post-industrial society in an increasingly global economy resulted in a much more consumption-oriented context, affecting attitudes to employment and leisure, but also threatening those like the labour movement and churches who were too attached to the Western male manual worker model of work and association. Wider economic change focused on 'the rediscovery of the market' which became 'a trademark of modernity' for globalization, a trend confirmed by the collapse of the only alternative of 'actually existing socialism' in 1989 (Sassoon, p. 615). The pivotal role played by the market in economic life, when allied to a consumption-oriented society, invaded the political and cultural fields. The state had made irreversible gains in its managing of economic affairs and the social welfare of its citizens. Corporate state and nanny state epitomized that stifling, intrusive power, as did their erosion of the part played by the institutions of civil society in providing opportunities for people's local involvement in the running of their and society's affairs. It resulted in the local state taking responsibilities away from voluntary bodies, including the churches, in education, leisure and welfare. The resurrection of the market, the eruption of individual choice-based consumption, and the rebirth of civil society witnessed not the end of the state at all, but certainly the conclusion of the state as 'an end in itself' (Blair, p. 1). Similarly, mass markets and media were increasingly accompanied by the rediscovery of the self, of the individual portfolio, of identity but in and through a multiplicity of choices, reinforced explosively by new advances in communication technologies. Movement from restricted traditional patterns of family living and lifestyles to much greater diversity, supported by growing recognition of the equal importance of women in decision-making, from the most intimate to most public realms, both reflects and contributes to these wider changes. It should not be surprising that religious life has undergone a series of changes matching those in every other field. Dramatic decline of mainstream Christian denominations in the West has been paralleled by the stubborn persistence of common religion and its transformation into the more 'pick-and-mix' variety of the more consumption-oriented post-modern society. As remarkable, in Britain and other Western nations, is the transition from the profound problems and challenges of intra-faith relationships between historic Christian denominations, to the greater challenges of inter-faith relationships.

When all these signs of transition are located in a global context, they are not just more pronounced. They are enlarged into worldwide concerns, with the increasing complexity of problems that brings with them. Yet also they are joined by challenges of a particularly new and global character, in terms of sheer scale, like population increase, or innovation, like environment. Influenced by, and in turn influencing, all these signs of change is the persisting, growing challenge of marginalization between and within nations.

Gathering together these indications of change, to address them all and not just one or two, is the task from now on. Globalization processes will demand no less. And their cumulative effect does begin to point in certain directions, suggesting what the new age should be called. And that, as before, will offer means of making sense of contemporary change and engaging purposefully with it. For it is becoming evident that no one grand narrative in politics, religion or economics, can describe or explain all this satisfactorily. No one sector, voluntary, business or state, can address these matters adequately. It is as though the new age is requiring increasingly our ability to construct connections between perspectives and with others. It is about finding ways of holding together often profound differences for our own self-sufficiency and for future living on earth. It is about an emerging age of partnership and reconciliation.

Defining and elaborating such a concept clearly has a substantial speculative content. Distilling it from signs of transition in the 1960s to the present is not to work primarily with historical evidence, as for the previous ages. It is to reflect on 'public events' which are 'part of the texture of our lives' today (Hobsbawm, 1994, p. 4). To extend these reflections into the next generation becomes even more speculative, and therefore provisional. Yet we can discern these signs of contemporary change emerging out of our study of the 1960s to the present, and it is such formative indications which suggest the development of the emerging future as an age of partnership and reconciliation. In other words, it is essentially an 'act of reflection on lived experience', but recognizing that reflecting on the practical affairs of society and world can and should lead us to ways of understanding or theorizing about it. It 'enables us to think about that real world of practice with a clarity and breadth of perspective often unavailable to the hard-pressed practitioner' (Forrester, pp. 60, 67). It represents a distillation and reformulation of emerging trends in society and world, in the light of a faith which has journeyed through detailed interactions of atonement and voluntarism, incarnation and state. It is about a major change in our thinking and practice as a response to continuing change, in order to affect change. It is to be embodied in wider processes of change, but with a purpose drawn from before, through and beyond it: 'The needed conviction will not come from a catalogue of policy recommendations. It can only emerge as a consequence of a new historical tide that induces a change both in values and conduct; in effect, out of a prolonged process of cultural self-re-examination and philosophical re-evaluation, which over time influences the political outlook both of the West and of the non-Western world' (Küng, p. 82). For distilling partnership and reconciliation from current change is transformed into conviction when confronted with such global challenges as population, environment and marginalization. We have no choice about facing up to them if we are to survive. 'There is one world and it is not endless and we have to work out among ourselves how we are to live in it together or we shall die in it separately' (Boyle, p. 119). And that is about partnership and reconciliation.

Promoting interaction as Christian obligation. Atonement and voluntarism, and incarnation and state have each contributed to changing society in their own right, as well as through their interaction in the sense of being both causes and effects. The novelty of the emerging age is manifested particularly in the growing importance for theology and society of that process of interaction itself, without detracting from the contribution of partnership and reconciliation in themselves. For the emerging context, in its nature and challenges, promotes and requires collaboration, seeking to hold together different perspectives, interests and resources. The persistence of two major identities, one secular and the other religious, is a reminder, too, that it continues to be essential, particularly for partnerships and reconciliation, to recognize appropriate and distinctive contributions in developing adequate interpretations of, and engagements with, the new context. Christians, members of other faiths or promoters of secular reason cannot claim with widespread support that faith or reason alone is necessary for adequate understanding of the contemporary situation and problems. There are therefore Christian as well as secular contributions involved in the interpretation of partnership in our context, just as there are secular as well as religious interpretations of reconciliation. Yet that commitment to partnership and reconciliation from each perspective, and therefore equally to their interaction, does not detract from the importance of connecting the Christian contribution, in clear and demonstrable ways, to faith traditions, narratives and communities. Indeed, the impact of plurality and diversity in the contemporary context makes that linkage even more important. Without clear embedding in traditions and communities, partnerships in such a plurality of competing insights and resources are likely to end in hostile or friendly take-overs by the stronger partner. It is another confirmation, too, of the recognition in all ages of modernity of the importance of the proactive character of the Christian contribution. We should expect, and the dangers of plurality require, recognition of the particular consequences of faith traditions for partnership and reconciliation including interaction with secular realities. That will both underwrite, and, at times, also move beyond the secular in criticism and construction. And yet, because the process of interaction is two-way between secular and religious, that also leads to the reformulation of Christian tradition and Church, just as society has been changed by them.

Dynamic interactions between partnership and reconciliation do more than affect their formation. They contribute equally to the growing significance of the interactive process itself. It is as though there is a dialectical relationship between thesis and antithesis which does not generate a synthesis, but is a continuing process of critical interaction. Rejecting the achievable goal of a socialist utopia, Bernstein came to a similar conclusion: 'I have extraordinarily little feeling for, or interest in, what is usually termed "the final goal of socialism". This goal, whatever it may be, is nothing to me, the

movement is everything. And by movement I mean both the general movement of society, i.e. social progress, and the political and economic agitation
and organization to bring about this progress' (Sassoon, pp. 17–18). Out of
this interactive, interdisciplinary 'movement' or process of clearly account-
able identities, we can, as in previous ages, promote a practical divinity and
ethic out of economic and other processes. This in turn will have a proactive as
well as reactive relationship with that context.

And, of course, the age of partnership and reconciliation will never aspire
to be a grand narrative. If no one sector or perspective can claim to explain or
engage the profusion of globalization, neither can this. Yet it can be seen as a
way of weaving 'the separate histories into one history in which the single
strands do not lose their original colour', but contribute to new understandings of Christian social thought and practice (Rieger, p. 140). It will therefore
provide essentially provisional but workable frameworks for interpreting and
engaging the emerging context. It is a recognition that in this age particularly,
but in the two previous ages as well, 'all serious theology must be public theology' (Forrester, p. 200).

Partnerships. Collaboration with others in ideas or practices is increasingly
recognized by our plural context and by the great global challenges. Partnership is about that, about taking part with others in influencing our context. It
is a term increasingly used in public discourse at all levels of society, from
smallest local project to great international alliances. It frequently refers to
co-operation between private, public and voluntary sectors. Such participation in our contemporary situation therefore reflects some of its key characteristics, particularly as various representations of diversity. In turn, through
such embodiments, it seeks to change the situation.

To be so involved in changing society and theology through partnerships
means taking seriously a number of features, including identity, resources
and outreach, for a partner to be effective in them. Without them, participation in partnerships in a plural competing market-place ends in take-overs, by
those who do incorporate them, or the collapse of the collaborative project.
For example, identity is that confident understanding of ourselves, as individuals and collectives, including where we have come from, where we are,
and where we are going. For Christians, it is informed by involvement in their
faith narratives, traditions and communities. Historically, the ages of atonement and incarnation contributed to that identity formation for Christians
from the eighteenth to the twentieth centuries, and still do so. The emerging
age of reconciliation's contribution to Christian identity will be explored, in
terms of practical discipleship, in Chapters 5, 6 and 7, as it has been in terms of
tradition and faith community or Church, in Chapter 1. Yet identity, without
the resources in which to embody it in the economic, political and cultural
materials of contemporary life, is not sufficient. Similarly, that sacramental

interaction between identity and resources is alone inadequate for effective partnership in and through the emerging context. A third property for partners is also required, the commitment and ability to engage in partnership itself, to engage with others as outreach and dialogue, and including ideas and practices. Partnership is the recognition that we cannot go it alone in terms of understanding and praxis, nor should we desire to. It is acknowledgement that operating in a global context requires a 'pragmatic framework' like partnerships 'to integrate significant elements of other bodies of explanation' into a relationship with the Christian traditions (Dicken, p. 137).

Two interpretations of partnership emerge from the contemporary context. First, it is engendering in patterns of family life, personal relationships, new social movements, and workplace an ethos of contracts between parties to achieve goals, often short-term and powerfully pragmatic. It is neither place nor time for continuing an exclusive emphasis on partnerships through abiding covenants. Yet despite their provisional character the contract culture is generating forms of obligations and rights since contracts cannot be sustained without them. In doing so, they also represent the need for a covenanting dimension. The furore over the Church of England's report on family life today, *Something to Celebrate* (1995), illustrated the inability or unwillingness of many in Church and wider society to grasp the validity and accuracy of recognizing both contractual cohabitation and covenantal marriage.

Partnerships are, secondly, now recognizing the central role of the interactive relationship between a self-interest, powerfully acknowledged in economic relationships and increasingly in welfare policies, and wider social purposes and values. Rarely should partnership be entered into unless our self-chosen purposes and interests are accommodated. Partnership for the sake of it is rarely successful in the longer term; it needs to serve your interests as well as wider interests, which include the other partners and the chosen project or challenge.

Two interpretations of reconciliation. The age of reconciliation encompasses both the Christian need to be actively involved in the age of partnerships, because that is what the context requires and demands, and the obligation to do so, because that is what Christian beliefs require and demand. For reconciliation is one of the greatest foundational theological themes of Christian traditions and communities. And note immediately that we are dealing with a plural understanding, with at least two major interpretations of reconciliation out of two great traditions.

For the Reformed tradition, reconciliation results from the atoning death of Christ, the person's justification by faith through the grace of such an act. Focusing on that atoning death also means seeing reconciliation as ongoing process in continuity with the saving works of God through history. Our sufferings, through engagement in reconciliation, are part and parcel of Christ's. We literally share in that process of redemption:

> While we were yet helpless, at the right time Christ died for the ungodly. Why, one will hardly die for a righteous man . . . though perhaps for a good man one will dare even to die. But God shows his love for us in that while we were yet sinners Christ died for us. Since, therefore, we are now justified by his blood, much more shall we be saved by him from the wrath of God. For if while we were enemies we were reconciled to God by the death of his Son, much more, now that we are reconciled, shall we be saved by his life. Not only so, but we also rejoice in God through our Lord Jesus Christ, through whom we have now received our reconciliation. (Romans 5.6–11)

For the Catholic tradition, reconciliation focuses on the love of God, poured out through Christ's death, and its inauguration of a new creation.

> Therefore, if any one is in Christ, he is a new creation; the old has passed away, behold, the new has come. All this is from God, who through Christ reconciled us to himself and gave us the ministry of reconciliation; that is, God was in Christ reconciling the world to himself, not counting their trespasses against them, and entrusting to us the message of reconciliation. So we are ambassadors for Christ, God making his appeal through us. We beseech you on behalf of Christ, be reconciled to God. (2 Corinthians 5.17–20)

The task in the contemporary context, as an age of reconciliation rightly obliges us to do, is to weave the insights of both traditions into a broad interpretation of reconciliation, drawing, as it were, resources from the previous ages of atonement and incarnation. The existence of the different traditions and the plural nature of a global context, require no less. The aim of this argument is to elaborate it as the preferred option.

Equipped with such a broad plural understanding of reconciliation, insights or fragments from it can be used to identify and promote the processes of reconciliation and partnership in our world. For Christian traditions have rich experiences of understandings and practices of reconciliation. Religions are recognized as important players in the contemporary situation, and the ages of atonement and voluntarism and incarnation and state reveal the powerful history of that religious contribution. The Bishop of London, Right Revd Richard Chartres, arguing for the rebuilding of the IRA-bombed ancient church of St Ethelburga as a centre for reconciliation and peace, rightly observed that 'If the potential of faith communities is not channelled into preventing and transforming conflict, then the vacuum will be filled by those who wish to manipulate religious energies for their own narrow political ends' (*The Times*, 30 June 1999).

There are two ways in which Christian traditions can use their resources of faith and community to identify and promote reconciliation in our contemporary context.

The first is rather broad based and general, and refers to the essential Christian task of holding together insights and practices in relationships which can be creative and disturbing, if not turbulent, particularly in an openly competitive environment. John S. Mill referred to this: 'It is only by the collision of adverse opinions that the remainder of the truth has any chance of being supplied . . . Truth, in the great practical concerns of life, is so much a question of the reconciling and combining of opposites, that very few have minds sufficiently capacious and impartial to make the adjustment with an approach to correctness' (Briggs, 1982b, p. 12). Such a reconciling of opposites is no longer pre-eminently binary, in the Christian tradition's experience of reconciling divine and human in Christ, of immanent and transcendent in God, but increasingly also multi-faceted given the nature of economic growth and globalization. 'Today's global society, even more than its predecessor sixty years ago, confronts the task of reconciling technological change and economic integration with political structures, national consciousness, social needs, institutional arrangements and habitual ways of doing things' (P. Kennedy, 1993, p. 330).

The second Christian contribution is much more focused and relates to the growing need, in an increasingly fragmented and multipolar world, for the promotion of processes of reconciliation in conflict situations, in for example, Northern Ireland, Rwanda, Chile, South Africa, and the former Yugoslavia. Reconciliation in such dramatic situations, but equally in much lower key, local, even family or community situations, presents two faces. On the one hand, there is the social face, 'providing structures and processes whereby a fractured society can be reconstructed as truthful and just'. It is about enabling people to come to terms with the awfulness of the past, punishing wrongdoers, and making reparation to victims, using such means as a Truth and Reconciliation Commission. In all these processes, the churches have played important parts, because of the need to 'create a secure space and an atmosphere of trust that makes civil society possible'. The churches can do that because they are both a foundation of civil society and credally committed to reconciliation.

On the other hand, there is an increasingly recognized spiritual face of reconciliation. For the social is in the end always also about rebuilding shattered lives. Without the healing of memories, and never their denial, and without forgiveness, social reconstruction can never become a deep-seated long-term reality. For that task, the churches and Christians are ideally suited, as governments and non-governmental organizations are increasingly acknowledging. For sharing and living in the Christian narrative is about putting our story inside Christ's story: 'If Christ's suffering was redeeming for a sinful and conflicted world, then perhaps my suffering can gain meaning by being united to Christ's suffering' (Schreiter, pp. 4, 5). Yet even here at the most intimate heart of the Christian gospel, that experience is, and has to be, shared with others from quite different traditions. It is also therefore about partnerships. The Bishop of London, observing 'the growing network of centres, worldwide, involved in conflict resolution', concluded that the proposed Centre for Reconciliation and Peace at St Ethelburga's would need to take account of the fact that 'a multitrack approach to diplomacy is developing in which faith communities may have a role with other partners in transforming conflicts' (*The Times*, 30 June 1999).

This should not surprise us, for there are two sides to the cross. Reconciliation on this side of the cross, set in Gethsemane, involves wrestling with compromise and even violence, because power can be exercized for constructive and divine purposes. It is messy and dirty, as well as creative and loving, and it is certainly part and parcel of trying to work in partnerships with people and groups from other traditions and experiences. And that has to be held in clear, challenging and tangible touch with the other side of the cross, with that atoning love on the cross confirmed by the resurrection. Holding together opposites drives us to acknowledge that their ultimate reconciliation can only be achieved through their participation in the benefits of Christ's atoning death. It is about the contractual relationships of the age of partnership being informed by the intimations of covenantal relationships of an age of reconciliation. A key Christian task is to promote the linkages between the two, but not at the expense of diminishing the value of the contribution of each to God's wider purposes.

Now reconciliation through partnerships with others is predominantly about this side of the cross, about living with tensions between different identities and integrities which cannot, and should not, be collapsed into each other. There is not, and can never be, a Christian economics or politics, as radical orthodoxy seems to suggest. There are Christian engagements with the secular, hopefully in constructive partnerships. That is the story of the ages of atonement and voluntarism, of incarnation and state, and now of reconciliation and partnership. It is a story of faith interacting with and in and through the context in which it is placed. It is about being influenced and influencing. It is about recognizing that life on earth will always be about living in the interim, with a Kingdom always on the way this side of the cross, but sustained and informed by a grace from the other side of the cross: 'That would remind us that, though Christ has come, although salvation has occurred, the classic Christian grammar of these things requires us also to say: salvation is occurring now and is still awaited, eagerly, in hope' (Lash, p. 362). It points to a broad and diverse understanding of reconciliation, intimately linked to partnerships yet distinguishable from them. It is about the reconciling of people to God, each other, and their environment, about a Christ who is 'before all things, and in him all things hold together' (Colossians 1.17).

Part 2
Practical Divinity in the Emerging Age of Partnership and Reconciliation

The task of theology, then, is to begin from common practice and examine its quality in open trial by the use of natural reason in order to discover the truth of this practice, by a truth-directed reason; and the fulfilment of this purpose requires reference to the author of practice and practical reason. And the outcome of the trial should be an agreement on the proper organisation of common life which would actually promote the practice of society. It is notable that throughout the concern is public, theology mediated in public practice, the use of public reason, open trial of the truth and the achievement of truly social existence. (Daniel Hardy, in Ford, p. 31)

The late sixteenth and early seventeenth centuries proved to be an opportunity for developing English, and particularly Anglican, theology. It was a period of continuing change, coming between the explosive events of Reformation and Civil War. Developing theology was a tricky business. It certainly meant avoiding pitfalls relying on single authorities for guiding Christian life, whether Church laws of Roman Catholicism or Bible of Reformers. Christian thinkers like Hooker decided to focus instead on 'present organized practice', as Church, Bible, tradition and Prayer Book, but also relating to the life of society, people and state. That 'common practice' emerged out of early seventeenth century England and led to the development of practical divinity. It is that concept I have chosen to elaborate with reference to contemporary tasks, and inspired by its origins. For the resonances between that early modern formulation and today's context are striking. We are dealing with traditions, communities and authorities, with interactions between God's word in Scripture and works in nature and history, between what we would now call secular ages like state, and theological ages like incarnation. And it is about a public matter, a public theology, so much so that 'it is the responsibility of anyone skilled to attempt it; and its purpose is closely bound up with the functioning of society'. But there the similarities end, because religion is no longer a foundation of debate and practice in society, and attempts to reinstate it are so unlikely to succeed as to be as wasteful of energy as intentionally going up a cul de sac. Yet despite that challenge to reformulate the nature and content of what it means to do public theology today, we will address our task in a global context in a similar spirit, 'beginning from practice and correcting it through historical and rational consideration referred to divine truth' (Ford, pp. 31, 33). This practical divinity will result from joining the practice of partnership with the traditions of reconciliation, inspired and informed by signs embedded in the emerging global context.

The task of the remaining chapters is to explore how partnership and reconciliation is emerging in that context. They do so emphasizing what this means as practical discipleship, and operating respectively across three levels: local, national and international. In each, the language and practice of partnership is playing an increasingly important and creative part. Each focuses on an important theme arising out of the earlier analysis of global change: Chapter 5 addresses civil society, Chapter 6 the market economy, and Chapter 7 marginalization.

The following three chapters, therefore, are vignettes of partnership and reconciliation operating at different levels of society; they are not exhaustive accounts of appropriate activities, not least because the future cannot be predicted in detail. What they can do is show ways of practising partnership and reconciliation. This is about changing society. It is about practical divinity.

5 Neighbourly Discipleship: Transforming Localities

In a world influenced by global processes and challenges, local concerns, like national ones, appear to be increasingly distant from the real action. Yet that is not the case. While those processes draw authority upwards from the nation to the international level, they also push it downwards to the sub-national level. The growing pressure for regional autonomy in Britain, Spain and Italy exemplifies that trend. In other words, in a global economy, the local symbolizes the continuing importance of particular places where people live, often work, enjoy their leisure time and die. Even with the great migrations of modern urbanization, which show no signs of abating, particularly in developing economies, the exodus is routinely from rural to urban locality. The local remains the place where global forces now converge and shape the lives of people, communities, associations and environments. Yet it is also a place where they can all, in turn, influence their situation and those forces most sharply and tangibly. It is the location where changing society and theology, in both senses of changing, can and does still occur. It therefore becomes a reformulation of what it can now mean to be neighbourly.

Of course, some argue that the emphasis at this level should be on community, a concept more than a reality much loved by modern communitarians like Etzioni, and by post-modernist philosophers and theologians like MacIntyre and Hauerwas. In the midst of the confusions of living in a plural context, the security of a community and its tradition becomes understandably attractive. Yet their commitment to community is as inaccurate and unsafe as their misreading of the contemporary context, which is certainly about plurality but also about the global forces of integration. For there is no community to which we now belong. At best, there are a number of communities. And community is a concept that can mean almost anything to anyone. It is a classic aerosol word.

To interpret locality as civil society is more helpful for our task, providing its limitations are acknowledged. For although civil society depends profoundly on local associational activities, its societal character also gives it a nationwide remit. Besides embracing too broad a canvas, it is also too restricted, for the local includes local government and business activities as well as voluntary ones. So we will stay with the concept and reality of the locality throughout the chapter, yet we will use civil society, thus amended, as an entry point into wider and more focused illustrations of what partnership and reconciliation mean at local level. For the concept of civil society particularly allows us to focus on those voluntary neighbourly activities of local people and their associations which are now reflecting and engaging global questions of economic change and marginalization explored in Chapter 2. Equally, they also exemplify what partnership and reconciliation are beginning to mean.

REBUILDING CIVIL SOCIETY

For some, current debates about civil society are 'full of nostalgic rhetoric seeking an entirely impracticable return to an idealized nineteenth century constructed on these assumptions' (Hobsbawm, 1994, p. 139). Much in secular and theological communitarian lobbies certainly makes that mistake. Yet such questioning, in turn, could reveal an undue reliance on the state. Despite these criticisms, civil society persists as 'that whole sphere of economic, cultural or political self-organization, independent of the state' (Shanks, p. 7). It has flourished through the disruptive history of urbanization and industrialization in Britain and the United States – witness its central role in the age of voluntarism – and it is re-emerging as a central part of the age of partnership and reconciliation. Above all, it reflects the continuing importance of the local for human living.

One of the most useful definitions of civil society describes it as 'all the intermediate social organizations, the autonomous and semi-autonomous institutions, the constitutional checks and balances, that lie between central government and individual citizens, that protect them from direct, and always potentially arbitrary, central interference, that give shape and substance and continuity to their lives, a focus for loyalty and a place of engagement with other citizens that is not simply an extension of the market-place – the fabric of society, in short, or, as Hegel calls it, "civil society" ' (Boyle, p. 18). In other words, it refers to all bodies, small and great, in which people associate to pursue their self-chosen purposes, from local football club meeting in the pub or group protesting over a local problem, to national, and indeed international organizations with local branches. And the churches and other great faiths are perhaps the greatest.

The support, enhancement and reformulating of civil society, encompassing all these non-governmental associations rooted in localities, not surprisingly, is at the centre of contemporary political and religious concerns. Historically, the British Conservative Party's origins, in the late eighteenth century, promoted the importance of voluntary local associations, what their leading philosopher Edmund Burke called God's Little Platoons, not least in reaction to the totalitarian Jacobin state of the French Revolution. That commitment has continued to this day, and figures large in the publications of the leading think-tank, the Institute of Economic Affairs, as the priority task of 're-inventing civil society' (Green). More significantly, it has reappeared to occupy a central role in the policy and philosophy reformulation of New Labour. In Prime Minister Blair's *The Third Way*, Chapter 4 is titled 'Strong Civil Society: Rights and Responsibilities,' and in his seminal book on *The Third Way*, Anthony Giddens again has a chapter on the 'State and Civil Society'. After generations of neglect of, and indeed hostility to, the voluntary associations of civil society, British Labour is returning to nineteenth-century roots in the mutuality of working-class organizations and friendly societies. But the contemporary political importance of civil society is also developing in new and essential ways. On the one hand, new social movements are engaging those issues which often lie at the heart of the challenges of globalization, particularly environmental and marginalization questions. That represents the new politics of post-modernism. On the other hand, the pressure to develop international structures to engage globalization is manifested most powerfully in the emergence of the greatest regional bloc, the European Union. Enshrined at the heart of its Maastricht Treaty, in its 1992 Preamble, is the foundational principle of subsidiarity, which includes civil society.

In all these examples from the political order of creation, there is growing recognition, not simply of the contribution of civil society to the emerging new political order, but of the indispensable role it does and must play in partnerships with state and business sectors. The language and practice of partnerships is becoming more and more influential. For Blair, it is about taking voluntary organizations, particularly at the local level, with a novel, refreshing and powerful seriousness, 'encouraging their growth to tackle new needs, in partnership' (Blair, p. 4). It is a recognition that neither the local and national state, nor business, should alone be responsible for ordering our affairs, but that their partnerships must now include participation by local people through their local associations. It is a profound conversion, with an equally profound obligation to ensure that political parties honour such commitments – their recent past histories should make us watchful of their welcome new language and practice of partnership. In the 1980s, the Conservatives under Mrs Thatcher conducted sustained assaults on all those intermediate associations which criticized, or stood in the way of, her revolution, whether trade unions or churches. The age of the state, particularly under socialism, again witnessed the centralization of power, functions and resources in the hands of local and central government. Churches and voluntary bodies, conversely, were stripped of many historic tasks, particularly in education and welfare. The old Left, still lurking behind many local Labour controlled fiefdoms, remains often implacably opposed to real effective partnerships. The results of these attitudes and policies, taken to extremes, have been exemplified in the command economies of the Soviet Union and Third World. The collapse of that politicization of life, which they so powerfully represented, has left a disturbing vacuum which is essentially the absence of civil society. Rebuilding that will be a key task on which their political and economic freedoms will depend.

Promoting civil society through its local associations is also a central feature of the major Christian denominations, particularly in the Reformed and Anglican traditions. William Temple expressed this conviction most cogently:

> Actual liberty is the freedom which men enjoy in these various social units. But most political theories confine attention to the individual and the State as organ of the national community; they tend to ignore the intermediate groupings. But that makes any understanding of actual liberty impossible; for it exists for the most part in and through those intermediate groups – the family, the Church or congregation, the guild, the Trade Union, the school, the university, the Mutual Improvement Society. (Temple, 1942, p. 70)

The Roman Catholic tradition is equally supportive of the intermediate associations of civil society, particularly in their more local form. The principle of subsidiarity, influential today in the European Union, particularly through this Catholic tradition, was enunciated by Pope Pius XI in 1931 in the social encyclical *Quadragesimo Anno*. It has been more recently elaborated as 'a principle of responsibility, according to which what the individual can do on their own initiative should not be done by the community, and what the smaller community can do of itself should not be done by the larger community or the state' (Küng, p. 202).

It is from such fundamental understandings of civil society that the new theological principle of partnership emanates, a complementary relationship for engaging the plurality of sectors of state, business and voluntary. It both supports, in terms of identity through tradition, and requires, in terms of contemporary needs and realities, the intentional and strategic commitment by churches to civil society and partnerships with it and beyond it.

One of the great values of civil society is recognition of the local as a fundamental basis for people's participation in society. Yet its natural wider connections with society as a whole, and increasingly internationally, including non-governmental organizations, is equally important in a global economy. It reinforces the emerging role of an international third sector as civil society, again in partnership with other sectors, yet always embedded in the local, without which it cannot be sustained, without which it is essentially meaningless. Within these frameworks, a number of important roles can be identified for it, including educational; openness to new insights and concerns, and the ability to respond quickly to them; a valued independence from political parties and business interests; giving a public hearing to the voiceless; and providing a framework or forum for dialogue. It is profound recognition that 'the quality of public ethical debate seems to be at its best wherever civil society in general happens to be strongest' (Shanks, p. 209). To these I would add more traditional functions which have gained new urgency and form in the emerging new age, from mutual aid and support, and leisure, to self-help groups covering a variety of needs and aspirations.

Yet the very principle of partnership which affirms and depends on strong civil society also requires recognition of its limitations. For partnership, inspired by reconciliation, is, and has to be, about more than voluntary bodies, about more than the churches, even where they are strongest, in localities: even there, local and central government is essential. It continues to have indispensable 'protective, redistributive and conflict-mediating functions' in modern society. The variety of groups in civil society, and their tendency to become prey to disruptive gangs, requires such roles to be effectively performed to prevent civil strife (Reader, 1994, p. 60). Neither new social movements nor churches can acquire political power without their character being changed in fundamental ways. For that is to idealize them, in ways some post-modernists attempt with community, including faith communities. It is to transfer them to the other side of the cross, when they can never be anywhere else than this side of the cross. The age of partnership, inspired by reconciliation, will always stand against such confusion by recognizing the obligation never to make our identities other than what they are and to include in that affirmation the equal obligation to relate to, and work with, other identities.

It is easy and comforting to be nostalgic about locality, and especially its associations. Much of New Right and religious thinking is of that kind, yet it seriously misreads the changing nature of localities. Even such central institutions of localities as churches and community economic initiatives are continually being transformed in relation to the changing context. For example, the accelerating availability of information technology is facilitating the networking of local movements and extending them into the international sphere.

However, the changing nature of local civil society is reflected both in the decline of many large old membership organizations and in the rise of high levels of self-organization, particularly in the United States and Britain. Wuthnow's research into small group movements in the US is especially illuminating. He concludes that '40% of Americans – some 75 million – belong to at least one small group that meets regularly' to develop common interests. Even more importantly, their sense of association is not as much about being part of a locality, as 'people with similar concerns' getting together 'to pursue a "journey through life"'. Therapeutic models have particularly influenced such groups, but they are in the classic tradition of the age of voluntarism's self-help. It is just that they now adopt a post-modern dress.

Research into the third or voluntary sector activity in Britain since the 1950s suggests a similar degree of change. Substantial expansion again reveals declining activity and membership of some traditional groups as being more than made up for by the rise of new groups, especially of self-help and environmental kinds, and with growing female participation. In 1991, there were over 160,000 registered charitable groups, with nearly 20% of the population engaging in some voluntary work each year, and about 10% on a weekly basis. That activity rate declines among younger people, and in more deprived communities, but the figures take no account of substantial levels of informal networking by individuals and small groups which are not classified as voluntary, but which contribute to the vigour of civil society in localities. Good neighbourliness and informal witness by individual Christians make important contributions.

PARTNERSHIPS INVOLVING LOCAL VOLUNTARY BODIES IN A GLOBAL CONTEXT

Changing civil society is about more than replacing some traditional models of voluntary activity by newer forms. There is now growing evidence that local movements are addressing globalization processes and problems in their local manifestations. Some of these have an international character either because they are appearing across the world or because they are also sometimes part of actual international networks.

Two such areas have been chosen for examination. The first relates to economic and social regeneration, particularly in more deprived localities. In the Church of England they are known as urban priority areas (UPAs), and include inner cities, inner urban areas of older industrial towns, and large public housing estates. These projects link to the complex issue of the contribution of marginalized communities to economic growth, particularly given rapidly changing labour markets in a global economy. They therefore illustrate some of the ways the local can contribute to addressing such issues and problems. The second area of concern focuses on the challenge of fragmentation and growing divisions in society (and world) with reference to crime and punishment, and of living with different groups and interests.

Both exemplify partnerships between local people and voluntary associations, state and business. There are strong connections between the two areas of concern in that the first, economic and social regeneration, can be regarded as addressing important causes of social division, fragmentation and unrest. Although the projects are principally in developed economies (particularly in Britain and the United States), they clearly resonate with experiences in the developing economies. Most importantly for the interaction between partnership and reconciliation, they will be tested against the three marks already identified as necessary for those wishing to participate effectively in the age of partnership in a plural and competitive market-place. These apply equally to the Church, in terms of what it means to be an effective Church in partnerships, through identity, resources and social outreach. It will be sharp reminder to many liberal Christians that in a plural context the interaction between reconciliation and partnership needs to be demonstrably two way, and certainly should include effects of the theology of the word, as reconciliation, on context, as well as the theology of God's works operating in and through that context, and particularly as partnership. It is about, therefore, participation and reconciliation as 'practical means of furthering the social and material refurbishment of neighbourhoods, towns and larger local areas' (Giddens, pp. 80–2, 79). It is about neighbourly discipleship transforming localities.

Economic and social regeneration of localities: partnerships at work

Globalization and economic growth, driven by the relentless engine of technological advance, 'cannot be wished away'. Nor can their complex nature, or tendency to generate winners and losers. From the late eighteenth century, gathering pace ever since, the trend has been to greater productivity, to produce more with less. Under 3% are now engaged in agriculture in Britain and the United States, growing more than ever before. So it will be with manufacturing, and then services. And so it is happening. Such technological advances as biotechnology and robotics will drive these tendencies further and further, aided and abetted by globalization processes and information and communication technologies. And reinforcing those changes, because of the population explosion worldwide, 'more than a billion jobs will have to be created over the next ten years to provide an income for all the new job entrants' (Drimmelen, pp. 27, 80).

How do we face up to that on such a global scale? Clearly, contributions of governments, transnational corporations, and international institutions like the World Trade Organisation and the International Labour Organisation will continue to grow in importance. That is about acknowledging the tide of economic growth and change. And clearly that will affect, for good and ill, localities.

But what of those multitudes of localities either not fully part or not part at all of those dominant economic forces? How do we enable such areas to participate constructively in economic change? Accounts from around the world, from inner cities of Britain to rural areas of Bangladesh, demonstrate that such participation is happening, at times parallel to mainstream formal economies, but yet complementing them in terms of income and social regeneration. They can suggest the emergence of a social economy, in which the third or voluntary sector plays an indispensable part, rooted as it is in the local. Sometimes they evolve into creative parts of the formal economy, sometimes they generate new ways of operating financial systems. And partnerships between people, organizations and sectors, sometimes across different levels, from local to international, are increasingly demanded as integral parts of effective performance. Churches and other religious and voluntary bodies in civil society are often at the heart of such endeavours.

There is now growing evidence demonstrating how local initiatives can help reverse economic and social decline, particularly when supported by sustainable investments from government, business and international institutions. They can create work skills and small enterprises, and contribute to producing more socially cohesive communities and societies. In this, they also provide necessary preventive measures to complement strong criminal justice policies, particularly in divided Western societies.

Classic examples of such partnerships involving funding arrangements, small groups, and economic and social regeneration in deprived localities, are revealed in the operations of the Church Urban Fund (CUF). As implementation of recommendations by the Archbishop's Commission's Report, *Faith in the City* (1985), raising a large capital resource for distribution to agreed local applications for funding was in itself a partnership between central agencies of the Church of England, dioceses and parishes, and the business sector. By the mid 1990s, £22.5 million had been granted to over 1,200 projects in UPAs across the country, with over £2.3 million for over 65 projects in the Diocese of Manchester. That partnership requirement also determines funding provisions for the local projects themselves. They have to raise the finance from a variety of sources: the CUF, the government's regional funding structure, the Single Regeneration Budget, the European Social Fund, charitable trusts and local business. All now invariably require local projects to put together a funding base from such a variety of partners, and demonstrate collaborative working with other denominations, faiths, voluntary bodies, government agencies and businesses.

The task of such local initiatives is to enable and empower local people, groups and communities to stand on their own feet. It is about promoting self-sustaining economic and social growth, in ways which have clear resonances with general patterns of economic growth on a global scale. It is about enabling the marginalized to be made full members of national and global economies, through the localities of civil society.

Besides a whole series of partnerships involving finance and practical working within a locality and beyond, these projects share a number of important features. They are frequently about identifying or generating and then fostering local self-help groups. They can develop from informal personal services into small business and income-generating organizations. They often focus on such signs of social dislocation as solvent, drug and alcohol abuse, car theft and unemployment.

Results of such activities are significant for local marginalized neighbourhoods in Manchester and beyond. They can be measured and can be substantial in income generation, jobs, training, crime prevention and criminal rehabilitation. Yet it is not just these necessary quantifiable results which are significant for Church and society. We must also recognize the daily unseen and unsung achievements of these involvements. A project in a particularly deprived inner city community of greater Manchester is based in a church school which serves the local community. A recent project report observed: 'There have been a number of developments which have come about unexpectedly, for example, less arguments and fighting amongst parents on the estate over children, as they now know each other and are willing to talk over problems. They are beginning to understand the importance of being assertive without the aggressiveness ... The parents are accepting the need to show greater responsibility towards their lives and those of their children, and in turn guide their children to this end' (St Philip's, Salford, unpublished, 1996). All that, with tangible yet unassuming and untrumpeted consequences for the quality of life, is achieved through such ordinary mundane means as coffee mornings for gossiping, parenting work shops, lunch clubs for the elderly, and first aid courses. Yet the prevention of social disease is not therefore better than cure. That is to slip back into old dialectics of either-or, which is inappropriate in a multicausal and multifaceted world. Prevention is rather one essential prerequisite for a just, orderly and peaceful and prosperous society, to be promoted in conjunction with a variety of other policies.

Local social and economic regeneration programmes through partnership and reconciliation, so graphically illustrated through the work of the Church Urban Fund, are examples of emerging partnerships on a global scale, and their contribution to the social and more formal economies. That is a welcome but also essential development given the progress of unremitting globalization.

Take St Illtyd's Family Centre in South Wales, 'a new concept in child care services' initiated by South Glamorgan County Council and the Diocese of Llandlaff's Board for Social Responsibility. Since mothers play an increasingly important part in the new labour markets, child care and family nurture are indispensable for changing patterns of relationships and employment. The project is explicitly regarded and organized as 'an exciting partnership which offers a wide range of facilities and support for children and families' (Llandaff Diocese, unpublished, 1996). Such small programmes remind us of the global importance of microenterprises operating in formal and informal sectors. They are principal providers of employment and essential contributors to family survival, to the social and economic regeneration of localities. For the 500 largest transnational corporations, the main engines of the global economy, with 25% of world economic output, only employ one twentieth of 1% of the world's population. 'About half of the paid jobs in the world are held by people who work in one- to five-person enterprises, and in some places the percentage is even higher'. More importantly, it is a worldwide trend uniting developed and developing economies. The UN's *Human Development Report 1996* recorded that the informal sector in which microenterprises operate accounts for nearly 80% of all employment in Ibadan, Nigeria, and 68% in Bombay, India. In Latin America and the Caribbean, 'more than 50 million microenterprises employ more than 150 million workers'. Yet the growth of microenterprises is also an important economic and social force in the United States. Between 1992 and 1996, while bigger companies shed 645,000 jobs, small and medium-sized firms created 11.8 million new jobs (Drimmelen, p. 147).

Historically, capital and financial provisions were at the heart of the economic processes of the industrial revolution, and are more and more influential in the emerging global economy. How can modern financial instruments be used in localities not simply in relation to the essential mainstream functionings of the formal economy, but in supporting the wide spectrum of microenterprises, and promoting local partnerships? Growing evidence suggests that microcredit is one such productive way of resourcing the economic and social regeneration of marginalized people and communities through partnerships. Essentially, microcredit is lending very small amounts of money, often without collateral, to poor aspiring entrepreneurs. 'Today, more than US$1 billion a year is being lent to some 8 million people in the South. Even the USA has about 300 micro-credit programmes.' All these schemes recognize that one of the major problems of being poor, of being marginalized, in a global economy, is lack of access to finance and capital for mutual self-improvement. Commercial banks are notoriously reluctant to lend to the poor in general and to their proposed small enterprises in particular. They are thought to present unacceptable risks to traditional mainstream financial institutions, and the administrative costs of supporting a multitude of microenterprises are regarded as prohibitively high. 'Women are especially affected by local customs and even national laws which discriminate against them in economic life.' Yet they constitute more than 60% of the agricultural workforce in Africa, and contribute up to 80% of small-scale food production. Despite such effort, 'they receive less than 10% of the credit to small farmers and only 1% of total credit to agriculture.'

The problem of the inability to obtain small-scale financing for local enterprises from commercial banks is compounded by exorbitant interest rates charged by moneylenders. It is precisely at that point of need, essential for promoting local economic growth and social cohesion, that microcredit plays such a central role. Moreover, existing schemes demonstrate that the poor are not bad risks, 'that they are prompt and reliable repayers (especially women) and that they successfully use small loans to increase their income. Leading micro-credit lenders around the world boast repayment rates of 97% and higher.' As important, because of the multifaceted nature of the challenges facing the global context, and which all enterprises and endeavours now need to engage, the schemes invariably promote partnerships through democratic and participatory ways of organizing, and particularly through co-operatives, but also apply social and environmental criteria for loans. Equally, they clearly reveal the importance of being complemented and supported by other strategies, since no one programme can address effectively such complex contemporary problems as economic growth and marginalization. For example, fairer world trading policies, international debt relief, supportive legal frameworks for small enterprises, co-operatives and credit systems all have a role to play if micro-credit schemes are to make more effective contributions to localities.

The best known micro-credit scheme is the Grameen Bank in Bangladesh, one of the poorest nations on earth. It is directed particularly at the needs of the poorest people, the landless, and gives training and support to aspiring borrowers, but uses stringent conditions for assessing credit-worthiness and project viability. Candidates for loans join groups of five borrowers, of whom only two are initially allowed to apply for loans. It is at this point that local weekly training is provided. 'Depending on their performance in repayment, the next two can apply and subsequently the fifth as well' (Drimmelen, pp. 148, 149, 150). Currently, the Bank serves one million rural clients, of whom over 90% are women; 99% of loans are repaid, way beyond the performance of commercial banks. The key is partnership between people, communities and organizations connected through mutually supportive networks. They all represent ways of facing up to contemporary global change, but are only effective in the long term if done in collaboration with other systems and sectors.

Partnerships addressing divisions and fragmentations in society

Much in social and economic regeneration is about dealing with the cohesive forces of globalization, including the multicausal nature of economic growth. Yet those same powers also generate divisions and fragmentations, adding to the already increasingly plural context of post-industrial and post-modern society. Two stories of local projects illustrate how people are living with such change through change. The first is from Manchester and concerns the disturbing problem of youth crime, a powerful symbol of the social consequences of a deeply divided society. The second is from rural Shropshire and relates how a local community has tried to make sense of a fragmented and plural context. In both, the church has played a leading part, but in partnership with other groups and people. Reflecting on their experience develops our understanding of what it means for the church to be effective partner through the three properties of identity, resources and outreach. That leads into elaborating how the age of reconciliation can interact critically and constructively with the age of partnership.

The Youth Justice Trust. Whenever I go to a local church meeting in the Manchester area and ask what most bothers the people, they invariably reply 'crime', and invariably focus on harsh punishment as the best way to tackle it. That is, until we begin to ask questions about what lies behind crime, what are the most effective ways to tackle it in the long as well as short term, and therefore how much can be prevented. Only then do we get into serious discussion of contemporary crime. Only then do we get beyond current populist media and political reactions to crime – what I call 'the one key to open all doors approach', be it harsher punishment or the latest American penal programme. The more I reflect on the complexities of our society in an emerging global economy, the more I realize that there is never one key to open all doors, whether that key be explanations of a contemporary issue or appropriate policy responses, and whether that issue be crime, unemployment or whatever.

It is in that spirit that I have come to see that facing up to crime is about far more than the issue of crime and punishment. It is about what kind of society we live in. R. H. Tawney's advice in the early part of the twentieth century in Manchester is still relevant, that in addressing a problem like poverty or crime, we would be wiser 'to start much higher up the stream than the point' we wish to reach. Addressing the issue of crime in Manchester or New York today cannot be divorced from wider matters relating to growing marginalization in society in an increasingly global context, which itself is also about growing inequalities and divisions. We are already in a new context of accelerating globalization and yet increasing fragmentation and tribalism, with the turbulence historically associated with such divisions. Patterns of marginalization, accentuated by the consequences of economic change, and elaborated in Chapter 2, revealed connections between those patterns and social disorder and imprisonment. Some 40% of the West Indian population in Britain live in households earning below half average income, with the average of 37% of children in such households, so why should we be surprised that we have so many young and black people before our courts, and that we commit more people to penal institutions than any other European country except Turkey? Some 20% of households are workless, and within them unqualified young men face a particularly difficult task securing reasonable employment, so why are we surprised at the correlation between increasing rates of unemployment and of committal of young people to penal institutions? It is clearly necessary for us to face up to crime, but we would be foolish if we thought simple monocausal explanations would be sufficient. The same applies to dealing effectively with the problem of crime. Justice policies have to be complemented by preventive measures, and that, among other things, links back into the social and economic regeneration of localities. And informing all these approaches, as with addressing any other complex contemporary problem, is the growing recognition that 'in order to work, partnerships between government agencies, the criminal justice system, local associations and community organizations have to be inclusive – all economic and ethnic groups must be involved' (Giddens, p. 88).

Addressing youth crime and disorder in a Manchester integrally part of wider processes of marginalization and disturbance, the Youth Justice Trust embodies these understandings and characteristics. Essentially a partnership body, it was set up by the Anglican diocese of Manchester's Board for Social Responsibility as lead agency, in collaboration with other relevant agencies, including the Home Office, Social Service Departments of local government, the Probation Service, the National Association for the Care and Resettlement of Offenders (NACRO), and other voluntary bodies. Why did the church lead such a partnership? Because no one agency could now tackle such complex matters. Within such an agreed collaborative effort, the church was regarded as a body involved in various relevant aspects of the youth crime problem, from participation in deprived localities and with young people, to being an organization with strong historic and ideological commitments to the pursuit of justice and practice of compassion. It had the respect of the other, at times contending, agencies, as a body of detached concern sufficient to 'hold the ring'. It also possessed the resources to provide office space and managerial support systems. It had, in other words, a clear identity, sufficient resources and a strong commitment to outreach, to working with others in partnerships.

What does the Youth Justice Trust do? First, it seeks to provide accurate, regularly updated information for agencies involved in youth justice services in Greater Manchester, from courts, Probation and Social Services, to police and local voluntary bodies. These agencies can then make more appropriate management and resource decisions.

Second, it seeks to bring together relevant agencies to develop policies and services for young offenders. Underlying these objectives is the Trust's concern to protect and enrich society by proactive as well as reactive policies. It works purposefully so that young people are brought from punishment for offences to a proper participation in society. It is concerned for both restorative justice and the redemption of individuals and societies.

Two projects illustrate this concern for developing the practice of partnership and reconciliation. The Trust is involved in a programme for young arsonists, crimes which have cost communities millions of pounds in damage, often to valued public buildings like schools and churches. Its aim is to provide an effective non-custodial alternative for convicted young arsonists. Instead of custody, and with the active involvement of fire officers, young people are given supervision orders with intensive special programmes, confronting them with their offending behaviour, thereby seeking to rehabilitate them and to protect the public against re-offending. Of the small number who have, as yet, gone through the programme, only one has re-offended, and that was not an arson offence.

The second project focused on persistent young offenders; the Trust was concerned to develop practical, stringent, condition-bound alternatives to penal institutions, both for their rehabilitation and for greater cost effectiveness. The price of incarcerating young people is astonishingly high – equivalent to over three full-time community or youth workers for each person imprisoned. More importantly for church and society, the short-term benefit to the public by taking the young person off the streets is more apparent than real. Imprisonment is often a further brutalizing experience for the young prisoner, who will encounter violent bullying, physical and sexual abuse and drug addiction. Instead of being rehabilitated, prisoners are frequently hardened and their criminal efficiency increased; it is damnation rather than redemption. And that is unacceptable to the church, with its clear commitment to love as well as justice, and its concern for the redemptive processes of reconciliation both of individuals and of societies. It is that gospel imperative which clearly and tangibly informs the practices and thinking of the Trust, theological fragments interacting with similar fragments from other traditions involved in the partnership, all promoting particular policies on the remand and incarceration of young people in penal institutions. 'Serious conversation with theology will be greatly limited if the voice of theology is not recognisably theological . . . Conversation partners must remain distinctive enough to be identified, to be needed' (Forrester, p. 31).

The Local History Group. How does the church make sense of increasingly diverse and plural localities? In situations where no one fragment, tradition or organization dominates, how do people live and work together more effectively? In the midst of diversity and collaboration how do people and groups maintain the integrity of their identities? What does the church's involvement in such localities mean for developing its identity in and through partnerships as the interaction of the age of partnership and reconciliation?

The Local History Group emerged out of a small group of rural communities in Shropshire, and brought together people with very different beliefs and concerns. It never adopted a name; it covered a range of interests, with none allowed to be dominant; it met in people's homes, the vicarage and a pub. The Vicar acted as convenor, because he knew all the people, and was a respected reconciler of interests. Essentially a forum for the free exchange of views around common concern for local narratives and history, the Group began to identify and develop shared interests. Some of these eventually took the form of practical programmes, including a play scheme and environmental project. By ranging across a number of issues, it avoided the narrow focus of single issue groups, and so had the value of trying to see things as a whole. It was never explicitly churchy or Christian, but included some committed church members, some on the fringes of the church (believers not belongers), and some who had no interest in the church at all.

Reflecting on the story of the Local History Group raises three questions about what form Christian involvement should take in such partnerships. Exploring responses to them elaborates further what reconciliation and partnership mean in that process, and their interaction. It is their sum total which begins to suggest the form which Christian discipleship can and should take in addressing the global economy through localities.

First, involvement in a forum containing a plurality of perspectives encouraged church members to develop their Christian understanding of identity. They began 'to clarify what their beliefs contributed to the discussions and how they provided a basis for the local action. This is what local theology became in this specific context – a process of reflective engagement that brought certain aspects of Christian tradition to life. For the first time, perhaps, we could begin to see what some of these words meant in the light of the very real problems we faced together.' It is where understandings of justice, love and reconciliation are discovered and appropriated within Christian tradition and faith community. An older woman, faithful member of a church in a deprived inner city community, regularly served tea and toast to local mothers in the church hall. It was a place to come and meet others, to relax and laugh together. A theological student on placement there sat and listened to her work, and helped her to see how her service connected to the Gospel stories of service, even to death on the cross. So she now saw what she was doing, and why. Not that it changed what she did. But it was now so different. She had appropriated the Christian story of reconciliation in and through her partnership involvement.

Second, however, membership of such groups begins to suggest that involvement in partnership itself now becomes part of the Christian task and discipleship. Since the church is no longer the centre of life, particularly in Western societies, its vocation is not to respond by retreating into inward-looking, congregationally based churches, but is about taking part with others in promoting better localities. That can be achieved by the church providing an open, 'no strings attached' forum for such a coming together of different perspectives and traditions: 'If it has a wider role, it can only be as an inter-network network, providing a forum or some common ground for other networks. It cannot do this if its declared aim is to capture all the other groups within its own net.' Christian involvement in partnerships requires commitment to sharing stories, to listening to each other. Yet this implies recognizing, and becoming at ease with, the Christian contribution of unearthing the questions behind the questions: 'Perhaps the greatest advantage that the church possesses is that it can legitimately initiate discussion of any issue at a moral or spiritual level.' A particular Christian contribution to partnership activities can therefore be 'to carve out spaces and opportunities for issues to be discussed in such a way that the moral dimension is included' (Reader, 1994, pp. 80, 78, 85).

Third, Christian participation in partnerships requires facilitating interactions between partnership and reconciliation. For example, such outreach clearly has a dimension engaging with people and serving communities for their own sake. It will always be about labouring and not asking for any reward. It will be about promoting peace, justice, mercy and love because they are signs of the Kingdom. And yet . . . Since everything is multifaceted, discipleship is about that, and more than that. It must also be about nurturing the Church in the locality. In the last five years, the Diocese of Manchester, in company with other dioceses and denominations, has lost 15% of its membership. There are a number of localities where it is facing extinction. If the Christian task does not also now include building up local membership, then there will be no Christian social witness through partnership, because there will be no organized Christian presence. There is a large store in the middle of Manchester which I used to visit as a child once a year to buy Christmas presents. It contained an amazing profusion of quality goods and services on floor after floor. It maintained its dominant position in retailing because it regularly surveyed its customers. Over the years, the numbers shopping there declined greatly. They still conducted surveys of their customers. What they did not do was to ask the views of those who had stopped shopping there. I now await their closure. That is what has happened and what is happening to the church in Britain and most of the West, a body no longer reaching out with appropriate purposes, which include clarity about particular identity, resources involving membership, and outreach as mission. That is what well-meaning liberal bodies like the Church Urban Fund have now to come to terms with. It is about interaction between partnership and reconciliation.

Having an eye to building up membership and being committed to collaboration with others is not easy. Most want to do one or the other, to use partnership as opportunity for conversion, or engage simply in practical projects. Neither should any longer be an exclusive influence in contemporary discipleship. How do we develop such a tricky balance? A story might help. In the 1970s and 1980s, the Church of England's Board for Social Responsibility produced a number of influential reports on major social issues including nuclear weapons, industrial conflict, economic life, homosexuality and the future of the welfare state. They brought together secular and theological expertise in the membership of working parties and in the way the reports were divided up. Consequently, the tradition was that they were written for the Church, with society looking over its shoulders. Christian discipleship in partnerships turns that tradition upside down. The Christian task now is to address society through partnerships, with the Church now looking over its shoulder to its traditions in clear, tangible and identifiable ways. So, from involvement in those partnerships, from the presence in such Christian participation of such signs as the concern for underlying moral and spiritual questions, and the commitment to justice, peace, and reconciliation, those fragments must be clearly traced back into the Church and embodied in its traditions. Through that, the two sides of the cross can and will be brought together, and in turn, inform the Christian contribution to partnerships. It becomes the Christian task of promoting more effective local churches in and through more effective localities. The one now hangs with the other, the interacting of the age of partnership and reconciliation. It is to enable Christians 'to grow into this dynamic mutuality through processes of faith development and critical exploration, so that the mission of God in Jesus may reach its fulfilment for the good of all humanity' (Hull, p. 13).

6 National Discipleship: Reformulating Politics

The changing context has had a particularly formative influence on political life and its role in the nation state. The evolution of global free market capitalism has put pressure on the ability of the nation state, and therefore politics, to control economic life and welfare policies. It seems a long way from the golden age of such management in the 1960s and 1970s. The lessons of inflexible command economies, the epitome of political control of life in general, and economy in particular, is stark and unequivocal. If you do not respond to change by changing in this context, you will disappear. That was the harsh, unremitting message for the socialist project, delivered by the events of 1989. If you do not reform, you will be 'blown away by the gale of global competition' (Gray, 1997). Facing that challenge, linked to the comprehensive changes of the 1960s to the present, therefore demands the reformulation of tradition. It is a task which is an obligation for all who wish to survive gracefully in this emerging age by seeking to change it, and integral to it is the reformulation of politics. For the erosion of politics by globalization processes and socialist failures does not reduce the necessity of politics for human living. Engaging globalization and global challenges, including the role of the nation, means changing politics in its changing national framework. That task will therefore be explored through three reflections on the importance of reformulation from a Christian and then Third Way perspective, the emerging practice of a cosmopolitan citizenship and nation, and the redevelopment of the social market economy and welfare state.

REFORMULATION AS A WAY OF LIFE

Responding to change constructively is classic test of human creativity. For people, social systems and wider creation, it can often contribute to survival and growth. Yet adapting to change effectively is not simply reacting to events, however necessary that is. In the world of ideas, practices and systems the process of adaptation can, in turn, influence the changing context. Reformulation is precisely about facing up to change by and through change. It is about interactive engagements with changing context. Two stories illustrate what such reformulation can mean. Both reflect struggles to address continuing transformations generated by industrialization and urbanization. The first is from the earlier stages of these processes in the late nineteenth century and focuses on the work of Charles Gore and the reformulation of Christian tradition as liberal Catholicism and Christian social reform. The second is from the late twentieth century and explores the work of Tony Blair and the reformulation of British socialism as a Third Way.

Interestingly, they are connected through the greater durability of the tradition of ethical socialism as Christian social reform over against the tradition of radical Christian socialism. Gore and the Christian Social Union made powerful contributions to the former's construction. Tony Blair, following in the steps of his predecessor, John Smith, has recognized this Christian tradition as an important contribution to reformulating socialism as a reformist Third Way. Both stories are significant because they generate insights into how people and systems, both religious and political, have responded to change. Blair illustrates how social democracy has sought to respond to the seismic changes endured by this generation, and what appeared to be the likely extinction of the socialist tradition. Gore exemplifies Christian response to change a century ago, the legacy of which still endures and is still influential in mainstream Christian social witness. That persistence of a tradition, relatively unchanged, may of course help to explain why Churches are experiencing such decline and maybe eventual extinction in the West. For facing up to change, particularly on the scale we are enduring, demands regular reformulation. Reflections on the Third Way, in critical interaction with our understanding of the emerging age of partnership and reconciliation, may therefore contribute valuable insights to that contemporary reformulation so integral to Christian survival and growth. And because globalization is proceeding apace, problems of Western Christians and socialists will also be experienced by those in developing economies in the not too distant future. Reformulating politics and Christianity have much to learn from each other.

By the later nineteenth century, the age of voluntarism and atonement was no longer engaging effectively the urban–industrial revolution, and particularly its disruptive consequences. New responses were called for; they emerged in the form of the mass politics of democracy and labour movements, reinforced by an intellectual and cultural environment moving from individualism to collectivism. Endeavours to humanize or replace capitalism were supported by growing belief in evolutionary or gradual change. Churches began to react to problem and response through a similar process of change, symbolized by the age of incarnation. At the heart of that Christian reformulation were the Christian Social Union and the collection of essays *Lux Mundi*, edited by Charles Gore. Indeed, so successful was this whole undertaking that it continues to inform the Christian social witness of mainstream

British churches, from the Anglican *Faith in the City* to the ecumenical *Unemployment and the Future of Work*. The problem, of course, is that new Christian reformulations should now be affecting that witness.

At first sight, Gore was an unlikely leader of reform. Nurtured in the Anglo-Catholic dogmatism of the Oxford Movement, he was groomed for leadership by Liddon. As first Principal of Pusey House and 'heir to the ideals of the lately dead Pusey' (Chadwick, p. 24), it was assumed he would simply continue that tradition. But Gore was both a rebel and authoritarian, and is reputed to have shaken his fist at Lambeth Palace, the epitome of establishment. He wore boots made by the Co-operative movement, and was buried not in a cathedral, as a bishop, but in the church of the Community of the Resurrection, Mirfield, Yorkshire, as its founder. He was an exception among bishops in that, rather than retiring or dying, he resigned in order to do more significant tasks. More importantly, he was alive to the changing context of the economic, political and social turbulence of the 1880s. For it was this which provoked the founding of the first socialist group, the Social Democratic Federation (1883), the radical Christian socialist Guild of St Matthew (1877), the Fabian Society think-tank of British socialism (1884), the general worker trade unions focused around the great dock strike of 1889, and the extension of democracy by the Reform Act of 1884. Intellectually, these developments were paralleled by the increasing influence of the Darwinian evolutionary mind-set on social, political and cultural ideas, the rise of philosophical idealism with its emphasis on the state and active citizenship, and the influence of historical and biblical criticism on the social sciences and religion. Gore's grasp of incarnational theology, of the embodying of the Christlike God in and through the realities of the world, drove him to try to bring together such social and intellectual change in the reformulated Christianity of liberal Catholicism and the Christian Social Union.

The seminal collection of essays *Lux Mundi* (1889) had a much more telling sub-title: *A series of studies in the religion of the incarnation*. Using the central theological commitment to incarnating the divine in the realities of life, Gore engaged constructively with contemporary developments to interpret Christianity through contextual change, including contemporary intellectual discourses. As liberal Catholicism, it was essentially a combining of catholic tradition and reformed criticism as evolving process. The result of that interaction was a reformulation of Christian doctrine, resourced by the acceptance of biblical criticism, and focusing particularly on the understanding of Christ through the kenotic theory, the self-limitation of Christ through the act of incarnation itself. This reformulation of doctrine as well as practice contrasts favourably with New Labour's unwise attempts to limit reformulation to practice and theoretical outworkings, and leave core traditional values untouched.

On the other hand, as important for Gore, interacting tradition and modernity required and informed his participation in the Christian Social

Union from its foundation in 1889. As the premier organization promoting Christian social reform, it was involved in such practical programmes, of significance still today, as the campaign against low pay, leading to the Trade Boards Act of 1909 and resourced by a consumer movement purchasing only from companies with fair wages and conditions. As Christian ethical socialism of the reformist kind, it had a deep influence on the churches, as the socializing of Christianity, and on social reform, as the christianizing of socialism. Its legacy is still traceable in the programmes of Tony Blair and New Labour, and in Frank Field's work on welfare reform. That continuing influence suggests that criticism of *Lux Mundi* and the reformulation of Christian beliefs and social practices, as simply accommodating the faith to modernity and so hastening its decline, is at best a half-truth, and at worst mischievous. For it neglects its social and political influence, and the far more decisive long-term corrosive effects of industrialization and urbanization on religious theories and practices. Gore's work rather stands in the tradition of reformulation as contribution to changing society and theology in and through their interaction. In that, he heeded the acerbic judgement of his disciple, R. H. Tawney, on the eighteenth-century Church of England, that 'the social teaching of the Church had ceased to count, because the Church itself had ceased to think' (Tawney, 1966, p. 188). Such a 'fundamental defect' could only be rectified by a reformulation of faith in categories sensitive to, yet in critical interaction with, the dominant developments of the contemporary context (Atherton, 1979, p. 186). Gore exemplifies that necessary endeavour at the turn of the twentieth century.

The 'Third Way', and its equivalents in Chancellor Schröder of the German Social Democratic Party (SPD), and the New Democrats of President Clinton in the United States, represents the necessary reformulation of social democratic political tradition, essential because of major continuing electoral defeats and the changes in the generation following on the 1960s. For Blair, acknowledging both causes of decline was an essential prerequisite for effective reformulation: 'society changed and we did not change sufficiently with it' (Blair, *The Guardian*, 10 September 1996). The Third Way as reformulation of social democracy emerges out of that recognition. It therefore offers a representative case study of the need for, and possibility of, change through the reformulation of centre left political thought and practice. It is of particular interest because it reflects, and contributes to, the language and practices of the emerging age of partnership and reconciliation. For it, too, acknowledges that 'politics is first and foremost about ideas . . . [and] ideas need labels if they are to become popular and widely understood' (Blair, p. 1). As important, such big ideas need to be sufficiently comprehensive to engage contemporary economic and social affairs. The Third Way, through stakeholder economy, company and welfare system, reflects that concern for a breadth sufficient to relate to the large forces of globalization.

As an exercise in reformulation, the Third Way is essentially a 'framework of thinking and policy-making that seeks to adapt social democracy to a world which has changed fundamentally over the past two or three decades. It is a third way in the sense that it is an attempt to transcend both old style social democracy and neoliberalism.' Now that movement beyond the traditional dialectics of Old Left and New Right is particularly important for understanding the contemporary task of reformulation. For the Third Way moves beyond the Old Left, with its commitment to the state as end in itself, high taxes, and producer interests. It rejects the socialist failure to modernize the economy by recognizing the capacity of capitalism to innovate, adapt and generate increasing productivity, and of social policy to reform the ideas and policies of the welfare state to reflect and engage changing labour markets and lifestyles. It is to reject a socialism which died with the ending of a bipolar world.

Yet equally, the Third Way moves beyond the neoliberalism of the New Right. For that tradition can no longer reconcile the conservatism of its commitment to family, nationalism and civil society with its commitment to market fundamentalism which continues to erode those traditional bonds. The Third Way therefore rejects that advocacy of efficiency and choice linked to growing social exclusion. It rejects, in particular, more extremist versions of neoliberalism, propounded by Buchanan in the United States, Le Pen in France and Pauline Hodson in Australia. Facing up to change by promoting an isolationist economic perfectionism holds no hope, in the medium to long term, in a globalized economy and world.

Rejecting, but learning from, failed alternatives, leads to a reformulation which therefore seeks 'to manage that change [of the global economy] to produce social solidarity and prosperity' (Giddens, pp. 26, 1). It is about 'reconciling themes which in the past have wrongly been regarded as antagonistic – patriotism and internationalism; rights and responsibilities; the promotion of enterprise and the attack on poverty and discrimination' (Blair, p. 1). Avoiding the old polarities of individualism against solidarity, 'counterpoised as opposites' (Giddens, p. 20), the Third Way now seeks to hold them in creative if turbulent relationship as 'the vision of a communitarian ethical socialism, combining individual empowerment with social solidarity' (Marquand, *The Guardian*, 3 February 1995). It is not concerned with splitting the difference between left and right, a kind of social democratic middle axiom, but about pioneering welfare reform to combat social exclusion; it is about engaging private sector and business in new partnerships with government, promoting, for example, a more effective science base through the collaborative investment of government and Wellcome Trust; it is about being tough on crime and on the causes of crime through welfare to work and other programmes to reduce the divisive effects of marginalization processes. It is an important example of what reformulating politics could mean in an age of partnership and reconciliation.

Developing tradition through change also requires that reformulation learn from mistakes of its tradition in the past, and achievements of opposing traditions in understanding the need for change and achieving it. The ending of the corporate state in Britain in the late 1970s led to the necessary Thatcher project of modernizing the economy and state. Brian Griffiths' argument for a biblically based market economy, when he was a leader of the Thatcher government and revolution, included the recognition that 'each family should have a permanent stake in economic life'. Even more important was his view that the equivalent of this principle today is the right to 'the opportunity not just for a formal education but for retraining and post-experience training in later life' (Griffiths, p. 94). That is precisely one of the foundations of New Labour's stakeholder society and economy, another sign of the Third Way's discerning use of effective responses to the changing context from a variety of political traditions, including a radical conservative one. It is a clear contradiction of that profoundly inaccurate liberal shibboleth, recently reaffirmed by the Bishop of Edinburgh, that 'the fundamental moral difference between the visions of socialism and conservatism is that the former has always sought to transform society while the latter has been content to justify it' (Holloway, *The Guardian*, 13 June 1997).

Reformulating politics, through the 'application of enduring, lasting principles for a new generation' and context, moves well beyond such old dialectics. It requires new formulations from experiences of effective engagement with change (Blair, *The Guardian*, 10 September 1996). It was precisely that task of reconciling, or holding together, previously regarded irreconcilable opposites, that the first Christian socialists attempted in the name by which they became so well known. Christianity was perceived as the complete opposite of socialism. To bring the two concepts into some kind of relationship was both to discern the signs of the times and through them to seek to engage them actively: in 1850, F. D. Maurice wrote, ' "Tracts on Christian Socialism" is, it seems to me, the only title which will define our object, and will commit us at once to the conflict we must engage in sooner or later with the unsocial Christians and the unchristian Socialists' (F. Maurice, vol. 2, p. 35). The task facing contemporary followers of Maurice, in the Christian Socialist Movement, is to change their title to reflect the Christian interaction with the contemporary context. It is unlikely they will attempt, in the spirit of Maurice, such a radical reformulation. Maybe the title-slogan has to emerge out of what I describe broadly as the exercise of practical divinity in an age of partnership and reconciliation. If so, learning from the political reformulation of the Third Way, it will pay serious attention to three principles.

First, promoting partnerships, so central to the Third Way, is a recognition of the importance of pragmatism in the practice of politics. It is about translating core values into practice, with the compromises that requires. In R. H. Tawney's words, it is about 'realistic and practical solutions for specific problems' (Atherton, 1979, p. 474). What that involves for Blair is rejecting the cynicism that politics and public life cannot improve society, the fatalism that the global economy is beyond our influence, the prejudice which rejects the contribution of the Other, and the social exclusion which denies effective participation in society to so many.

Second, pragmatism without the vision of core values can rarely achieve effective long-term change. The Third Way's 'mission', for Blair, is 'to promote and reconcile the four values which are essential to a just society which maximises the freedom and potential of all our people' – the equal worth of each individual, recognizing talent and effort, and opposing discrimination; opportunity for all, and therefore opposition to the marginalization of people and communities, and the acceptance of variety in welfare provision; responsibility clearly linked to rights; and community as an enabling force for individuals, through partnerships (Blair, pp. 3–4).

It is that combination of vision and pragmatism which is an example of practical divinity, of holding together partnership and reconciliation, essentially as a way of life, as praxis. And that is in the tradition of Gore, who commented in 1928 that 'I must insist that what He offers to men is not first a doctrine about God . . . to be apprehended by the intellect, and afterwards, it may be, applied to life. It is the opposite. It is a life which He teaches, a way of living to which He points men, which involves or is based upon theology' (Gore, 1928, p. 14). It is about practical divinity.

But third, that praxis is essentially a continuing process, engaging the ongoing changes of modernization now in a global context. It is about being open to repeated reformulation, facing new needs and problems, increasingly on a global scale. It is about the necessary but always insufficient searchings of ethics and politics for more appropriate and effective expressions in always emerging new ages.

Learning from two stories of reformulating traditions in changing contexts takes our argument into the following sections on citizenship and economy. They will elaborate that principle of reformulation with respect to the developing practice of politics in the age of partnership and reconciliation. They will address problems and tasks identified in the analysis of the contemporary context in Chapter 2. They will continue a constructive but critical relationship with the politics of the Third Way, not least because this inextricably includes dialogue with Thatcherism, but also because partnership and reconciliation is not the Third Way at prayer. They are a reminder that the practice of politics will continue to be essential for human living in a global economy. Even more so they are a recognition that political discipleship will require involvement in the reformulation of politics for its effective survival, for political vocation in today's world is under threat from a number of quarters. For example, there has been a virtual collapse of trust in government in Europe and the United States, in the latter from 76% in 1964 to 25% in 1994. The appallingly low turnout of voters in recent elections in the United States and Britain, in the latter particularly for the European Parliament and local government, certainly calls into question the value of democratic politics today. The power of global economic processes will also put more pressure on the essential principle of democratic governance that the political dimension of life is not reducible to the economic (and vice versa, of course). That leads us into what may well be the central task and problem facing the reformulation of politics in the global context. For economics will continue to be at the centre of that world – indeed, more so. The problem is if that trend becomes over-influenced by neoliberal, deregulated free market forces. 'Globalization discriminates against modes of economic governance that require public intervention . . . it favours national systems like those in the United States and Britain that historically relied less on public-political and more on private-contractual economic governance' (Strecck, *The Guardian*, 7 September 1996). If that judgement is correct, then the erosion of political functions and virtues, secured over generations by labour movements, mass politics and states in the West and now in South East Asia, will be under grave threat, and with them, the managing and civilizing of market forces. That could be a recipe for further marginalization, divisions, and conflicts, but increasingly on a global scale. Addressing that agenda is the key political task, the managing of global economic forces for wider human, social and environmental purposes, yet without returning to an overactive state or a neoliberal free market. It is about the reformulation of politics in an age of partnership and reconciliation.

Changing National Politics: Towards Cosmopolitan and Ecumenical Citizenship

The secular practice of politics and nation state are intimately linked to the modern era, developing particularly out of the two great revolutions at the end of the eighteenth century. They are therefore a relatively recent phenomenon, signalled by the rise of such nations as France, the United States and Britain. The rush to decolonialization after 1945 produced a dramatic increase in the number of sovereign states. As such, nation states have shared a number of characteristics including a coherent geographical area encompassed by clear national boundaries; recognition of their sovereignty in international law; a variety of symbols of national identity from flags and anthems to common traditions and histories; a core of institutions, including an army and police force; and a financial nucleus of national bank, treasury department, and taxes and currency.

Nation states shaping international and domestic politics in the short twentieth century were equally an integral part of the processes of turbulent change affecting the 1960s to the present. In many ways these changes have diluted the powers of the nation state and consequently eroded the practice of politics. The challenges have been twofold: on the one hand, pressures from globalization processes have moved the political and economic agenda from national to supranational levels. Economic, and especially financial markets, transnational corporations and new international divisions of labour and production, have taken authority from national governments. Emerging global challenges of demographic explosions and migrations, and environment are increasingly recognized as problems for the international community. On the other hand, challenges have also arisen from below the nation state with growing demands for local and regional autonomy in developed and developing economies. It is the cumulative effect of all these challenges which requires the reformulation of our understanding of nation state and political task. What is equally clear to most commentators is that arguments about the future shape of nation and politics assume their continued central role in the protection and enhancement of human living and environment in a global context. For example, the historic task of civilizing capitalism is a persisting and indeed expanding obligation but of increasing complexity and sophistication. The contribution to that task of the Christian democratic tradition on the continent of Europe, social Christianity in Britain, and the Federal Council of Churches, the New Deal and the Great Society of the 1960s in the United States have been of some significance, but global challenges to their successors are even more daunting. Emerging pressures for reformulation will therefore take account of continuing (although changing) requirements for protecting and resourcing citizens in the face of global economic turbulences, including income transfer systems as welfare benefits, education and health care. Complementing the economic and social task is the continuing requirement for the nation state to act as reconciler of interests at national and local levels. Recognizing and promoting the institutions and practices of civil society and new social movements makes it even more necessary for the state to act as a 'dyke against sin' and an active facilitator of reconciliation in an increasingly plural context. The cost to people and environment when that fails is enormous, as Russia and African nations demonstrate. By 1994, Russian industrial output had dropped to 45% of the 1990 figure, with population falling by about one million a year and poverty reaching almost endemic proportions: 'the Russian state has been unable to maintain social order, to establish a legally regulated system of banking and exchange, or, most fundamentally perhaps, to define property rights so as to create confidence in the future' (Boyle, pp. 45–6). A strong state, able to maintain order and stability, continues to be an essential prerequisite for effective involvement in the global economy. For China and other developing economies, facing particularly sharply the full force of environmental and demographic challenges, it becomes indispensable for actual survival.

Reformulating nation and politics requires, however, more than recognizing the continuing need to protect and enhance the lives of citizens. Increasingly, new tasks are demanding the attention of the political agenda. Addressing issues of marginalization, the international level and the demand for greater local autonomy will begin to transform the practice of politics. The first, engaging growing marginalization within nations, is essentially a recasting of the wider project of civilizing market forces. In the form of the underclass, it presents particular challenges to political life, including social democracy as the Third Way. The remaining section of this chapter will explore the contributions which reform of the market and welfare system can make to this objective. What is clear is that a regurgitated mixed economy or corporate state of the 1970s are not serious options in the new context.

The second clear requirement for political change is the need to take the international dimension increasingly seriously. John Smith, leader of what had been the poorest European-minded socialist party, acknowledged this in 1993: 'Whether we like it or not interdependence is the reality of the modern world. Matters of vital importance to our lives such as our economic prosperity and the protection of our environment all depend on international collaboration. These days no country can go it alone' (Sassoon, p. 770). And effective working at the international level involves the transfer of some sovereignty to it.

Third, and complementing political movement upwards from the nation state, is the pressure to devolve power to regional and local levels. It is as though some problems in today's world are too large and some too small for the inherited nation state. Consequently, pressures are for 'a relocation of authority' by the state, both up and down, in order to create more effective political structures for facing up to change (P. Kennedy, 1993, p. 131). Yet implementing the principle of subsidiarity in a multipolar world, whether as Scottish parliament or regional devolution, means also avoiding the misuse of relative independence to promote ethnic rivalries and reinforce local political fiefdoms. Democratizing democracy will therefore presumably include electoral systems of proportional representation to reinforce political plurality and partnerships, and the mandatory requirement on local authorities to work in collaboration with private and voluntary sectors. These mechanisms are necessary to ensure subsidiarity is about increasing democracy at the peripheries, and not their politicization. Processes for reconciliation between rival groupings will be examined at the end of this section.

Despite the dual pressures on the nation state, which will certainly change the political environment, it remains a central and indispensable part of political scene and task. Arguments that the borderless world of the global economy of international finance and transnational corporations have rendered obsolete national boundaries and entities do not measure up to the complexity of the contemporary situation. For example, transnational companies retain powerful roots in parent countries, with key functions like financial control and research and development remaining under tight domestic control. The nation state, despite global change, persists as 'the primary locus of identity for most people'. When faced by the local impacts of the global challenges, whether environmental threat or creative destruction of technological change, the nation state remains 'the organizing unit that people normally turn to when challenged by something new'. Current panic over genetically modified foods, a powerful mixture of irrational and rational factors, illustrates people's dependence on national governments to address, on their behalf, international threats and challenges. 'The global demographic explosion, atmospheric pollution, and technologically-driven change each have their own transnational momentum; but it is national governments and assemblies which decide whether to abolish currency controls, permit biotechnology, control factory emissions or support a population policy' (P. Kennedy, 1993, pp. 134, 122).

Yet even the tenacious persistence of national politics, when faced by accelerating global changes, requires major reformulation to guarantee its effective survival into the next generation. On the one hand, it is likely to involve the reinvigoration of democracy, particularly in the light of the growing disenchantment of Western societies with political processes. This will almost certainly mean moving beyond traditional formal political systems to encourage participation of individuals, their organizations and communities, in partnerships in localities and regions, covering such fields as education, health care, social services and welfare systems. Proposals for welfare reform will reinforce this greater resort to civil society, working in partnerships with local or regional government, and business sector. Support for new social movements, and their ability to read the signs of emerging problems and challenges, often up to an international level, would be another healthy sign of citizen participation in self-governance. For unless it works in localities, as democratic politics in this broader sense, there must be the gravest doubts whether constitutional reform at national levels will do anything other than maintain present alienation from political processes. To help reduce that gravest of problems, presumably entails greater dispersal of power in formal political processes by eroding the dominant positions of major hegemonic parties and business interests. Systems of proportional representation, citizen access to the European Court of Human Rights and the vigorous control and restriction of party finances, could all contribute to the introduction of greater diversity, accessibility and plurality in the practice of politics, with the equal commitment to finding practical ways of purposefully holding that together in the face of global challenges. But that is what partnership and reconciliation means in the practice of politics in the nation state.

On the other hand, the reformulation of national politics will equally require more plural understandings of nation and therefore of citizenship. For the nation state will be increasingly locked into regional blocs like the European Union, and international organizations like the IMF, World Bank, World Trade Organisation, and the various agencies under the United Nations. For Giddens, the conscious promotion of such trends leads to the cosmopolitan nation: 'The "strong state" state used to be one well prepared for war. It must mean something different today: a nation sure enough of itself to accept the new limits of sovereignty.' Building on that development is an interpretation of citizenship as cosmopolitan. And that is a matter of particular interest and importance for the English. For as the United Kingdom develops a plural constitutional framework, with devolved government to Scotland, Wales and Northern Ireland, the issue of what it means to be English, and what citizenship means, becomes a representative case study for developing cosmopolitan citizenship. Fortunately being English has always meant accepting a diversity of origins from Saxon to Norman, Viking to Celts, and immigrant Jews to migrants from the Caribbean and Indian sub-conti nent. Accepting that is what it means to be English, learning to develop an identity with which we are comfortable, yet also accepting 'ambiguity and cultural diversity'. It should not be difficult to move from that to a recognition that we are also British citizens, citizens of the European Union, and increasingly of an emerging global order. It is about holding on 'to the principle of nationality, while striving to forge national identities that can accommodate the pluralism and mutability of contemporary culture' (Giddens, pp. 130, 137, 132). It is about being English through a cosmopolitan citizenship. Holding all that together in and through a series of political identities will be a turbulent experience. It will certainly be about struggles for reconciliation as much as for partnerships.

Again, looking at the English story can help. One of the earliest contributions to understanding what it meant to be English through narratives of its origins, always a key contribution to identity and community, was the work of a monk, the Venerable Bede. If you drive up the A1, turn right just before entering the tunnel under the river Tyne, and within a mile you will come across the beautiful little church of St Paul, Jarrow. The chancel is Saxon, and formed the basis of a monastery, where Bede spent most of his life. Although living in an isolated and turbulent part of Britain, 300 miles from London, he was in contact with continental as well as indigenous scholarship. Out of those modest sources he constructed the great *Ecclesiastical History of the English People* (AD 731), in which he recorded the history of the English up to his own day, and the complex development of Christianity in England. It was a seminal contribution to the construction of the English identity. Yet it was a plural identity, even then, because of its constitution out of a variety of peoples, traditions and systems. And Bede's Christian identity reinforced it, linking Celtic, English and Roman. A multitude of identities, moving outwards to the national and international, bearing the marks of that plurality even locally. And all located within the framework of eternity, recognition that even the global is not the ultimate.

As his death approached, the great scholar insisted on finishing the last sentence of his translation into English of St John's Gospel. 'And so upon the floor of his cell singing "Glory be to the Father and to the Son and to the Holy Spirit", and the rest, he breathed his last' (Bede, p. 302). That is a stark conclusion. Yet the other side of the cross is always beyond this side, reminder of our finitude and its location in the totality of God's providence. Understanding the church as local, national, international and as the whole company of heaven confirms that multilayered interpretation of reality. That is why we should hold the secular reality of our cosmopolitan citizenship in sharp and yet comforting interaction with our truly ecumenical citizenship, a citizenship which includes the cosmopolitan but within the even wider and more ultimate framework of eternity.

Accepting the pivotal role of the cross in elaborating our understanding of political discipleship and nation is also reminder that practising politics in a fragmented multipolar world is likely to continue to generate conflicts particularly within nations. Indeed their very localness and intimacy frequently imbues them with a pitiless ferocity which plumbs the depths of inhumanity and wickedness. Processes of reconciliation are therefore likely to become more and more indispensable parts of political discipleship.

Reflecting on the experience of people and nations, Daan Bronkhorst, an Amnesty International worker, noted how societies (and groups below the national level) go through three phases in moving from the trauma of conflict to the promotion of reconciliation.

He describes the first as the genesis phase, the early signs of a shift in power relations in the conflict-ridden society. A growing militancy confronts the oppressing authorities, as in South Africa in the late 1980s. Calls for reconciliation, often from churches, are too early and inappropriate for what the context can bear.

Beginning the transition of power inaugurates the transformation phase, and this second stage can be marked by a particularly symbolic event, such as the fall of the Berlin Wall in 1989. That heralds the end of any return to old ways, and events can unfold in rapid succession, leading to the accession to power of the opposition. Reconciliation is now regarded as part of the possibility of a reconstructed future, but cannot be addressed as yet because of the sheer pressure of events.

The third and final stage is the readjustment phase, the reconstruction of society. It is a time for consolidating change, often with the old oppressive leadership still around (like Pinochet in Chile). It becomes the time to implement visions for a future society, with wrongdoers brought to justice, reparation to victims, but all with a shortage of trained personnel (there were no judges in Rwanda) and structures. It is the occasion for a Truth and Reconciliation Commission as in South Africa in 1996–7, of facing up to crimes, survivors and pardons, of a fragmentary realization of reconciliation, of the realization 'how difficult a complete turn-around of a society will be'. It is precisely at that point that reconciliation, as the interaction of both sides of the cross, becomes an indispensable part of the processes of reconstruction by understanding 'how they interact with the work of God and how they can become instruments of God's work in all this' (Schreiter, pp. 7, 9, 12). It points us to the role of spiritual as well as social reconciliation in the lives of individuals, families, communities and groups, whether Christian or not. It becomes embodiment of all those other processes of partnership and reconciliation, in personal and social relationships, and at all levels of society and beyond. The politics of discipleship are restored to their God-given place in the divine and human order.

PROMOTING THE SOCIAL MARKET ECONOMY

In the light of my growing understanding of globalization processes and problems, I have become much more aware of the dominant position of the global economy, instead of its being only one characteristic of the market economy. Yet much of what I argued for in *Christianity and the Market*, at the beginning of the 1990s, still holds good, in that the market plays the central role in what is to a large extent a global market economy. For many reasons, I have become more convinced that a principal task of Western Christianity, in developing a public theology for a global economy, will be to argue the case for that market economy to be developed, quite intentionally, as a social market economy. It is a central charge on what must become a reformulated Christian political economy. For the latter's historic concern for 'the causes of the wealth and poverty of nations', so powerfully expressed by Malthus as one of its great founders, has been translated into a global context more able to generate wealth than ever before, yet inextricably linked to unprecedented marginalization. Add to that the challenges of technology, population and environment, and the pressure is to continue to create wealth but to recognize that without the adequate participation of people in these processes and the security of the environment, economics becomes of doubtful value.

Letting people sink or swim, for the first time in recorded history in their billions, is not an alternative for Christian, religious or civilized opinion. To try to find ways of holding together market forces and these wider social purposes is therefore the key task for political economists. That is what I mean by the need to argue for an intentional social market economy on the national, and inevitably, given our context, on the international stage. And it will, again, require reformulation in terms of Christian opinion and in itself, since the changes of the last thirty years are unlikely to allow any kind of return to the corporate mixed economy states of the 1960s and 1970s. Seeking to achieve that, through the interaction between secular and theological, partnership and reconciliation, will clearly be the intention.

Such a commitment will represent a significant change of direction for Christian social thought and the teaching of the official churches in Britain and the United States. For example, even in 1991, the Church of England's report on Christianity and contemporary culture, *Good News in Our Times*, associated the revival of market economies with the libertarianism of laissez-faire capitalism. It therefore equated the enterprise culture with 'naked individualistic competitiveness', and denounced it as a 'moral evil which undermines values of stability, fidelity and other family and community-building values' (p. 60). That was only to repeat the historic charge against capitalism made by social Christianity since the mid-nineteenth century. For example, it was to continue Bishop Westcott's charge, in 1890, that 'the method of Socialism is co-operation, the method of Individualism is competition . . . The aim of Socialism is the fulfilment of service, the aim of Individualism is the attainment of some personal advantage' (Atherton, 1994, p. 81).

This inclination of the English Churches to side consistently with the corporatist, welfare state model of the golden era of the 1950s to the 1970s makes it seem as though deep in Christian tradition, including in the Scriptures, the commitment to divine governance produces an 'instinctive tendency to desire some kind of Command Economy' for the allocation of resources (J. Kennedy, p. 18). When that is allied with the ascetic tradition, and its deep questioning of the value of wealth, it produces an essentially critical view of the market economy. It at least distances itself from the economic activities and values of the market economy, so central to the whole modernization project since the late eighteenth century, with their recognition of decentralized decision-making, economic mechanisms, competition, self-interest and inequalities.

It has therefore contributed to the effective marginalization of the churches from how the world has necessarily and increasingly worked since the emergence of modern economics and economies. It is to neglect the insights of the great incarnational theologian F. D. Maurice and his advocacy of the realities of contemporary life as in themselves constituting an essential part of the theological task. In a lovely passage, he observed how 'the steadfastness of Balaam in refusing to turn aside when the creature on which he rode refused to go forward, is precisely the steadfastness of our country gentlemen, be they High or Low Churchmen, and false prophets. They do not believe that facts are the angels of the Lord, saying "Thus far shalt thou go and no farther" ' (F. Maurice, vol. 1, p. 441). It has ruled out the development of an effective and adequate public theology for such a world as part of the general apologetic task.

The church's distancing itself from the market economy is symptomatic of opinion considerably wider than Christian. It prevailed in much of British society, particularly in the intellectual and political establishments of the age of the state until the late 1970s. Both Crosland's seminal *The Future of Socialism* (1956) and eventually Heath's 1970 Conservative administration were essentially corporatist, relegating the market mechanism to a profoundly subordinationist role, to what dominant theological opinion in Britain has regarded as 'a serviceable drudge' (Preston, 1987, p. 154). Even in the 1980s, changes in policy and economic performance, despite being more market-oriented, have not been fundamental nor broad enough to sustain the development of an effective social market economy. Skidelsky rightly observed that there is a world of difference between, on the one hand, coming to terms with market mechanisms or accepting their use where appropriate, and on the other hand, the commitment to the market economy as a preferred social institution. What has dominated Britain has been rather old-fashioned neoliberal capitalism or post-war corporate welfare state Keynesian socialism. It has not developed into an intentional partnership commitment to the social market economy 'as a social institution', embedded above all 'in social arrangements regarded as "fair" ', and embracing industry, government, civil society and culture (Skidelsky, p. 4).

What would such an intentional commitment to the social market economy involve? Learning from contemporary developments in Britain, Germany and South East Asia begins to identify the social market economy not as fixed goal but as dynamic process. This acts as criticism of our existing practices and as a signpost for a way forward. Yet the social market economy is not simply a challenge to existing institutions and practices, it is also a recognition that its survival will depend on its ability to meet new challenges. It is a call for the transformation of British society, and the continuing reformulation of the social market economy. It is about the conscious commitment to participate fully in a dynamic process of changing political economy. Not to do so will result in the continuing relative decline of Britain. Indeed, for one commentator, the social market economy may well represent 'the only sort of free economy likely to survive in the years to come, and the only sort that deserves to survive' (Gray, 1992, p. 93).

In what ways will a social market economy call for the progressive changing of British society? It certainly means the decisive rejection of neoliberal laissez-faire capitalism and command economies. Both have been tried and found to be fundamentally flawed – the former because it denied the strategic importance of the social fabric for ensuring sustainable economic growth, the latter because it was incapable of coordinating efficiently and productively the myriad of consumer and producer decisions. The adoption of the social market therefore becomes replacement, in the global market economy, for the increasingly redundant language of capitalism and socialism. More importantly, it reflects the reasoned conviction that a modern social order has to hold together, to reconcile, on the one hand the most efficient way of allocating scarce resources among competing needs, and on the other hand the wider concerns of society, and now world, as a whole. Between these two sides of the same coin there will always be great tension; they will always be in a process of constant interaction. They can never be collapsed into each other without devastating threats to economic prosperity and democracy, and consequently to peace itself. They combine to form the modern social market economy.

At the heart of the social market economy, then, there lies the practice of market economics as the decentralized and collaborative decision-making by individuals, households and firms in the creation of goods and services and in the distribution of the product. It achieves this, essentially, by making 'the pursuit of individual plans the means of satisfying the plans of others' (Skidelsky, p. 10). As the market mechanism, it relies on certain indispensable virtuous elements: on competition, to promote efficiency and innovation, and to limit overbearing power by giving alternatives to producers and consumers; on prices, to signal consumer and producer preferences; on profits, to stimulate and increase efficiency, and to fund essential investment for future production; and on private property rights, to resource and safeguard individual plans as essential for the effective operating of a price mechanism. It can be summarized in 1998 as 'competition where possible, regulation where necessary' (Blair, p. 10), continuing the tradition of the German Social Democrats Party's Bad Godesberg Programme from 1959: 'As much competition as possible, as much planning as necessary' (Sassoon, p. 250).

Despite the central and indispensable part played by market economics in the social market economy, it has been recognized from Adam Smith onwards, and is now evident with renewed concern, driven by the damaging effects of globalization, that market economics need to be in an interactive relationship with such non-market or extra-market realities as law and order, values and customs, and an enabling state limited by its relationships with the private sector and civil society. So the state, for example, has come to occupy an increasingly central, essential, and at times problematic, role in the development of the market economy in general, and social market in particular. It provides the legal framework for market operations by defining and protecting property rights, contracts and competition; it seeks to correct defects of the market, including in key areas like social goods and externalities; and it seeks to ensure that the market is politically and culturally acceptable by embedding it in fair social arrangements. The contribution of the latter, in particular, is acquiring new relevance and urgency in a context deeply informed by the turbulence of globalized and more deregulated economies, the conflicts of multipolar politics, and the demographic and environmental explosions. Commitment to an achievable just social order is primarily a political acknowledgement that free markets erode the bonds on which societies depend for their effective operation, and therefore need correcting. It is a recognition that 'no economy can flourish in the long term without a minimal social consensus' (Küng, p. 181). To that general task of wider social sustenance and regeneration, and to the particular role of justice in it, Christianity has a major contribution to make. Its historic experience of engagement in struggles for justice, informed by rich and provocative insights of a theology from both sides of the cross, have played and will continue to, often indispensable parts in liberation movements, both great and small. Such involvement also reflects the increasing importance of partnerships between state, private and the voluntary sectors, and the indispensable role of civil society, including the churches, in those relationships. It is their promotion of greater participation in decision-making in economic life and the role of fairness as motivation and regulative principle in it, which will make an essential contribution to the chances for survival of a reformulated social market economy.

That constitution of political economy should therefore represent the need for a 'social order . . . set alongside the market economy which must take over those things in regard to social security which the market economy of itself cannot achieve' (EKD, p. 25). It is an acknowledgement that the market economy alone has never intentionally provided either a socially acceptable social order for the sick, the unemployed and other vulnerable people, or a comprehensive civil spirit, both of which lie at the heart of Christian concerns. For the market economy to operate effectively in delivering goods and services in a modern society does require civic and political programmes promoting high employment levels, education, health care, housing and infrastructures, basic incomes, and insurance against health risks like ill-health, old age and unemployment (risks which will increase given the growing turbulence associated with rapid global, economic and technological change). Complementing and often inspiring and organizing these requirements is the democratic political order, since democratic practices are both supportive of and in critical interaction with, the market economy. Gray is right to argue against the too comfortable associating of capitalism and democracy, promoted by Michael Novak in his *Spirit of Democratic Capitalism*, and particularly by Fukuyama in *The End of History*. Democratic principles and processes will not tolerate for long the marginalizing and diseased social consequences of unbridled neoliberal laissez-faire capitalism: 'Democracy and the free market are rivals, not allies', even though it is essentially an interactive and therefore generally reconcilable relationship (Gray, 1998, p. 17).

It all adds up to promoting and safeguarding the socio-political security of the great majority of the population as essential for effectively operating the market economy in a global economy. Without it, the market's production of, and dependence on, risk-taking, mobility and training, becomes more unlikely to be attained. It is this integral relationship, yet necessary distinction, between market economics and wider socio-political concerns, which constitutes the social market economy. Both are indispensable. Market economics is essential for efficient delivery of goods and services needed to sustain and enhance life. The practices of politics and civil society are an essential 'constitutive part of the whole integrated order' (EKD, p. 25). The former is absolutely necessary for sustaining life today, but not sufficient for abundancy of life. The latter is not an appendix to, or repair shop for, the effective functioning of market economics; it is its precondition.

The economic and social orders therefore represent different competencies which have to be held in constructive relationship. It is an equilibrium which requires constant clarification, modification and reformulation, since it can be endangered by either side. For example, social investment can be reduced for narrow reasons of economic efficiency, but damaging, in consequence, long-term socio-economic viability; greater social entitlements can be demanded without the corresponding increased economic contribution required for survival in an increasingly internationally competitive context. Maintaining such a balance represents the continuing and essential struggle to reconcile principles of efficiency and competition with the principle of solidarity, the indispensable constitutive elements of any adequate social market economy. It involves commitment to a constantly moving and evolving equilibrium.

Promoting a reformulated social market economy therefore involves facing up to internal and external challenges. On the one hand, is it sufficiently plural and dialectical, in Mill's words, to combine and reconcile such 'opposites' as fairness and efficiency? General Motors, one of the largest transnational corporations in the world, was managed very effectively in terms of shared moral goals in the 1970s. However, the commitment to fairness was no protection against the more efficient Japanese corporations. Balancing efficiency and fairness is essential for a social market economy; achieving that interaction is much more difficult and complex. For example, the new Clause 4 of New Labour's constitution appears to accept, rather blandly, these conflicting features of modernity by declaring its commitment to 'a dynamic economy, serving the public interest, in which the enterprise of the market and the rigour of competition are joined with the forces of partnership and co-operation to produce the wealth the nation needs and the opportunity for all to work and prosper' (Sassoon, pp. 738–9). Yet it is precisely features like the dynamics of competition and the economic system which have contributed to that enfeeblement of community and social solidarity which are necessary for a healthy society, for the public interest and good. Holding together efficiency and justice will always be at best an uncomfortable experience and most difficult of tasks.

On the other hand, living with unfulfilled interactions applies equally to the relationships between social market and wider global challenges. For example, increasing disturbances associated with a globalized and frag-mented world reinforce the central importance of the maintenance of peace and order in a nation, and the contribution of an effective economy to it. Pro-moting a social market economy on the world scene reflects its position as the likely least harmful way of operating a political economy providing it is able to maintain successfully that relationship between peace and prosperity, and increasingly on an international as well as national basis. That commitment to peaceful legal order and economic achievement is illustrated by the experi-ence of the German people and churches. For without the two, the threat of neo-fascism or religious fundamentalism arises. A recent report of the German Evangelical Church (EKD) comments incisively on these relation-ships: 'This is what gives the social market economy its binding significance: social peace and a democratic regulation of conflicts can be maintained only if long-term unemployment, an unjust division of income and wealth, and the pauperization of particular groups among the population can be avoided' (EKD, para. 69). For the turbulence we face includes the increasingly impor-tant impact on our economy of structural change and greater international competitiveness. It therefore also includes the disturbing growth of social security claimants and the persistence of long-term unemployment, particu-larly in continental Europe. All combine to require careful and urgent redressing of the balance between efficiency and solidarity, with implications for social investment and active partnership between government, industry and civil society, and yet to do so sensitive to the demands of global competi-tion. Keynes understood this need for reformulation in response to change when he observed, in a period of similar turbulence, that: 'It is certain that the world will not much longer tolerate the unemployment which is associated . . . with present day capitalistic individualism. But it may be possible by a right analysis of the problem to cure the disease while preserving efficiency and freedom' (Keynes, p. 20).

An external challenge to the market economy, of similar gravity to the threat of disorder, is represented by environmental concerns. It exemplifies a new and perhaps ultimate challenge to the social market economy, since human purposes ultimately depend on a sustainable environment. Fortu-nately, there are important developments in economic theory and practice which are engaging with this challenge. They are suggesting market solutions for some ecological problems, but not as market fundamentalism. There is a growing concern, represented by the Brundtland Commission Report (1987), to promote sustainable development and ecological modernization. The task for this generation is 'to ensure that it meets the needs of the present without compromising the ability of future generations to meet their own needs'. The aim is to promote partnerships between governments, businesses, scientists, environmentalists and civil society to restructure 'capitalist political economy on more environmentally defensible lines'. Yet to reconcile those two great interests will be extremely difficult, and at times impossible, since 'the one is bound sometimes to come into conflict with the other' (Giddens, pp. 56, 57, 58). Meeting that challenge, along with the question of global marginalization (to be addressed in the next chapter), will require further reformulation of social market economies as part of the history of change achieved by market economies. They suggest that the order of change will have to be at least as great as the Keynesian reforms of the 1930s and 1940s if the social market is to survive gracefully. Engaging in that task is the vocation for political economists. It is about national discipleship.

STAKEHOLDER WELFARE: REFORMULATING THE WELFARE STATE

Welfare, as the protection and promotion of the well-being of its citizens, remains a fundamental part of the agenda of the nation state and of political discipleship in the contemporary context. The inevitable disruptive consequences of globalization processes for people and communities, historically associated with industrialization and urbanization, continue apace and provoke people's demands for protection. As stakeholder welfare, this support is an integral part of the contemporary political scene, and is linked to arguments for a stakeholder economy, company and society.

Such developments in current political language and practice reflect the intimate relationship between the greatly changing context and the shape of welfare provision. For many of the astonishing changes in the global and national context from the 1960s have direct implications for welfare, and therefore the need for change, for the reformulation of welfare. Revolution in the labour market, with the decline of full-time male manual worker jobs, the rise of part-time jobs and women's participation in the labour force, the reality that many of the new jobs are so low paid that they cannot compete with welfare payments, and the growth of no-work households have clear and substantial consequences for the existing welfare state. In addition, changing patterns of family life, and particularly the growth of one-parent families and their link with poverty, along with an ageing population in the West, again put particular pressures on welfare systems. Running through all these changes, but focused especially on the cultural context, and epitomized by postmodernism, is the rise of the individual, of the pursuit of self-chosen purposes as the preferred style of living affecting all sectors of society from political to religious.

Such a changing context has, not surprisingly, led to an accelerating criticism of welfare provision as being out of tune with the 1990s. Across many nations, the reform of welfare is now an agreed central task of the political agenda. The world is littered with nations reforming their welfare systems, and certain convergencies are evident – witness the resonances between the reform proposals of neo-conservatives like Michael Novak in the United

States, and New Labour advocates in Britain, like Frank Field and Anthony Giddens, and their collaboration within nations, again in the United States and Britain. The movement from welfare state to stakeholder welfare summarizes many of these resonances, epitomizes the need for reformulation in a central area of social policy, and provides a means for developing the understanding and practice of partnership and reconciliation in the nation. Four convergencies particularly exemplify the more significant characteristics of stakeholder welfare: the contribution of civil society, inclusivity, a more balanced reflection of human nature, and a more proactive view of welfare.

Civil society

A renewed and reformulated understanding of civil society has a fundamental part to play in the transition to stakeholder welfare. It reflects, for example, an acknowledgement of plurality, including the necessary roles played by different sectors in society, and the need for partnership between them. This commitment to subsidiarity is another aspect of the end of the age of state domination of welfare services. Promoting the contribution of the private sector and civil society to welfare delivery is now an indispensable part of the political task. The involvement of the third sector in welfare has been particularly important in Germany, especially in child care; and in Holland, Belgium and Austria they have made considerable use of non-profit organizations, with profit going back into the organization and not to the shareholder. The voluntary sector has also played an indispensable part in mutual support, in Britain, in the late nineteenth and early twentieth centuries, again with important Christian contributions. It reinforces the likely increasing role of civil society in future welfare services.

An inclusive society

Stakeholder welfare is also about promoting an inclusive society; it is not about reducing provision to a safety net for the most disadvantaged. In the words of one of the best Christian social witness reports, *Not Just for the Poor* (1986), the Church of England rightly affirmed that any reconstructed welfare system had to touch all citizens. Involving the marginalized was the priority but not at the price of excluding the advantaged. It was about promoting an inclusive citizenship, since: 'Only a welfare system that benefits most of the population will generate a common morality of citizenship' (Giddens, p. 108). Yet a comprehensive interpretation of welfare including all groups and persons, is not a return to the old state welfare system of post-war years. Its reformulation would, therefore, combine benefit provision with individual and household effort to deliver adequate living standards. By ensuring that all participated it would contribute to a peaceful social order. The marginalization of large parts of a nation's population is not conducive to an orderly society at ease with itself. It produces fear and panic among the advantaged. Stakeholder welfare is therefore 'intended to do away with the sort of economic conditions in which that threat is greatest'. It is about promoting a large view of citizenship against the divisive minimalist view of neoliberals like Nozick (Shanks, p. 209).

An adequate anthropology

At the heart of any political, economic and social system is a view of human nature. Stakeholder welfare is no exception, reflecting and promulgating an understanding of the human which engages more accurately with the changing context and reflects a more balanced view of human nature. On the one hand, stakeholding takes seriously the social autonomy of people, the growing importance of the self, which is such an influential characteristic of the contemporary context. It is a feature that emerges in the labour market and training, with the individual portfolio approach to jobs and education. It is powerfully part of the post-modernist scene, and figures large in the works of Derrida and Foucault, and in their critics' responses, such as Giddens and Habermas (Reader, 1997, Chapter 6). And, of course, it is an integral part of the emerging 'pick and mix' approach to religion in the West. Summarizing these concerns and insights, Giddens observes, 'We have to make our lives in a more active way than was true of previous generations, and we need more actively to accept responsibilities for the consequences of what we do and the lifestyles we adopt' (Giddens, p. 37). It is a view of social autonomy that translates into the politics of welfare reform in terms of people building up and owning their own welfare capital fund through their contributions and their employers. Stakeholding welfare, in pensions and other major benefits, is about 'compulsory membership with personal ownership of the welfare capital which results'. It is a movement away from both the old welfare system of benefits paid with no obligations required, and the newer scheme of guaranteed incomes for all, with their payments of cash benefits for all, regardless of work effort.

On the other hand, stakeholding represents a more balanced view of the human than that represented in the old welfare state. Instead of the overemphasis on welfare as institutional expression of altruism, there is a recognition of the individual as responsible, driven by proper self-regard or self-interest. Halsey, sensitive to the Christian socialist tradition of social policy making, has expressed this rediscovery of a more realistic view of the human by advocating 'the doctrine of personal responsibility under virtually all circumstances. People act under favourable and unfavourable conditions but remain responsible moral agents'. It is an understanding that connects with the tradition of working-class mutual aid societies and movements of the late nineteenth century, combining self-improvement with collaborative effort. It is a recognition of R. H. Tawney's Christian acceptance of individual responsibility and sin, and a rejection of the unbalanced emphasis on the human as altruistic, full of rights, and productive of progress, without that corrective of duty and sin. It points to 'a community based on reciprocal duties and shared effort, prudence and mutual responsibility' (Field, pp. 4, 64–5, 101). And because it acknowledges the 'obligation collectively to ensure each citizen gets a stake in society' (Blair, *The Guardian*, 9 September 1996), it can introduce a conditionality, it can require the acceptance of responsibility, of active participation in return. Contracts with citizens in education, housing, training and employment represent that move from post-war welfare's dependence on altruism and universalism, to also harnessing self-interest and sin, through conditionality. The Christian understanding of the individual's relationship and responsibility to God, of sin and finitude, and therefore of the importance of character balancing altruism and self-interest, powerfully interacts with these emerging interpretations of welfare stakeholding.

Proactive welfare

Finally, stakeholder welfare reflects the transition from a more passive view of welfare, of support when ill or unemployed, befitting an age of a more closed economy with its stabilities of employment as full-time male manual work. Instead it promotes, given the dynamic nature of the global economy, a more proactive understanding of welfare encouraging individual participation and enterprise, and providing support if and when things go wrong. It is about drawing people into the national wealth creating project, rather than treating people as passive recipients of a redistributive welfare state. The welfare to work programme, linked to a statutory minimum wage, with benefit enhancement for working families, provides both unskilled work that is more attractive than welfare and an obligation to contribute to society and family through employment. It therefore represents a necessary attack on an old welfare system that encouraged dependency characters at ease with idleness, mendacity and profligacy, attempting to replace them with work, honesty and saving. The task is to liberate the poor, to erode the underclass by breaking the cycle of deprivation through education, training, and conditionality, and by ensuring everyone has an effective stake in society. Without that, people will not easily survive the gales from an increasingly competitive global economy. The politics of reformulating welfare is to ensure all citizens have that right, recognizing the obligations that necessarily now have to accompany it. It is certainly about enacting a variety of partnerships between sectors and people. It is equally about reconciliation as at least holding together very different insights into human living as required by the changing contemporary context.

7
International Discipleship: Programming for Ecumenical Liberation

> The more these debates themselves become genuinely transnational the better. (Giddens, p. 155)

Globalization is the new foundational context within which we now live, move and have our being, but now in necessary partnership with the whole created order. It is a complex of realities increasingly impinging on every aspect of our already complex lives. And because it is associated with those daunting challenges of environmental and demographic explosions and marginalization, it appears to overshadow our lives as a distant but approaching apocalypse. It can communicate a truly millenarian sense of foreboding, as though inaugurating the judgemental rule of Christ on earth. I certainly have that sense when I lie awake at night and reflect on world population trends and their likely implications for people and environment. I have that clear visual awareness, too, of being overshadowed every time I look at a large painting of Pendle Hill which dominates my room. Its commanding presence, the largest feature in the landscape of north-east Lancashire, bestrides the changing context of the post-industrialization of great textile manufacturing towns, and an equally turbulent historical context, darkened by the narrative of the Lancashire witches, their supposed dark deeds and terrible deaths at the beginning of the seventeenth century (Ainsworth). Much more significant for the lives of people and communities is another story of that domineering hill. A generation after the execution of the Lancashire witches, George Fox walked that moorland. In his Journal for 1652, also full of apocalyptic foreboding and hope that 'the day of the Lord . . . was coming upon them', he wrote:

> As we travelled we came near a very great hill, called Pendle-Hill, and I was moved of the Lord to go up to the top of it; which I did with difficulty, it was so very steep and high. When I was come to the top, I saw the sea bordering upon Lancashire, and there, on the top, I was moved to sound the day of the Lord, and the Lord let me see in what places He had a great people to be gathered. (Fox, pp. 59–60)

From Pendle Hill the founder of the Quakers gathered in a great Society of Friends which soon bestrode continents, and particularly in the United States through the leadership of Penn and Woolman. Within a hundred years, members occupied significant positions in the early industrial revolution as merchants, bankers and manufacturers, even in the emerging great textile manufacturing towns of north-east Lancashire, lying in the shadow of Pendle Hill. Often reformers, often witnesses for God's peace, liberation and justice, they became leaders in the struggles for penal and factory reform, for the defeat of marginalization and war and their harmful consequences for people and economies. They addressed the great questions of their day and ours. So Pendle Hill no longer overshadowed the context, as an ever-darkening presence. Instead, it bestrode the context as sign of the movement to God's Kingdom.

Facing up to globalization, to the international character of our lives, means engaging with change as Fox did. It will mean recognizing *pressures* and *possibilities* for developing international institutions to deal with global challenges, facing *problems* associated with the international creation of wealth and poverty, and finally, constructing *programmes*, embodying the age of partnership and reconciliation, to achieve change through marks of that changing global context. It therefore represents a journey back to localities where change has to be seen to be achieved, but only because it has travelled through national and international arenas. For globalization incorporates such linkages between levels and across disciplines and interests. Changing theology and society therefore reflects these realities but seeks to move through and consequently beyond them. It becomes a challenge to the global to realize its true potential, to become what it is, truly ecumenical, truly economic, true to the whole inhabited political and environmental economy. It is about putting to work the age of partnership and reconciliation, about practical divinity. It is so that the divisive overshadowing becomes the inclusive bestriding.

The Pressures for and Possibilities of Global Governance

Our generation has experienced the emergence of the challenges of environment, population, technology, the global economy and marginalization to a prominence which is now compelling the development of new responses. As such, they represent a departure from previous experience, because by their very nature they can only be addressed effectively at international level. It has taken over a decade for sheep farmers in the hills of North Wales and the Lake District in Britain to overcome the disastrous pollution of land from the Chernobyl disaster. And that occurred over half a continent away, travelling across half a dozen nations, leaving havoc in its wake. It is not surprising that there is a growing recognition by nation states that unless they learn to collaborate to address such global challenges, there is unlikely to be a sustainable future for any of them.

Fortunately for people and created order, there are substantial signs of the rapid development, since the 1970s, of forms of global governance for promoting international action on global questions. These activities are generally located in two main groupings. On the one hand, there is an increasing tendency for sovereign powers to devolve more authority to such supranational regional trading blocs as the European Union (EU), NAFTA and the ASEAN. The EU is developing into an important example of transnational governance. On the other hand there are a plethora of international bodies from the IMF and WTO to the United Nations and ILO. There are now over 300 such international governmental organizations, joined by the great transnational corporations of the private or secondary sector. In addition, civil society is also developing an international third sector of over 4,500 non-governmental organizations (NGOs). Representing a cosmopolitanism from below, through such bodies as Greenpeace, Amnesty International and the churches, their presence at the World Summit for NGOs at Beijing in 1995, with over 50,000 delegates, illustrated the need to extend collaboration between international governmental bodies and transnational corporations to include the international third sector. Like the West German acceptance of the Soviet Union in the 1980s' radical but necessary development of Ostpolitik, facing up to global questions now demands partnerships involving all three sectors: 'It requires that each side grants the other side its right to exist and its ability to live in peace' (Sassoon, p. 719). Effective engagement with the global challenges will require no less. Despite disenchantment with the practice of politics at national and local levels, there really is no alternative to developing forms of global governance if we are to survive together on this planet. It is as well that 'there already is global governance and there already is global civil society' (Giddens, p. 140). The task of political discipleship is to transform what exists, not to waste scarce energy on trying to reinvent it.

However they are organized and whatever form they take, the varied institutions for global governance will need to address the kind of global issues which Richard Falk of Princeton University has developed in partnership with colleagues from around the world. Their cumulative effect is to suggest an 'essential vision' for a 'humane governance', and includes: 'restraining war, abolishing war, making individuals responsible, collective security, the rule of law, non-violent revolutionary politics, human rights, the stewardship of nature, positive citizenship, cosmopolitan democracy'. It leads, in von Weizsäcker's thinking, to a 'world domestic policy'. It means that such 'a politics which in the perspective of this world domestic policy does not ask under what basic conditions human beings can survive on a habitable earth and give their social life a human form will not achieve its goal' (Küng, pp. 64, 68). Nor would it deserve to. But that is what effective engagement with the great global challenges will require of us all.

Of all the supranational regional trading blocs emerging on the world scene in recent years, the European Union particularly embodies the possibilities and problems of this movement towards more global governance. Living through the 'age of catastrophe' (Hobsbawm, 1994) and at the centre of its two World Wars, globalization processes confirmed and accentuated the acknowledgement that undue focusing on the nation state was recipe for disaster. A new way of practising politics had to be discovered which promoted economic and political integration as of value in itself but also as means of constructive involvement in the emerging world economy. Such a route, it was intended, would also allow the incorporation of European traditions, deeply rooted in Christian democracy, to protect and enhance citizen welfare and solidarity in the face of global turbulences. It can therefore be seen as part of capitalism's transition from an international economy with nation states as primary regulators, and where transnational corporations have their main base, to a truly global economy freer of its various national entanglements. Yet the difference is that, because of the surrender of some national sovereignty to the EU, it may well be able also to develop an international social policy to establish basic norms of welfare and working conditions, and survive in a globally competitive environment. The Maastricht Treaty's Social Charter in 1992 exemplifies this great project. The risks are enormous, the reward treasure beyond compare, for 'to create European institutions and norms, replacing those of each nation-state, will be a momentous enterprise whose outcome is uncertain' (Sassoon, p. 770). A similar journey beckons the other great regional blocs of NAFTA and ASEAN.

As a model for bodies with worldwide responsibilities, the EU has two features which particularly reflect the nature of the changing context, but which also illustrate how it can, in turn, be used to effect change. On the one hand, its essential character is not bipolar since it is neither superstate nor mere organization of states. It therefore achieves the economic benefits of a fundamentally co-operative way of living together, yet encouraging competition both within and between regional blocs, but, one hopes, in a more co-ordinated way. On the other hand, as evolving federal governance, it offers the world an organizational form for grappling with the global challenges of the twenty-first century. It suggests that 'a federation of democratic, wealthy, socially diverse, mixed-economy societies would be a powerful force on the world scene' (Huntington, 1988, pp. 93–4.) As an interrelation of states, it begins to do justice to the degree of economic interpenetration of nations occurring so dramatically since 1945. It has achieved an integrated Europe, with no barriers to the flow of goods and services, with a common currency, an increasingly strong Parliament, and an emerging common defence and foreign policy. It now has a third of world trade, seven of the ten top trading nations, powerful financial institutions, major industries, the largest market and world class performance in culture and education. 'The Community is becoming rather less a collection of nation-states and rather more a coherent entity which the rest of the world recognises as a power in itself' (P. Kennedy, 1993, p. 268).

Not surprisingly, for a necessary but hazardous journey, the development of the EU faces particular problems in engaging the contemporary context. For example, it is finding it difficult to overcome people's alienation from the practice of democratic politics at national level, and to encourage their commitment across the continent to that international governance which the EU so manifestly represents. Combining a proper recognition of local, national and international citizenship in a cosmopolitan and ecumenical form is a necessary ideal for the practice of politics today and the immediate future. Tackling these problems of integration cannot any longer be done aloof from global challenges. For example, demographic changes of the greying of Western Europe and population decline in some nations, like Germany and Italy, link to population explosions in poorer nations and growing floods of immigrants from Africa, Asia and Yugoslavia seeking jobs and security. One of the great tasks facing the EU is to hold together integration and diversity, reconciling those internal developments with the challenges of global change. Reformulated structures may well be needed, with less time spent on integration and more on how to meet global challenges through integration. Yet despite achievements and problems, the EU remains 'the most complex and advanced political response to the existence of a transnational economic system that the world has to offer at present' (Boyle, p. 88).

Partnership for its own sake is no recipe for its survival, and international partnerships are no exception to that operating principle. Global governance is evolving, and necessarily so, because global challenges demand no less and nation states offer increasingly less. Four particular items are appearing on that international agenda: the globalization of financial life, environment, security and marginalization. The latter will be addressed in the final parts of this chapter.

The globalization of financial life. The global economy is illustrated especially by the rise of global financial markets, encouraged by the collapse in the early 1970s of the Bretton Woods system of financial regulation, the central feature of successful post-war reconstruction, and by the consequent deregulation of capital markets. The result has been excessive volatility in foreign exchange markets with, for example, a turnover of over $1 trillion per day, equivalent 'to the total currency reserves of the world's central banks' (Drimmelen, p. 64). These astonishing flows of finance, resourced by electronic communication systems, are increasingly unrelated to trade, and increasingly speculative. They represent 'the enormous practically unknowable virtual economy of financial derivatives' (Gray, 1998, p. 198). As such, they constitute one of the gravest threats to peoples and nations.

Since capitalism is now fundamentally an international reality, effective responses to it need to be increasingly on an international basis. This is the case not least because capitalism has never been a totally self-regulating entity, despite its technical claims to self-equilibrium, claims rightly questioned from Malthus to Keynes and beyond. The need, therefore, is for institutions and practices of global governance to manage world markets, to promote greater cohesion of societies through global regulation of currencies, capital movements and trade. There is growing agreement that such objectives will require progress in at least three areas.

First, the need to calm excessive currency movements. Some, including the arch-speculator Soros, are suggesting the need to co-ordinate links between the major currencies of the euro, yen and dollar in formal partnership rather than open competition, in order to stabilize exchange rates for the good of necessary long-term investments.

Second, the need to discourage enormously disruptive short-term speculation and protect and encourage long-term investment, has led some to promote the Tobin Tax of a 0.1% tax on all international financial transactions.

Finally, new challenges of globalization are putting increasing pressure on existing international financial institutions and pushing them through the necessary process of reformulation. Proposals for reform include more equitable representation on the World Bank and IMF, greater accountability and transparency in their operations, including to NGOs, and more devolution to regional multilateral development banks.

Environment. Threats to environment by the combination of demographic explosion and economic growth clearly require to be addressed at local and national levels. Promoting a social market economy is integral to these programmes. Yet the sheer scale and extent of population and economic growth and its consequences for environmental damage now mean that international action is becoming the *sine qua non* for any other effective environmental polices. The problem now is that 'whole countries may be deforested in a few decades, most of a region's topsoil can disappear in a generation; and critical ozone depletion may occur in as little as twenty years' (P. Kennedy, 1993, p. 346). The demand for international response is therefore now so urgent that it has to work with a variety of economies, of which the market economy is only one. Yet it is still likely to be the preferred way of operating because of its recognition of the importance of capital and scientific knowledge in any response, and the need to promote sustainable growth rather than oppose growth in itself. However, reconciling growth and environmental sustainability becomes all the more difficult as challenges accelerate and focus on the global level. If China, with its population of over one billion, succeeds in reaching Deng Xiaoping's aim of raising GDP per capita to $1,000, and in each household having a fridge generating CFCs, then the consequences for the environment will be devastating.

Market solutions and global rather than national programmes are clearly both possible and required, but we must not forget that unless the United States faces up to its responsibilities as the biggest polluter, global action will not succeed. It is also likely that achieving sustainable economic growth will depend on controlling if not reducing the rate of development by reconciling the needs of humanity, renewable and non-renewable resources consumed, and effects on the environment. If that is the case then any reformulation of global practices will have to include radical as well as realistic measures. Radical realism becomes part of adequate involvement in the age of partnership and reconciliation.

Security. The issue of a secure peace will occupy a central place on the international agenda as it did on the national and local. The movement from a bipolar to a multipolar world, characterized by intensive local conflicts, has been exacerbated by pressures of population, urbanization and environment, seen in the struggle for water and land resources. It has provoked a new intensity and scale of consequences, with the development of modern technologies of warfare, including nuclear proliferation. After the ending of the Cold War, we do not face the 'new world order' which some hoped for in 1990, but rather a 'troubled and fractured planet' (P. Kennedy, 1993, p. 349). Bosnia, Kosovo, Rwanda, Sierra Leone, Indonesia and Chechnya have raised fundamental questions of citizenship, identity, human rights and freedom through the destructive consequences of uncontrolled fragmentation. That fragility is revealed, too, in the West through unemployment, social divisions and crime. No wonder many in the Church of England are returning to the Prayer Book's collects for peace at Matins and Evensong, with new awareness. Their authors in the early sixteenth century knew, like citizens of Kosovo today, that without order, the rest, including economic progress, would never follow. No wonder they prayed 'give unto they servants that peace which the world cannot give'. Like Shakespeare, a generation later, we are being made aware of how thin is the veneer of civilization:

> Take but degree away, untune that string
> And hark! What discord follows.
> *(Troilus and Cressida)*

The international political task therefore becomes seeking peace and stability as prerequisite for that economic development, so essential for the poorest nations to become members of the community of the global economy. Yet 'contriving terms of peaceful and productive coexistence among peoples and regimes' will always be different and so difficult (Gray, 1998, p. 132). Indeed, perhaps the greatest task for Christian and human discipleship is to come to terms with the plurality of the great challenges which the global context now presents. It will mean, for example, accepting that not all regimes will be democratic, so there is no Fukuyama 'end of history' with all being liberal democracies; it will mean coming to terms with not all being rational, given the presence of religious and political fundamentalisms; yet it will also mean that despite such competitive and conflictual variety, all have to learn to work in partnerships. The alternative is the way of global death. If the challenge of global marginalization is added to that agenda for international governance, then practising partnership and reconciliation becomes a fundamentally global discipleship. 'The more these debates themselves become genuinely transnational the better.'

MARGINALIZATION AS A PROBLEM OF THE INTERNATIONAL

The growing chasm between rich and poor countries is a dramatic exception to the increasing output of goods and services by the global economy. Yet it is misleading if we then claim that marginalization is the only great problem of the global economy, and do not connect exclusion processes with other great challenges. For inequalities between nations are linked to demographic problems, in that unless population in the poorer nations begins to moderate in relation to economic growth, then the former will not be sustainable and the latter will have little effect. Similarly, marginalization has damaging consequences for environment in terms of pressures on the resources of land, water and air. Technological innovations, too, exacerbate divisions particularly at the expense of the poorest, whether as biotechnology or robotics. There is a powerful set of interconnections between these challenges, and they combine to heighten the scale of global marginalization; it embodies problems facing the international dimension of contemporary living; it becomes paradigmatic test of effective engagement with our changing global context.

Accepting the necessity and inevitability of these various forms and problems of international governance, leads to redrawing international discipleship as finding ways of 'reincorporating those whom the economic system, the system for satisfying our mutual needs, threatens to exclude' (Boyle, p. 175). It will involve reconciling varieties of interests and insights, including pre-eminently economic and social purposes, resourced by a whole series of partnerships at all levels of global living. It becomes what Adam Smith and Thomas Malthus saw as the task of how to create and distribute a sufficient wealth of nations, but it is now in an immensely more complex global economy.

If that becomes the pre-eminent task of international governance, where do you begin? In the words of the old farmer, when asked the way by a confused traveller, if you want to get to there, don't start from here! Facing up to global marginalization is not about promoting neoliberal free markets on a world scale. They only express needs and wants through purchasing power, and they have a long history of undermining ethics and responsibility through extending the commodification principle to every area of life, from human kidneys in India to televangelists in the United States. Neoliberalism is a recipe for growing divisions and conflicts within and between nations. The fact is that market-dominated regimes of the 1980s and 1990s have not trickled wealth down, and the poor are getting poorer. The answer is equally not found at the other end of the political economy spectrum, with command, state socialist type economies. 'The rejection of market exchange as the central organizing practice of a modern economy leads inexorably to heavy reliance on state coercion' (Gray, 1998, p. 137). That again has devastating consequences for people as free citizens and valued consumers, and even more so for the environment. Additionally, rejecting command economies repudiates the way of revolution in modern economies. As Sassoon observed in surveying a century of European socialism, after 1917 there was a 'marked absence of *any* possibility of a working-class revolutionary insurrection on the Bolshevik pattern'. To fail to see that was to be 'condemned to complete political insignificance, or to utter defeat' (Sassoon, p. 56). That warns all theologians of public life tempted by the utopian, transformationist yearnings of liberationist movements. Invariably they end up promoting a Christ against globalization by encouraging isolationist purity, and being associated with such strange bedfellows as terror regimes in Cambodia and Maoist China, the alternative economics of local self-sufficiency of Cobb and Daly and the small religious communities of MacIntyre and other post-modernist theologians. They all hold in common 'that they sought to seal off the nation from what was represented as a corrupting outside world' (Boyle, p. 235).

If facing up to marginalization is not about all that, what has it to recognize and engage? Essentially a paradox: if there is no feasible alternative to working with global processes, then unless their intrinsic problems and their interaction with the global challenges are addressed, they are unlikely to survive. Accepting the global market economy means therefore coming to terms with the relative competitiveness of global economic growth as essential for delivering a decent standard of living for an ever-expanding world population. It is clearly not everything, but it remains the basis of what people deem important, from education and health care to food, clothing and housing. Yet equally, the most effective system of wealth creation in world history is not so for two thirds of the world's population, or for the bottom 20% in the developed world. The two just do not add up, therefore suggesting that the way forward will require the reform of the global market economy. We are driven 'to consider, once again, the built-in defects of capitalism. What changes in the system would their removal require? Would it still be the same system after their removal? For, as Joseph Schumpeter had observed, apropos of the cyclical fluctuations of the capitalist economy, they "are not, like tonsils, separate things that can be treated by themselves, but are, like the beat of the heart, of the essence of the organism that displays them" ' (Hobsbawm, 1994, pp. 574–5). Essentially, that way of reform will involve a clear choice between 'the control of the economic system by the market' with 'the running of society as an adjunct to the market', or embedding the economy in social relations.

Given the task of facing up to marginalization as entry point into engaging with all the global challenges, then the latter, embedding the global market economy in social relations, must be the preferred option. And that will involve reforming the global market economy, and then interacting it with national and regional social market economies.

Reforming that international global market economy will therefore mean accepting and promoting its variety in two ways. On the one hand, it will involve accepting 'a diversity of cultures, regimes and market economies as a permanent reality'. Consequently it will stand against the hegemonic tendencies of a Western, particularly United States, free market which is essentially intolerant of plurality. Asian religious traditions are supportive of such a programme, since 'Asian freedom from economic theology allows market institutions to be judged, and reformed, by reference to how their workings affect the values and stability of society'. They suggest an important 'appeal to economic policies' in the wider tradition of practical divinity. On the other hand, allowing 'the world's manifold cultures to achieve modernizations that are adapted to their histories, circumstances and distinctive needs' leads to the development of 'indigenous kinds of capitalism', following the experience of South East Asia, China, Japan and maybe Russia in the future (Gray, 1998, pp. 12, 20, 192, 20, 195). It is about countries achieving modernity by renewing their own traditions in interaction with the requirements for economic growth. It is not about imitating the West, but about a multiform global market economy interconnecting with different cultures and regimes. In the language of contemporary social ethics, it generates a patchwork quilt interpretation of the global market economy, 'a reasonably peaceful coat of many colours, each portion of which develops its own distinct cultural identity and is tolerant of others' (Stout; Gray, 1998, p. 195).

Equipped with such a plural view of the global market economy, engaging global challenges through marginalization will require further reforms informed by the commitment to 'a global market economy which is politically obligated to humane and social goals, which does justice to future needs and risks, and reckons with the natural foundations of life' (Küng, p. 215). We now know, from the material emerging in the argument so far, that achieving such reform will involve a number of policies. Some have been noted already, and can be transposed onto the level of the international market economy.

These vary from a politically enforced competitive order, reformed financial markets, stakeholder welfare to promote and protect citizen participation in the global market place, and the security of a peaceful social order, to an environmentally sustainable economic growth. Three additional areas require further elaboration, namely transnational corporations, trade, and arguments for a global ethic. The issue of international debt will form the basis of the final section of this chapter.

Transnational corporations. The issue of organizations, with particular reference to companies, was raised in the examination of the contemporary context in the second chapter. Many now argue for a more plural inclusive interpretation of organizations, exemplified by stakeholder corporations (Kuhn; Atherton, 1995). Yet none of these arguments about organizations addressed the international arena, particularly the challenge of the transnational corporation (TNC), a key player in globalization processes, not least because TNCs are frequently larger and more powerful than nation states in the developing world. For since TNCs cross national boundaries, they are much more difficult to control; they can play off one state against another for tax, price and investment purposes; weaker, poorer states are especially vulnerable to their activities and powers. It is not surprising, therefore, that vulnerable developing economies demand mandatory codes of behaviour for TNCs, and strong developed economies prefer voluntary codes. The areas of TNC life which they both seek to regulate include the disclosure of information, tax evasion, employment protection, industrial relations, and anti-competition behaviour. So far, codes have been developed by the OECD, ILO, the UN and the EU.

Achieving the reform of such organizations requires, however, more than the endeavours of multinational organizations. The contribution of NGOs is increasingly important in the total reform process. For example, church-related organizations in Switzerland persuaded the massive Migros supermarket chain to press Del Monte to improve working conditions on their pineapple plantations in the Philippines. This links into the increasingly important role of civil society in promoting change in the global business sector. In these discussions and activities, the churches' contribution is essential, and includes such bodies as the Interfaith Centre on Corporate Responsibility (ICCR). Importantly, this is a classic partnership body, bringing together churches, Jewish communities, judiciaries, pension funds and health care systems. In 1996, in the United States, they initiated 185 resolutions 'on corporate policies related to social justice, military production and the environment with 126 companies'. The model of the ICCR has been followed particularly in the Netherlands and Britain.

Trade. Market economies, including global ones, are about consumption, about producing goods and services to meet consumer needs and wants. In a post-industrial society that becomes even more the case. In highly populated modern societies those purposes can only be met by trade, and increasingly between nations. So often, such world trade has exacerbated the growing gulf between rich and poor nations. Because of that influence, reforming trade as part of reforming the global economy therefore becomes high priority. Among other measures, it will involve reformulating the link between consumers and producers, so both are pressured to promote more 'socially and environmentally responsible consumption'. In the earlier tradition of the Christian Social Union, it is about provoking consumers to become more alive to the working and living conditions of producers, and their relation to the environment. For example, 75% of US shoppers say they would be prepared to pay higher prices for clothing and shoes (especially trainers) with 'no sweat' labels (Drimmelen, pp. 140, 149, 138–9, 140). As important, potentially, is the development of alternative trade organizations to address the gap between producers in developing economies and consumers in developed economies. By purchasing directly from small producers, and selling their products through Churches, shops, and mail order companies, the organizations are able to pay the producers a fair price. The retail value of fair trade between South and North is now reckoned to be about US$ 300–500 million per annum. That is now being greatly extended by the growth of fair trade products and companies selling through supermarkets. Christian Aid's Global Supermarket Campaign in Britain is a good example of this development of partnerships between civil society and the business sector, producers and consumers, rich and poor.

In order to support these programmes there is a need for the continuing reform of the World Trade Organisation, the premier player in international trade. Sadly, it has refused to develop formal relationships with the NGOs, but in the end it will have to work in partnership with civil society if it is going to deal effectively with marginalization from a trading perspective. Fortunately, it has been prepared to begin work on key trade-related clauses on social and environmental issues. The social clauses seek to make access to world markets conditional on the recognition of workers' fundamental rights, and the latter seeks to ban imported goods produced in environmentally destructive ways. Unfortunately, both can be misused by the richer nations, particularly the United States, to justify protectionist policies against the trading needs of poorer nations. However, despite these problems, the principle and necessity of fairer trade remains a major imperative in the reform of the global market economy.

A global ethic. The final part of the reform we need to work for relates to arguments about the nature and role of ethics in such strategies. It has already become evident that ethics play a central part in discussions about trade, codes for TNCs, and the relationship between efficiency and wider social purpose in the social market economy. Essentially, therefore, developing the ethical dimension is a recognition that global systems, in matters of economy and governance, are required, among other things, to face up to global responsibilities. The challenges of population, environment, and technology are steeped in ethical issues. Tackling marginalization will not be effective without acknowledging that dimension and elaborating it as an indispensable part of the political and economic task. And that takes us right into the heart of what partnership and reconciliation mean.

Constructing a wide ethics for global responsibilities initially involves developing our understanding of fairness, toleration and human rights, and building on international partnerships as a means to that end.

What we have in common, globally, is the unavoidable necessity of addressing the great global challenges. What divides us is histories, cultures and traditions. Reconciling those competing claims, embodied in so many different ways, and at all levels of society, involves an ethical responsibility, particularly as expressed in the search for fairness or justice. Yet fairness cannot dominate the ethical programme, because of the proper requirements of efficiency in the necessary promotion of economic growth. What is clear is that we can never make progress without giving justice a formative role in addressing the marginalization problem. That will be the case for at least as long as 'the liberal capitalists pass over in silence that the system in which they and their friends satisfy each other's needs keeps whole nations in poverty in some distant continent' (Boyle, p. 227).

Living in a global economy has to include living with differences in cultures, religions, politics and economies. 'It is to voice a hope that Enlightenment thinkers have in common with all those religions and philosophies, ancient and modern, that recognize the ideal of toleration.' Yet living in a world of increasing competition for scarce resources will put the virtue of toleration even under more pressure. The continuing importance of the practice of politics, in conjunction with the fast-growing role of science and technology, will also therefore reinforce the importance of a 'critical rationality' (Gray, 1998, p. 207). The task of reconciliation is therefore likely to include both virtues, toleration and critical rationality.

Hovering around all these practices and values is the issue of human rights, of our estimate of human worth in a global market economy. Taking over two centuries to implement fully in the West, they acknowledge that there can be no justification for violating the fundamental rights of the person 'to life, freedom (not slavery), protection from torture and arbitrary deprivation of freedom; and there is a need for a ban on discrimination on racial, religious and similar grounds'. Although of principally Western provenance in their modern form, they resonate with insights in most cultures and religions. That is a necessary reminder of the importance of the Universal Declaration of Human Rights (1948), and the worldwide struggle for them, from Aung San

Suu Kyi in Burma to Ken Saro-Wiwa in Nigeria. Yet the Christian and religious concern for the person requires even that fundamental ethical declaration to be judged according to context. For human rights are not above human beings, but are there for human beings. Unless that is acknowledged, then rights become absolutized into the supreme right, which then becomes the occasion for new hatreds and war and inhumanity. Conversely, 'wherever nations or ethnic groups remain aware that right, too, is there for human beings, they relativize positions which are theirs by right; they facilitate giving and taking, those concessions and compromises without which politics is quite impossible' (Küng, pp. 87, 79). They enable, indeed require, the pursuit of partnership and reconciliation in the promotion of ethics in the reform of the global market economy.

Two recent international conferences illustrate how such collaboration can work on such agendas. The United Nations Commission on Global Governance (1995) rightly rejected the forced utopia of global government, but also rejected a 'world without systems or rules'. The challenge was rather to promote reconciliation 'to strike the balance in such a way that the management of global affairs is responsive to the interests of all people in a sustainable future, that is guided by basic human values, and that it makes global organisation conform to the reality of global diversity'. Supporting that general programme with more detailed proposals on global security and the management of economic interdependence, was the powerful ethical imperative, of global dimensions because it is prominent in all religions, that 'people should treat others as they themselves wish to be treated' (Küng, pp. 224–5). It is suggested that such a Golden Rule could form the basis of a global civic ethic for cosmopolitan citizenship.

The second international commission was on culture and development, and recognized the paradigm shift from eurocentric to polycentric. Again, the emergence of a new diversity highlights and requires the role of partnership and reconciliation in the process of developing the contribution of ethics to international programmes addressing great global challenges. And that takes us ultimately to the other side of the cross. For sustaining the human struggle with marginalization and other global challenges requires underpinning by the 'unconditional duty for man to exist . . . Thus here we are dealing with a duty which is not a counterpart of another right – unless it be the right of God the creator God over against his creatures, to whom, with the bestowal of existence, he has entrusted the continuation of his work' (Küng, p. 249). Without that unconditional duty of man to survive, linked to God's rights, it is much more difficult to see how the human will be driven to collaborate with the Other, in terms of different cultures, religions and traditions, recognizing that without these partnerships, the great challenges will not be overcome.

The final contribution to reforming the global market economy must come from the promotion of intentional social market economies. The nature of that contribution has already been elaborated with regard to the national level. The task now is to advocate it on the international stage as paradigm for facing up to global marginalization and other challenges. As already recognized, that will continue to depend on its reform. Substantiating the feasibility of that obligation is its tradition of reformulation, including, more recently, the Keynesian revolution and the development from old heavy industries to information technology-based production and services. The collapse of command economies was related partly to their inability to do precisely that. An even greater support for the social market's vocation is provided by its foundational commitment to reconciling wider social purposes and economic values. For a 'socially committed market economy' links a fundamentally pragmatic embrace of the market economy with 'the attribute "social" as an ethical obligation'. In the German tradition, so powerfully expressed by Professor Müller-Armack, the significance of the social market economy is that 'it combines the principle of freedom in the market with that of social equilibrium'. It is an acknowledgement that ethical criteria have at least as big a part to play in the global market economy as economics, for 'fundamental though the economy and politics may be, they are individual dimensions of the all-embracing world of human life which . . . must be subjected to ethical and human criteria for the sake of human beings' (Küng, pp. 198, 200, 214). Without that additional dimension of the social ethical, it is unlikely that the global market economy will engage successfully the great challenge of marginalization.

Yet such regulatory principles, admirable as they may be, are of little use unless brought practically to bear on the complexities of globalization and marginalization. This can be achieved in a variety of ways. For example, calculating the costs and benefits of economic transactions is central to the task of modern economics and market. Indicators like Gross National and Domestic Product (GNP, GDP) only include in their calculations goods and services exchanged for money, and make no qualitative judgements. Consequently, work not paid for, like the voluntary endeavours of civil society and women in the home, is not measured, and no distinction is made between the cost of child care and landmines. Not surprisingly, other indicators are now being promoted, including the Human Development Index (HDI) of the UN Development programme. 'Since 1990 this list has annually ranked 174 countries by a measurement that takes account of such factors as life expectancy, educational attainment and basic purchasing power' (Drimmelen, p. 124). The results vary considerably from the league tables following GNP indicators. It is an extremely tangible embodiment of the challenge to the paradox of traditional wealth creation and the resultant marginalization. For if such economic growth is so clearly connected to poverty, inequality and environmental degradation, and these are priority questions we must now address more adequately, then there is a strong argument for adopting ways of measuring effectiveness in tackling poverty, inequality and environmental degradation as well as economic growth. A Human Development Index, given equal weight with Gross Domestic Product, would be a better way of addressing those questions, precisely because they seek to reconcile social and economic purposes. It is a powerful example of practical divinity at work.

PROGRAMMES FOR THE INTERNATIONAL: EMBODYING LIBERATION

It has been exciting to preach the Lord's Jubilee year of 2000 CE, and its hoped for deliverance of people from the slavery of marginalization through debt. For so it was recounted in the Scriptures: 'And you shall hallow the fiftieth year, and proclaim liberty throughout the land to all its inhabitants; it shall be a jubilee for you' (Leviticus 25.10).

All very noble, and rightly befitting the ancient Holiness Laws of the Jewish people, and properly recognized and advocated by later Christian and Islamic religions, including Jesus at his first address in the synagogue:

> And he came to Nazareth, where he had been brought up; and he went to the synagogue, as his custom was, on the sabbath day. And he stood up to read; and there was given to him the book of the prophet Isaiah. He opened the book and found the place where it was written,
>
> 'The Spirit of the Lord is upon me,
> because he has anointed me to preach good news to the poor,
> He has sent me to proclaim release to the captives
> and recovering of sight to the blind,
> to set at liberty those who are oppressed,
> to proclaim the acceptable year of the Lord.'
>
> (Luke 4.16–19)

What more fitting tribute to these ancient origins of the cry for liberation from the oppression of historically endemic poverty, than for churches to stand up and preach that demand for justice and freedom for the world's poor, which is the natural biblical consequence of the call to holiness?

Yet it is easy to preach good news to the poor. It is immensely more difficult to deliver it in practice. The problem, of course, is that it was never fully delivered when the great jubilee principle was first formulated in the millennium *before* the birth of Christ. How much more difficult is it to achieve in this immeasurably more complex world of the global economy in the third millenium after the death of Christ.

Any really constructive encounter with global marginalization should be a journey of biblical liberation. In Chapter 2 we saw that the biblical Greek word for stewardship, *oikonomia*, means managing the household ('economy') and the whole inhabited world ('ecumenical'). These two meanings opened up and then challenged what is happening in our world. So they illustrated the growing importance of economic life and the increasing trends of globalization, and how they are converging as the global market economy. These developments can be summarized as the movement towards a single more integrated economy, with money, technology, trade and ideas bringing us closer and closer together.

Yet these decisive trends have been accompanied by increasing polarization between and within nations, reflected in the characteristics and causes of globalization itself. The plight of sub-Saharan Africa, 'the Third World's Third World', most clearly epitomizes the disastrous consequences of marginalization processes in a global market economy. It is as though the nations of sub-Saharan Africa are being allowed to fall off the map of the world, off the map of the emerging global economy. It is a rejection of the biblical principle of stewardship, of household and economy including the whole inhabited world.

Now it is within these processes of marginalization from the global economy that the issue of international debt is most prominent, and particularly in sub-Saharan Africa. Its catastrophic effects on the poorest nations, savagely eroding their ability to resource even basic education and health care for their people, is linked to the draining of those resources to the wealthiest nations in debt repayments. It becomes a stark account of marginalization, poverty and injustice, one of the greatest challenges to the biblical principle of stewardship and its commitment to the welfare of the whole global household.

How, then, do we make sense of stewardship in such a global market economy? The campaign of Jubilee 2000 to remove the unpayable debt of the poorest nations on earth is a prime example of how we can practise discipleship in an age of partnership and reconciliation in response to global challenges.

How we respond is of supreme importance. So often the idealism of liberation ignores the realities of life, and either becomes utopian irrelevance or degenerates into the tyranny of enforced panaceas. Avoiding these options is the way of wisdom, because in rejecting such temptations it still recognizes that the problem of global-scale poverty remains and yet must be addressed with radical pragmatism because it represents one of the greatest challenges to our common humanity and concern for the vulnerable. Can we, as human beings, ignore the deep distress and death of millions of children, mothers and the elderly simply because of their poverty, without thereby losing an essential part of what it means to be truly human, to be created in God's likeness?

Such poverty must also be addressed because it challenges our self-interest. Large-scale endemic poverty in developing economies threatens our prosperity and security in the affluent, developed economies, and therefore drives us to find remedies for our shared predicament. For remember, marginalization also occurs within all nations, including the prosperous.

Proclaiming liberation, or what the Bible calls 'the year of the Lord', as a realizable hope is therefore profoundly about how we translate vision into reality. It is about how we embody concern for stewardship, as managing with efficiency and justice our complete global household, in the realities of our global context today, and thereby seeking its reform. It is about taking God's world seriously as vehicle for putting God's word to work. What does that mean in practice as the exercise of practical divinity?

Well, it involves recognizing that in an increasingly global economy, showing increasing signs of fragmentation and turbulence (manifested, for example, in the growth of world poverty and debt), no one explanation can account for such diverse trends and characteristics. Incorporating the marginalized into the global economy will therefore take into account lessons learned from examining the processes of wealth creation. So it will note that conditions for initiating and sustaining economic growth include material factors of capital, technology, trade, infrastructure and sound government, but equally education and training and those non-material factors of self-help, the entrepreneurial spirit, critical enquiring dispositions and the recognition of women's role in development.

For example, women are at the heart of the demographic challenge in terms of birth control and local economic regeneration. Yet they are frequently intentionally disadvantaged in education compared to men, and marginalized from economic and political decision-making. In Somalia, adult male literacy was 18% in 1986 whereas the equivalent female rate was only 6%; 37,000 people were in secondary education. In South Korea the figures were 96% for males and 88% for females, with five million citizens in secondary education. Unfortunately, we are aware of the inverse correlation of adult female literacy rates and total fertility rates. The role of women in sub-Saharan Africa is therefore a fundamental cause and symptom of its dire problems. And that is a most powerful challenge to traditions and religions, particularly Islam and Roman Catholicism.

Similarly, although the World Bank has failed to acknowledge the state's role in promoting social cohesion, it is now recognizing the importance of a modern state for economic growth, in providing peace and security, the impartial and incorrupt administration of justice and the protection of property rights. Few developing economies, especially in sub-Saharan Africa, have such a basic minimum state, yet without it they cannot hope 'to reconcile the imperatives of global markets with the needs of social cohesion and environmental conservation' (Gray, 1998, p. 202).

The search for answers to social problems today cannot be achieved by simplistic appeals to single solutions or radically different alternatives to the global economy. It will require a variety of responses, addressing issues of fair trade, commodity prices, labour conditions, population growth, environmental protection, exchange rates and the multicausal nature of economic growth. Proposals for debt remission must be part of such a bundle of policies reflecting the complexities of the problems. Campaigning for the debt remission of

the poorest nations acknowledges these realities and seeks their transformation. Liberation from global marginalization will demand realism and radicalism – realism because economies have to be rebuilt and the existing
international financial system preserved, and radicalism in calling for remission of international debt and not mere rescheduling.

It is important to note that the problem of contemporary debt emerged in
that period after the 1960s which has witnessed so many changes and played
such a decisive part in our arguments. Initially it was linked to the lending policies of commercial banks in the 1970s, with surplus capital from the rise in oil
prices. It became a major problem when costs of repayment rose dramatically,
due to increasing interest rates and unfavourable exchange rates for borrow-
ing nations. This was compounded by the equally dramatic fall in the ability
of those same debtor nations to repay their debts, due to collapsing commodity prices and the consequent worsening terms of trade. The result was that
the poorest nations struggled simply to pay the interest, with no hope of
repaying the capital. Indeed, they were compelled to resort to the International Monetary Fund and World Bank because they could no longer even pay
the interest. They were driven to ask for their rescheduling. The international
bodies, in turn, inflicted on them structural adjustment programmes which
required debtor nations to follow austerity programmes through the liberalization of trade, the privatization of state enterprises, and balancing their
budgets. Sadly, resourcing such programmes has been achieved by diverting
resources from basic social programmes for the poorest people. It has resulted
in the destruction of environments, including rain forests, compelling governments to spend even less on their people, the growth of economic and
political instability, and at the same time, an increase in the flow of money
from these poorest debtor nations to richest nation creditors.

Such debt is both a form of slavery and destruction, and a reflection of profound injustices, since the poorest are compelled to pay the richest far more
than the original sums borrowed, at an appalling cost to the most vulnerable
people in the world. For national debt cannot be treated like personal or business debt, written off as bankruptcy. Nations are compelled by the IMF and
World Bank to go deeper and deeper into a debt which literally becomes
unpayable. The idea of Jubilee 2000 was to campaign for the remission of such
debt, for freedom from such slavery as a one-off redemption to celebrate the
millennium, recognizing that these liberation processes are inevitably part of
longer-term programmes. The idea was to treat the year 2000 as *kairos* time, a
focus of opportunity, in God's extended programme for our fulfilment.

The concept of Jubilee, as we have seen, is taken from those sacred Scriptures shared by Jews, Christians and Muslims, and refers to the declaration
that every fifty years, slaves and debts should be redeemed. It recognized that
debt was itself a potent form of slavery, from which men and women required
redemption. It acknowledged the need to correct periodically the inevitable

accumulation of those inequalities which enslaved the poorest and enriched the most powerful, and thereby contradicted the basic claims of justice. Every fifty years, therefore, the Jubilee of the Lord was to be proclaimed as a rare act of grace, consonant with God's great mercy. The fact that it was to be declared every fifty years was also an acknowledgement that every economic system was fallible, and would need periodic correction and reform. Jubilee did not establish a once-for-all utopia. It was never achievable in history. It was always a goal to be aimed for repeatedly, it was always about a continuing realistic programme to attain achievable reform.

The Jubilee 2000 campaign was launched with the aim of celebrating the millennium by focusing the minds and policies of governments, banks and international institutions on the one-off remission of the unpayable debt of the poorest nations on earth, so that they could enter the new millennium with some realistic hope of standing more on their own feet. It united such bodies as Oxfam, Christian Aid and CAFOD, with serious support from governments in developed and developing economies, and such international bodies as the European Union, the World Bank, ILO and Unicef, for partnerships have a central role in addressing such global challenges as marginalization. 'In order to emerge from the international debt crisis, the various partners must agree on an equitable sharing of the adjustment efforts and the necessary sacrifices' (Drimmelen, p. 71). For whole peoples and nations must not be allowed to fall off the map of the emerging global economy; stewardship includes the whole inhabited world. Even the poorest nations must be enabled and empowered to pursue self-sustaining economic growth so they can participate in the global economy. It is in the interest of richer nations to contribute to debt remission, but altruism and justice, as well as efficiency, must also be part of economic, political and social policies.

This telling mixture of idealism and realism takes seriously the global economy, with all its complexities and pluralities. Realism and idealism have to be held together, reconciled in a necessary but difficult tension, in the biblical tradition of good stewardship. Vision and ideals are involved in the call for the total remission of massive unpayable debt – those debts which the poorest have incurred 'which either physically cannot be paid or whose repayment would cost such human suffering that no honourable creditor would seek to exact it' (Peters). But realism requires such remission of unpayable debt to be orderly and unrepeatable, if only to maintain the loan discipline on which necessary future banking and lending will depend, and such remission must not be seen to reward bad payers and neglect good ones.

How such remission of the unpayable debt of the poorest nations is achieved is therefore crucial if it is to reflect that necessary commitment to visionary pragmatism. Jubilee 2000's Charter began to set out how this remission would operate in terms of criteria for remission and then procedures for implementing them.

Essentially, eligible nations are those whose debt is such a highly dispro-portionate part of their Gross National Product, their exports or government revenues, that they will never be able to repay the capital borrowed, and will always have, and increasingly so, great difficulty, and at great cost to their people, in even servicing the debt. In addition, since the remission of debt cannot be allowed to sustain elites in oppressive and parasitic policies and life-styles, and must be used to develop self-sustaining economic, political and social growth for the whole people, what are the conditions which should determine which nations should qualify for debt remission? It is argued, and convincingly, that the following features of debtor nations should be taken into account: their recent history and record as debtors, their broad economic policies past and present, the record of probity and concern for their citizens' well-being, concern for political and human rights, and proposals to use money released by debt remission to deliver health care, education, water and sanitation for all their people. (In 1996, there were 47 countries – 36 of them in Africa – which met only some of these criteria. Their total debt amounted to US$ 341,052 million.)

Jubilee 2000 proposed that the remission programme should be imple-mented country by country, case by case, with decisions about details of remission, including calculating the unpayable backlog of debt, decided in consultation with the debtors and creditors of each debtor country. The actual remission of debts could be agreed in each case by a small committee of arbitrators, a kind of partnership, nominated equally by creditor and debtor, with debtor representatives including at least two from civil society. The whole process would be overseen by the UN, and implementation of each debt remission package would be the responsibility of the debtor government, rather than creditors, though clearly in co-operation with them.

This would be an achievement of inestimable benefit to the citizens of the poorest nations, and to the rest of the world. For the ultimate credibility of the inexorable movement to a global economy depends on including all nations. Globalization, the development towards one world, cannot, by its very nature, be allowed to exclude the 47 poorest nations. Indeed, the remission of their debt would be an achievement comparable to that other great and his-toric process of redemption, the remission of slaves in the early nineteenth century. Its success would demonstrate the continuing great importance of visionary pragmatism, of radical realism, for human life. In other words, it would proclaim the acceptable year of the Lord, announcing good news to the world's poor, and it would also be to take effective steps to begin to put these noble hopes into practice. It would be a truly sacramental act, embodying great spiritual concerns in profoundly material policies. It would be a truly incarnational act, enabling the word, the Jubilee word of the Lord, to become flesh in the contemporary context. It would be an exercise in practical divinity through pursuing liberation in the global market economy.

The exploration of international discipleship began with the story of George Fox and Pendle Hill. There is another story which Fox would have thoroughly approved. After a long lifetime of dynamic Christian ministry, John Wesley wrote a letter, a week before he died on 2 March 1791, to the young campaigner for the abolition of slavery, William Wilberforce. It is a reminder that changing the international economy can be achieved against quite enormous odds. It is a reminder that it can be best achieved if set in the most inspirational and widest context of all, in God's good providence:

My dear Sir,

Unless the Divine Power has raised you up to be an *Athanasius contra mundum* I see not how you can go through your glorious enterprise in opposing that execrable villainy which is the scandal of religion, of England, of human nature. Unless God has raised you up for this very thing, you will be worn out by the opposition of man and devils; but, if God be for you, who can be against you? Are all of them together stronger than God? Oh, be not weary in well doing. Go on, in the name of God, and in the power of His might, till even American slavery, the vilest that ever saw the sun, shall vanish away before it. That He who has guided you from your youth up may continue to strengthen you in this and all things is the prayer of, Dear Sir, your affectionate servant –

John Wesley

(Hylson-Smith, p. 224)

It is all that, encompassed in this chapter and book, ending with Wesley's words, which can now address that challenge of 'the causes of the wealth and poverty of nations – the grand object of all enquiries in Political Economy' which Malthus set before us in 1817.

Postscript

In 1912 the Federal Council of Churches in the United States produced a memorable social creed. It came at a pivotal point in American and indeed world history. After two generations of industrialization and urbanization, a more mature industrial capitalism and urban community were beginning to emerge. In that struggle to civilize market economy and society, the churches had played a leading role through the social gospel. The production of a social creed by an ecumenical partnership of churches symbolized the practical programme for changing society which it sought to promote. As important, however, it also led forward into the next generation, playing an important role in the New Deal, acknowledged by its author, President Franklin Roosevelt, which again represented another stage in the long continuing journey to civilize capitalism.

Maybe we are at another similar pivotal stage of history as we move from national industrial societies to a global society. I have therefore produced a simple social creed for today's emerging world:

Our Christian and human task is now about:
Being truly global in our thinking and acting wherever we are;
Being good stewards of our political economy and environment;
Seeking the social well-being of every citizen.
And doing all to the glory of our capacious and dialogic God.

To do that of course, is about partnership and reconciliation; it is about a public theology; it is about a practical divinity. And that is because it helps us 'to see the world as it is, and as it will be or might be, more clearly' (Forrester, p. 259). And for that to happen is about changing theology and society.

Bibliography

*denotes books of particular importance to the author's argument.

Ainsworth, W. H. (1884), *The Lancashire Witches: A Romance of Pendle Forest*. Routledge: Printwise Publications, 1992.
*Appleby, J., Hunt, L., and Jacob, M. (1994), *Telling the Truth about History*. Norton.
Atherton, J. R. (1979), *R. H. Tawney as a Christian Social Moralist*. Manchester University PhD.
— (1992), *Christianity and the Market: Christian Social Thought for our Times*. SPCK.
— (1994), *Social Christianity: A Reader*. SPCK.
— (1995), 'The Individual and the Organisation', in Rodd, C. (ed.) *New Occasions Teach New Duties*. T & T Clark.
*— (1997), 'Church and Society in the North West, 1760–1997', in Ford, C., Powell, M., and Wyke, T. (eds.), *The Church in Cottonopolis*. Lancashire and Cheshire Antiquarian Society.
Beckford, R. (1998), *Jesus is Dread: Black Theology and Black Culture in Britain*. Darton, Longman and Todd.
Bede (1994 ed.), *The Ecclesiastical History of the English People*. Oxford University Press.
Blair, T. (1998), *The Third Way: New Politics for the New Century*. Fabian Society.
*Boyle, N. (1998), *Where are we now? Christian Humanism and the Global Market from Hegel to Heaney*. T & T Clark.
Braybrooke, M. (1992), *Stepping Stones to a Global Ethic*. SCM Press.
Briggs, A. (1982a), *Victorian Cities*. Pelican.
— (1982b), *Victorian People*. Penguin.
Bryant, C. (1996), *Possible Dreams*. Hodder and Stoughton.
Buber, M. (1968), *Between Man and Man*. Fontana.
Carey, G. (1993), in Gillett, D., and Scott-Joynt, M. (eds), *Treasure in the Field*. HarperCollins.
Carr, E. H. (1946), *The Twenty Years' Crisis, 1919–1939*. 2nd edn. Macmillan.
Chadwick, O. (1987), *The Victorian Church, Part Two 1860–1901*. SCM Press.
Cobb, J., and Daly, H. (1989), *For the Common Good*. Merlin.
Cocks, H. F. Lovell (1943), *The Nonconformist Conscience*. Independent Press.
Crosland, C. A. R. (1956), *The Future of Socialism*. Cape.

*Davie, G. (1994), *Religion in Britain since 1945*. Blackwell.

Demant, V. A. (1952), *Religion and the Decline of Capitalism*. Faber and Faber.

De Tocqueville, A. (1945 edn), *Democracy in America*. New York.

*Dicken, P. (1992), *Global Shift: The Internationalisation of Economic Activity*. Chapman.

*Drimmelen, R. van (1998), *Faith in a Global Economy: A Primer for Christians*. WCC Publications.

Engels, F. (1969 edn.), *The Condition of the Working Class in England*. Panther.

Etzioni, A. (1968), *The Active Society*. New York: Free Press.

Evangelische Kirche in Deutschland (1991), *Common Good and Self-Interest: Economic Activity and Responsibility for the Future*. EKD.

*Field, F. (1996), *Stakeholder Welfare*. IEA Health and Welfare Unit.

Finn, D. (1996), *Just Trading*. Abingdon.

Ford, D. (1989), *The Modern Theologians, Vol. 2*. Blackwell.

*Forrester, D. (1997), *Christian Justice and Public Policy*. Cambridge University Press.

Fox, G. (1924 edn), *Journal*, ed. N. Penney. Dent.

Fukuyama, F. (1992), *The End of History and the Last Man*. Free Press.

*Giddens, A. (1998), *The Third Way: The Renewal of Social Democracy*. Polity Press.

*Gilbert, A. D. (1976), *Religion and Society in Industrial England*. Longman.

Good News in our Times: The Gospel and Contemporary Culture. Church House Publishing, 1991.

Gore, C. (1889), *Lux Mundi*. Murray.

— (1928), *Christ and Society*. Allen and Unwin.

Gorringe, T. (1996), *God's Just Vengeance: Crime, Violence and the Rhetoric of Salvation*. Cambridge University Press.

Gray, J. (1992), *The Moral Foundations of Market Institutions*. IEA Health and Welfare Unit.

— (1997), *The Times Literary Supplement*. (9 May).

*— (1998), *False Dawn: The Delusions of Global Capitalism*. Granta.

Green, D. (1993), *Reinventing Civil Society: The Rediscovery of Welfare without Politics*. IEA Health and Welfare Unit.

Griffiths, B. (1982), *Morality and the Market Place*. Hodder and Stoughton.

Gustafson, J. (1981), *Theology and Ethics*. Blackwell.

Handy, C. (1990), *The Age of Unreason*. Arrow.

*Hastings, A. (1991), *A History of English Christianity 1920–1990*. SCM Press.

Hauerwas, S. (1984), *The Peaceable Kingdom: A Primer in Christian Ethics*. SCM Press.

*Hilton, B. (1988), *The Age of Atonement: The Influence of Evangelicalism on Social and Economic Thought, 1785–1865*. Clarendon.

Hobsbawm, E. (1962), *The Age of Revolution: Europe 1789–1848*. Weidenfeld and Nicolson.

— (1975), *The Age of Capital: 1848–1875*. Weidenfeld and Nicolson.

— (1987), *The Age of Empire: 1875–1914*. Weidenfeld and Nicolson.

*— (1994), *Age of Extremes: The Short Twentieth Century 1914–1991*. Michael Joseph.

*Hull, J. (1999), 'Christian Boundaries, Christian Identities and the Local Church', in *International Journal of Practical Theology*, vol. 1.

Huntington, S. (1988–9), 'The U.S. – Decline or Renewal?' in *Foreign Affairs*, vol. 67, no. 2.

— (1996), *The Clash of Civilizations and the Remaking of World Order*. Simon and Schuster.

Hylson-Smith, K. (1997), *The Churches in England from Elizabeth I to Elizabeth II, vol. II: 1689–1833*. SCM Press.

Iremonger, F. (1948), *William Temple: His Life and Letters*. Oxford University Press.

Jenkins, D. (1979), 'Doctrines which drive me to politics,' in Willmer, H. (ed.), *Christian Faith and Political Hopes*. Epworth.

John Paul II (1991), *Centesimus Annus*. Catholic Truth Society.

Kennedy, J. (1992), 'The Wolf, the Goat and the Lettuce: The Church and the European Model of Political Economy.' Unpublished paper, *God and the Market Place* Conference, University of Newcastle.

Kennedy, P. (1989), *The Rise and Fall of the Great Powers*. Fontana.

*— (1993), *Preparing for the Twenty-First Century*. HarperCollins.

Keynes, J. (1936), *The General Theory of Employment, Interest and Money*. Macmillan, in *The Social Market Economy* (SDP Green Paper, no date).

Kuhn, J. and Shriver, D. (1991), *Beyond Success: Corporations and Their Critics in the 1990s*. Oxford University Press.

*Küng, H. (1997), *A Global Ethic for Global Politics and Economics*. SCM Press.

*Landes, D. (1969), *The Unbound Prometheus*. Cambridge University Press.

*— (1998), *The Wealth and Poverty of Nations: Why Some are So Rich And Some So Poor*. Norton.

*Lash, N. (1992), 'Not Exactly Politics or Power?' in *Modern Theology*, vol. 8, no. 4.

Leech, K. (1981), *The Social God*. SPCK.

Long, D. (2000), *Divine Economy: Theology and the Market*. Routledge.

MacIntyre, A. (1985), *After Virtue*. Duckworth.

Markham, I. (1994), *Plurality and Christian Ethics*. Cambridge University Press.

Maurice, F. (1884), *The Life of Frederick Denison Maurice*. 2 vols. Macmillan.

Maurice, F. D. (1842), *The Kingdom of Christ*. J. Rivington.

Meeks, M. (1989), *God the Economist*. Fortress.

Milbank, J., Pickstock, C., Ward, G. (eds) (1999), *Radical Orthodoxy: A New Theology*. Routledge.

Moltmann, J. (1981), *The Trinity and the Kingdom of God*. SCM Press.

Northcott, M. (1999), *Life After Debt: Christianity and Global Justice*. SPCK.

Not Just for the Poor Christian: Perspectives on the Welfare State. Church House Publishing, 1986.

Novak, M. (1998), *Is There a Third Way?* IEA Health and Welfare Unit.

Oppenheimer, H. (1983), *The Hope of Happiness*. SCM Press.

Owen, R. (1969 edn), *Report to the County of Lanark: A New View of Society*. Penguin.

Peters, B. (1995), *An Introduction to the Jubilee 2000 Campaign for International Debt Remission*. Jubilee 2000.

Preston, R. (1979), *Religion and the Persistence of Capitalism*. SCM Press.

— (1981), 'Not Out of the Wood Yet: a Recent Christian Socialist Manifesto' in *Theology*, vol. LXXXIV, no. 698.

— (1983), *Church and Society in the late Twentieth Century*. SCM Press.

— (1987), *The Future of Christian Ethics*. SCM Press.

*Rack, H. (1989), *Reasonable Enthusiast: John Wesley and the Rise of Methodism*. Epworth.

Ramsey, A. (1960), *From Gore to Temple: The Development of Anglican Theology between Lux Mundi and the Second World War, 1889–1939*. Longman.

Reader, J. (1994), *Local Theology: Church and Community in Dialogue*. SPCK.

*— (1997), *Beyond all Reason: The Limits of Post-Modern Theology*. Aureus.

*Rieger, J. (ed.) (1998), *Liberating the Future: God, Mammon and Theology*. Fortress.

Robinson, J. (1971), *Economic Heresies: Some Old-Fashioned Questions in Economic Theory*. Macmillan.

Ryan, J. (1996), *Economic Justice: Selections from Distributive Justice and a Living Wage*. Westminster John Knox Press.

*Sassoon, D. (1997), *One Hundred Years of Socialism: The West European Left in the Twentieth Century*. Fontana.

*Schreiter, R. (1998), *The Ministry of Reconciliation: Spirituality and Strategies*. Orbis.

*Shanks, A. (1995), *Civil Society, Civil Religion*. Blackwell.

Sheen, H. (1965), *Canon Peter Green*. Hodder and Stoughton.

Skidelsky, R. (1987), *The Social Market Economy*. Social Market Foundation.

Smiles, S. (1859), *Self-Help: The Art of Achievement Illustrated by Accounts of the Lives of Great Men*. Murray.

Something to Celebrate: Valuing Families in Church and Society. Church House Publishing, 1995.

Stout, J. (1988), *Ethics after Babel*. Clarke.

Sugirtharajah, R. S. (ed.) (1993), *Asian Faces of Jesus*. SCM Press.

Sumner, J. (1838), *A Practical Exposition of the Gospels of St. Matthew and St. Mark*. Hatchard.

Tawney, R. (1966 edn), *Religion and the Rise of Capitalism*. Penguin.

— (1979), *The American Labour Movement and Other Essays*, ed. J. M. Winter. Harvester.

Temple, W. (1939), *Readings in St. John's Gospel*. Macmillan.

— (1942), *Christianity and Social Order*. Penguin.

Tillich, P. (1967), *On the Boundary*. Collins.

Vidler, A. (1948), *The Theology of F. D. Maurice*. SCM Press.

Williams, R. (1995), *A Ray of Darkness*. Cowley.

*Winch, D. (1996), *Riches and Poverty: An Intellectual History of Political Economy in Britain, 1750–1834*. Cambridge University Press.

Wogaman, J. (1985), *Faith and Fragmentation: Christianity for a New Age*. Fortress.

Wolffe, J. (1995), (ed.) *Evangelical Faith and Public Zeal: Evangelicals and Society in Britain 1780–1980*. SPCK.

Yeo, S. (1976), *Religion and Voluntary Organisations in Crisis*. Croom Helm.

Index